Political Consequences
of Crony Capitalism
inside Russia

CONTEMPORARY EUROPEAN POLITICS AND SOCIETY

Anthony M. Messina, Series Editor

Political Consequences of Crony Capitalism inside Russia

Gulnaz Sharafutdinova

University of Notre Dame Press

Notre Dame, Indiana

Library of Congress Cataloging-in-Publication Data

Sharafutdinova, Gulnaz.
    Political consequences of crony capitalism inside Russia /
by Gulnaz Sharafutdinova.
        p.   cm. — (Contemporary european politics and society series)
    Includes bibliographical references and index.
    ISBN-13: 978-0-268-04135-9 (pbk. : alk. paper)
    ISBN-10: 0-268-04135-0 (pbk. : alk. paper)
    1. Corruption—Russia (Federation)   2. Capitalism—Political
aspects—Russia (Federation)   3. Democracy—Russia (Federation)
4. Post-communism—Russia (Federation)   5. Russia (Federation)—
Politics and government—1991–   I. Title.
    JN6529.C6S53   2010
    320.947—dc22

                                                                2010033408

∞ *The paper in this book meets the guidelines for permanence
and durability of the Committee on Production Guidelines
for Book Longevity of the Council on Library Resources.*

CONTENTS

LIST OF TABLES

AND FIGURES

Tables

Figures

ACKNOWLEDGMENTS

The story of any book develops along with the story of its author's life. This book is special because it is the first one in my career and because its writing has been associated with years of intensive learning and growth. The project started in the U.S. capital, and many people and institutions were crucial to its development. I first want to thank the faculty of the political science department at the George Washington University (GW). Not only topnotch scientists, they are foremost a wonderful group of individuals who have a sense of humor and integrity and who provided me with a model of how a community of scientists should relate to each other. Lee Sigelman, Chris Deering, Susan Sell, Martha Finnemore, Michael Sodaro, Susan Wiley, Jim Goldgeier, Bruce Dickson, Forrest Maltzman, James Willson-Quayle, and Paul Wahlbeck all supported me and taught me a great deal.

Most special to me in this group are my dissertation advisers, Harvey Feigenbaum, Peter Reddaway, and Nathan Brown, whose enthusiastic support and encouragement and constructive comments and intellectual input have allowed me to progress from the first painful steps of elaborating this project through various chapter drafts to the defense of my dissertation in 2004. Harvey Feigenbaum's mentorship, personal support, and faith in my capabilities have been especially crucial in my professional career. His role was critical not only in this study but also in my career choice and in instilling self-confidence and faith in my future as a political scientist. Peter Reddaway continuously and generously supported this project, and it benefited enormously from his intimate knowledge of Russian politics, his attention to detail, and his careful reading of various drafts of this book. Nathan Brown set a great scholarly example with his quick, sharp, and constructive comments on various drafts as this book evolved. The book would have been different without his constant call for conceptual clarity and sharpness of arguments.

I would also like to thank my fellow travelers, the Ph.D. students at GW, especially Sophia Moestrup, Gregg Bucken-Knapp, Zsuzsa Csergo, Jackie Miller-McLaren, Alix Howard, Tricia Mulligan, Todd Andrews, Michael Macleod, John Donaldson, Erika Prenzlow, Michael Spring, Jason Macdonald, Lan Chu, Stephanie McNulty, Liang Sun, and Lee Ann Fujii. Sophia Moestrup, in particular, generously gave her time and energy to read drafts of this book, contributing both to big ideas and small articles that are so hard to get for someone coming from a culture and languages that do not use those articles. I leaned on her encouragement and support at the moments of skepticism and doubt about the project.

The story of this book continued at Miami University (MU) in Ohio, where I started my first real job. I would like to thank the faculty of the political science department at MU for welcoming me to the department and supporting and encouraging me through my first years of work here. It has been a good home for finishing this book. Karen Dawisha, Jeanne Hey, Shiela Croucher, Walt Vanderbush, Abdoulaye Saine, Laura Neack, John Rothgeb, Brian Danoff, Brian Marshall, Gus Jones, and Clyde Brown have all contributed to making MU an exciting and challenging workplace. I owe a special debt of gratitude to Adeed Dawisha and Venelin Ganev, who read drafts of this book at its final stages; to Jeanne Hey, who contributed to the book prospectus; and to Karen Dawisha, whose personal support and inspiring leadership of the Havighurst center has made Miami home to me and my family.

Various institutions supported this project financially and otherwise. The Kellogg Institute for International Studies, where I spent the spring semester of 2006, provided me with a superb place to revise my dissertation into a book. The Columbian School of Arts and Sciences gave me a dissertation award, and a George Hoffman Dissertation Award from the Institute for European, Russian, and Eurasian Studies allowed me to complete my dissertation. A dissertation award from the Institute for the Studies of World Politics made it possible for me to do fieldwork in Russia. I am also thankful to the editors of *Comparative Politics* who extended their permission to use data from my essay "What Explains Corruption Perceptions? The Dark Side of Political Competition in Russia's Regions,"

Comparative Politics 42 (2) (January 2010): 147–66. Finally, I would like to thank Rebecca DeBoer, the managing editor of the University of Notre Dame Press for offering a kind and professional hand in the final stages of this book's production.

I am indebted to my friends—in the United States, Russia, and other countries—for their unfailing support, encouragement, and love: Marijke Hallo de Wolf, Noori Janjani, Larisa Ainutdinova, Vagiz Sultanbikov, Rais Mazitov, Natalia Jacobsen, Wasi Khan, Manisha Tharaney, Alix Arbore, Najia Badykova, Neringa Klumbyte, Elena Lariuhina, Alexei Trochev, Stephen Deets, and Irina Aervitz. I would also like to express gratitude to Elise Giuliano, who read the manuscript at its initial stage; Lee Sigelman, who edited one of the chapters and thereby gave me the best writing lesson I have ever received; Henry Hale, who provided useful comments and advice as this project evolved; Conor O'Dwyer, who provided comments on the book prospectus; and Vladimir Gelman, who became a great companion during my fellowship at the Kellogg Institute and read the manuscript. Many people supported me during my fieldwork in Russia, especially in Kazan and Nizhnii Novgorod. I would like to thank Aleksandr Prudnik, Rustem Bikmetov, and Sergei Borisov in Nizhnii Novgorod for their kindness and support and Larisa Ainutdinova, Rashid Akhmetov, Marat Safarov, Ilgiz Mingaleev, and Vladimir Krylov in Kazan.

I could not have finished this book without my husband, Jevgenijs Steinbuks. Not only generous with emotional support and love, Zhenia has become my best critic and editor. We now share the new joy of our lives, our son, Rafael, who has been an incredible source of energy and inspiration for both of us. Finally, my greatest gratitude is to my parents, Gulia and Chulpan Sharafutdinov, and to my grandmother Raïsa for their unfailing love and generosity and the life they gave me; this book is dedicated to them.

It is what we think we know already that often prevents us from learning.

—Claude Bernard

What is the relationship between elections and democracy? What happens if the electoral choices are deemed ineffective for projecting the popular will? What is the link between political competition and democracy? What happens if political competition undermines the legitimacy of political elites and even the government? These are not abstract questions originating behind the protective walls of the academic ivory tower. They trouble, unfortunately, too many countries around the world. Even the United States—a mature democracy that has apparently resolved these issues—has recently been pressed to face some of these questions. After all, the strategy of promoting democracy around the world—the centerpiece of U.S. foreign policy in the past decade—was driven by an understanding of democracy that privileged the electoral mechanism and elite competition for power as its central elements. The striking failures in American foreign policy in different parts of the world in the past few years have stirred widespread criticism of the U.S. strategy and a debate about its underlying assumptions.[1] One of the questioned assumptions is whether the installation of competitive elections in a country results in a democracy and what the United States should do if democratic elections bring to power hostile politicians and governments.[2]

Russia is another country that had to face these questions, albeit from a different angle. For several years after the collapse of communism scholars and politicians in the West nurtured illusions about democracy

1

and free markets springing up at the end of the "transition period." After
all, political and economic reforms undertaken in most countries in the
region instituted elections as the main mechanism for power transfer
and allowed for the flourishing of private property and wealth accumulation. After almost two decades of transition, however, only a handful of
countries—the new postcommunist members of the European Union
(EU)—can claim that democracy and markets are gradually taking shape
in their country. For many others, democratic institutions appear as a fa-
çade legitimizing mostly unaccountable elites, corrupt political-economic
systems, and markets that are not free. The necessity of studying the factors that turn the wheels of such systems has become by now very obvious, spurring a wave of innovative scholarship, new concepts, and fresh
approaches.[3] Numerous accounts have tried to explain why and how democracy got derailed in Russia and in many other postcommunist states.[4]
This book adds to those accounts by attempting to interpret the democratic failure in Russia as a reflection of a more general problem of democracy's coexistence with crony capitalism: what happens when democratic institutions are imposed on a political-economic system lacking the
rule of law and stable property rights. Based on the experience of political transformation in the Russian regions, I develop new analytical lenses
for understanding the political dynamics in the countries that have not
been "transitioning" but rather got "stuck" between democracy and dictatorship, between corruption and the ongoing struggle for property,
between unfair elections and recurrent crises of succession. To do that I
employ insights from the literature dealing with crony capitalism and informal institutions and explore the consequences of political competition and electoral struggles in the context characterized by the prevalence
of informal elite networks.

Cronyism in politics is an old problem: public officials have often
used their power to benefit and enrich their friends and supporters outside of government. When a close connection between state officials and
economic elites dominates policy making, traditional cronyism becomes
"crony capitalism"—viewed in this study as a distinct institutional order
characterized by the domination of informal elite groups. In such a system selected economic elites receive preferential treatment and privileges, making support from the state rather than market forces a crucial

factor for maintaining and accruing wealth. It is not a secret that the years of postcommunist transformation in Russia and many other states undergoing similar transformations resulted in the emergence of such a system. I argue in this book that the coexistence of crony capitalism with such democratic institutions as political competition and the electoral mechanism produced a distinct pattern of political evolution in Russia, its regions, and, possibly, various other states combining democracy with crony capitalism.

The new political system established in Russia after the collapse of communism involved public participation in politics through elections. Neither public participation nor elections per se resulted in the legitimate government, however. Postcommunist economic reforms resulted in elite fragmentation, and the electoral mechanism paved the way for an intense contestation for power among the elites. Massive financial resources flowed into electoral campaigns and the invention of cunning strategies and tools of political struggle. The candidates aspiring to win hired political consultants (referred to as "political technologists" in Russia), who waged informational warfare and created other elaborate tools of public opinion manipulation.[5] The mass media and corruption scandals turned into the most potent instruments used in these struggles. The competing media outlets poured into the public realm tons of compromising materials aiming to discredit the competitors. Eventually, not only specific candidates were discredited but the whole "body politic" as well; the entire system fell victim to such methods of political struggle, with especially damaging effects on the electoral process. Far from being seen as the focal point of democracy building or an exercise of citizens' right to determine who governs them, the elections were perceived as the means to elite access to power and wealth and an elite tool rather than the means of projecting the public will. As "the baby is thrown out with the bathwater," the very idea of democracy, political competition, and the electoral process became discredited.

In any democracy politicians are confronted with a strong incentive to use corruption as a political tool for obtaining power. This incentive expresses itself in a milder form through the strategy of negative campaigning, commonly employed in the United States and many other established democracies.[6] As discovered by scholars of American electoral campaigns, the amount of negativity is determined by the degree of electoral contestation: the closer the race, the meaner the campaign.[7] In crony capitalist systems the degree and character of political contestation is even more intense due to the higher stakes involved in controlling a state office. Political and economic spheres under crony capitalism are tightly intertwined, so access to power means access to property and vice versa. In crony capitalism, a system based on privileges rather than rights, economic elites must maintain connections to the state in order to obtain and keep their privileges. For political elites, on the other hand, obtaining a state office means getting control over rule making, specifically with regard to the ongoing redistribution of wealth. With such high stakes for both political and economic elites, there is a strong inclination to use tricky, conniving methods to obtain victory.

Governed by a winner-takes-all mentality, competitive politics under such a system knows no respect for legal or civil boundaries. The methods of political struggle go beyond mere slandering of opponents, as occurs frequently in more established democracies. Competitors engage in a host of other, blatantly dirty political practices that involve provocation, fraud, and the use of legal means as well as administrative resources associated with the state. The logic of using corruption as a political tool plays out most ferociously in a competitive environment because politicians face electoral incentives to publicize corruption and provoke scandals. In the course of well-publicized and scandalous interelite clashes all parties become discredited, including the official authorities that try to "fix" the vote, or interfere in elections by using all means possible to achieve the desired outcome. Faced with successive dirty electoral campaigns played out as violent information wars among the candidates, the voters turn away from politics, distrusting the elites and the political institutions that are perceived as wasteful political games. The public not only disengages from public politics but also becomes inclined to support an authoritarian "solution," which seems a more attractive option than a manifestly corrupt system. Ironically, democratic institutions work in such systems but in a perverted way. When functioning in the competitive environment, the electoral mechanism not only ensures power transfer but also, unintentionally, uncovers the predatory nature of crony elites and undermines the legitimacy of the political-economic order crafted by a self-serving and unchecked ruling class.

The authoritarian solution is being now tried in Russia. In its radical expression, the turn toward authoritarianism under Putin manifested itself in the abolition of the gubernatorial elections in September 2004. What was really puzzling about this major reform of regional power formation is that Russian citizens did not seem to mind the change. Judging from the perspective of democratic theory, through this reform, Putin, in effect, deprived the country's people of their democratic right to elect regional leaders. At the very least, people could be expected to react negatively to this abrogation of their rights. The public opinion polls conducted by the well-regarded Levada Center a few days after this decision, however, produced rather shocking results: 44 percent of the respondents supported Putin's decision; 42 percent disapproved.[8] The majority of Russians seemed to support the curtailing of their right to participate in regional government formation. This attitude seems especially troubling in the face of studies demonstrating that regional-level elections have actually worked to hold governors accountable.[9] To complicate matters further, public opinion polls have also shown that the Russian people hold dearly the values of freedom and democracy.[10] Why, then, would they relinquish the right to form their own regional governments, which have a great effect on their day-to-day lives and concerns?

Rejecting ideas about the inherent authoritarian nature of Russian political culture, this book investigates more proximate causes behind the development of public attitudes in Russia. It argues that there are more evident factors that contributed to the rise of negative perceptions of regional elections and competition in Russia. The scandal-driven politics during the successive rounds of competitive electoral campaigns, regionally as well as nationally, tended to result in the public retreating into political apathy and protest voting. Reacting to perceived (and real) lawlessness and corruption among the elites promoted by scathing media reports, people voted increasingly for the candidate "against all" or abstained from voting entirely. The act of voting and the elections themselves were being progressively devalued as the arsenal of elite tactics to "manage" the electoral results grew.

Paradoxically, the new political momentum characterized by a rejection of democratic institutions and a desire for a strong central authority brings together the elites interested in self-preservation and the public agitated by the successive rounds of dirty electoral campaigns and belligerent, unaccountable elites. The common understanding that un-hindered political competition cannot or should not be sustained without endangering the very existence of the overall system creates a momentum for a shift away from competition. This is, I argue, what was happening in Russia after the turn of the century and the advent of the new era of Putin's politics. The authoritarian turn associated with Putin and supported in large part by the public should be viewed as a political response to the exigencies imposed by the interaction between crony capitalism, political competitiveness, and the electoral process.

The argument advanced in this book goes against the conventional wisdom. The widely used and respected institutional theories of democracy view competitive elections as one of the cornerstones of the democratic system of government. The classic procedural view of democracy advanced by Joseph Schumpeter, for example, defines the democratic method as an "institutional arrangement for arriving at political decisions in which individuals acquire the power to decide by means of a competitive struggle for the people's vote."[11] People's vote (i.e., elections) and political competition are thus the bedrock of democracy. Such a view expects the electoral mechanism to fulfill several functions. Elections are supposed to legitimize the political system and the government in the eyes of the citizens, encourage mass participation, and enhance popular interest in politics. Elections are also meant to ensure government accountability by keeping the elected officials under the threat of being removed from office. Political competition, on the other hand, is supposed to give voters a chance to choose among alternative candidates, alternative programs, and alternative priorities and to elect a government responsive to their needs. This is the dominant theory and the prevailing expectation as to how these institutions *should* work. The puzzle presented by post-communist Russia has been that the institutional forms are not always invested with the expected content and, therefore, do not result in the expected outcomes. At least in the short run, political competition and elections in the case of Russia did not ensure governmental accountability, encourage political participation, and legitimize the political system. Even when present—thus allowing theorists to refer to Russia of the 1990s as a democracy—these institutions were not sufficient to make the citizens believe that they live in a true democracy. To the contrary, played out in the context of crony capitalism, their functioning resulted in their own imperilment and devaluation. In the absence of legitimizing elections, the ruling elites had to look for other sources of legitimacy. The consequences for a fragile Russian democracy were devastating. The devaluation of democratic institutions opened the door for political centralization aimed at enhancing the system's stability and sustainability.

Legitimacy under Crony Capitalism

Crony capitalism confronts governments with special challenges for maintaining their legitimacy and exercising political authority. As cogently stated by Rose in 1978, "The central concern of every political system, however its leaders are chosen, is the exercise of political authority."[12] Political authority is closely linked to power but differs from it in one respect. Authority is power that is accepted and recognized as legitimate by those over whom it is exercised. This implies that any political leadership or government has to care about its legitimacy, or at least some minimal acceptance by the public, some minimal degree of voluntary compliance and consent. The reasons for this are simple. In the absence of consent, the government needs to spend more resources and develop additional enforcement mechanisms to ensure compliance. In the absence of generalized consent, the government will find it much more difficult to govern. Without legitimacy there is no political authority.[13]

Although the ideas expressed above do not appear controversial, the scholarship on postcommunist politics and especially that focused on Russian transformation, tends to ignore the inherent link between the government and the governed in accounting for political change in the region. There is a strong preference given to elite-centered explanations of political change, which do not leave any space for the role of the masses. The transition paradigm focused on the elites and pacts among them; the more recent cyclical approach to explaining the dynamics of political change also focuses on elite-level analysis.[14] Such a tendency seems understandable, especially with regard to Russia, which historically has been ruled by autocratic leaders and lacked democratic traditions. However, the central political dilemma of any government, as noted above, concerns the exercise of political authority and, therefore, ensuring some level of public consent or legitimacy. In Robert Michel's words, even "the despotism of the leaders does not arise solely from a vulgar lust of power or from uncontrolled egoism, but is often the outcome of a profound and sincere conviction of their own value and of the services which they have rendered to the common cause."[15] This inherent link between the rulers and the ruled needs to be integrated into our understanding of the dynamics of political change in the postcommunist region, especially because the examples of and the problems posed by delegitimized postcommunist governments such as Yeltsin's in Russia or Kuchma's in Ukraine abound.[16]

The term *legitimacy* is frequently used in political analysis but is infrequently defined (except in political theory) and is even less frequently agreed on. Because both concepts—authority and legitimacy—involve the relationship between the government and the governed, I rely on Lipset's conception of legitimacy as "a capacity of the system to engender and maintain the belief that the existing political institutions are the most appropriate ones for the society."[17] Such an understanding aptly brings to our attention two sides: legitimacy is about people's beliefs about rulers and institutions, and it is also about claims made by rulers. As posited by Beetham, "a given power relationship is not legitimate because people believe in its legitimacy but because it can be justified in terms of their beliefs."[18] In its search for legitimacy, a government has the choice of justifying its rule in terms of existing popular beliefs or trying to mold those beliefs. In either case, it faces a challenge. With regard to the first option, popular beliefs change as the socioeconomic and political situation changes, making the old claims for legitimacy outdated or mismatched. The second option requires special circumstances that would enable the government to play a significant role in shaping popular beliefs and perceptions. In the absence of the "ministry of truth" or "thought police,"[19] this indeed is a daunting task. However, this task becomes much easier if the government controls the media, which play a powerful role in shaping citizens' perceptions and attitudes and, therefore, the regime's legitimacy. The media's role becomes especially crucial during elections; this factor therefore has to also be integrated into the analysis of postcommunist regime dynamics.

What happens when legitimacy wanes? One immediate impact of low legitimacy is on governmental performance, specifically with regard to such governmental functions as law enforcement and tax collection. Another consequence of diminishing legitimacy is the opening of the political system to challengers. When people do not trust or consent to the government, there is an opportunity for outsiders to step in and offer an alternative vision. Hence waning legitimacy indicates a changing political opportunity structure for other political actors. Furthermore, depending on their understanding of the reasons for declining legitimacy, the new political actors have a window of opportunity for making corrections in the system. There is an opening for redefining the political system and transforming the political regime, if that is seen as necessary for avoiding the problems of the previous political system.

The accounts for declining legitimacy in such postcommunist countries as Russia or Ukraine in the 1990s have most often focused either on the effects of a "shock-therapy-type" economic reform, resulting in sharp economic dislocation for the population,[20] or on the inadequacy of the state to deliver collective goods.[21] The political mechanisms that could affect popular beliefs and perceptions have been accorded less attention. In this study I draw attention to the role of political factors—in particular, the workings of political competition and its reflection through the media—in shaping popular perceptions and, therefore, the legitimacy of ruling elites and political institutions.[22]

Political competition under crony capitalism undermines the legitimacy of elites and institutions via two channels. First, the rulers' potential to claim legitimacy gets undermined as a result of widespread blackmailing and negative campaigning in a "war of all against all," so that no credibility can be attached to any claim. Second, popular attitudes and beliefs about the system and the rulers spiral down, driven by revelations and claims leveled by political opponents against each other. In the end, after repeated rounds of political competition played out in public through competitive elections in the atmosphere of widespread corruption and its use as a political tool, the public sees no other alternatives but to opt for so-called color revolutions or support a shift toward authoritarianism.

The argument advanced here opposes the objectivist-type analyses of the sources of regime legitimacy that draw a direct link between popular dissatisfaction and objective conditions such as worsening material conditions or the state's failure to deliver public goods.[23] Popular perceptions, including those concerned with regime legitimacy, are mediated by various mechanisms that affect the type of information available to the public, as well as the individual's capacity to process information. These mechanisms include, for example, the impact of elites and the media, both of which have the power to limit public access to information, manipulate the type of information publicized, or frame information in specific ways, thus setting the agenda for the public.[24] In addition, institutions and social context have an impact on how the public perceives objective reality. As I argue in this book, for example, political competition in the context of crony capitalism constrains the capacity of the government to claim legitimacy as competing elites try to undermine each other using compromising materials and dirty tricks. The coexistence of crony capitalism and the electoral mechanism for power transfer creates, at least in the short term, a strong destabilizing dynamic that undermines public faith in the system.

Methodological Considerations

Why Russian Regions?

The argument advanced in this book originates in the analysis of scenarios of political-economic transformation playing out in the regions of the Russian Federation. The testing of the argument is also done on the subnational level. I used the subnational comparative method mostly for practical reasons. Investigating the informal relationships that play a key role in politics is a challenging task. Its accomplishment is more manageable on the subnational than national level. The type of knowledge required for this study is more accessible on the lower political level, which has a more restricted number of key players, than on the level of the federal center in Moscow. At the same time, looking at the subnational rather than national level enables a comparative study of postcommunist transformational outcomes in which many key variables (e.g., history, culture, and institutional legacies) can be kept constant. No comparative state-level study can allow for such a degree of similarity as the comparative study of regions. The potential problem with generalizability from a within-nation comparison is addressed in this study by using the subnational comparative method in conjunction with cross-national comparisons.[25] The argument developed here is not limited to the subnational level, however; it is also applied to the analysis of political transformation in Russia at large.

Even after the collapse of the Soviet Union, Russia remains huge. It is organized as a federation that is currently divided into eighty-three constituent units.[26] In the aftermath of the Soviet implosion, during the 1990s, the Russian Federation decentralized greatly. The terms *regionalism* and *asymmetrical federalism* were widely used to describe Yeltsin's Russia and discuss challenges to the country's territorial cohesion.[27] Indeed, the sweeping process of regionalization and the devolution or in some cases even seizure of decision-making prerogatives by the regions made it difficult to treat Russia as a monolithic entity. The reforms of the 1990s resulted in national disintegration and subnational integration.[28] As the central government divested itself of many previous obligations, the regional level has become the primary field in which state and society encounter each other. Absent a strong unifying influence from the federal center, regions went their own separate ways both in political and economic development. Even a quick look into the internal political developments at the regional level reveals a wide diversity of political trajectories. As noted by Moses, "a weak central Russian government since 1991 has provided both the incentives and opportunities for the leadership of regions to strike out on their own and to develop their own political identity and unique combination of political models."[29] These varying regional political models and identities have attracted much scholarly attention.[30] An entire subfield of Russian regional studies came into being that treated regions as separate political entities, not unlike states.[31]

The process of regionalization was reversed under Russia's second president, Vladimir Putin, who aimed to recentralize the Russian Federation under the new "power vertical." Although different regional models still remain, their number has decreased considerably as the role of the federal center and its interference in regional politics has increased progressively starting in 2000.[32] The diverging regional developments of the 1990s, however, enable a comparative study of the various economic-political models that emerged under Yeltsin. This study undertakes that task by examining two regions of Russia: Nizhnii Novgorod *oblast* (region), and the Republic of Tatarstan.

I argue that regional polities in Russia are best comprehended using the concept of economic-political networks (EPNs). These informal elite groups are the key actors and structures on Russia's regional political scene.[33] Characterized by close ties between government officials and big-business representatives, they are the embodiment of crony capitalism and manifest the systemic character of cronyism. The main feature of such a system is the absence of the rule of law and an impartial state that is capable of providing and enforcing a uniform set of rules for the various political and economic actors and of maintaining stable property rights. This political-economic system represents a distinct institutional order that entails a strong role played by informal institutions and relations and that must therefore be assessed on its own terms.[34] The various elements of this system interact differently from what could be expected in the systems characterized by the rule of law and an impartial state based on the domination of formal institutions.

In the politically fragmented Nizhnii Novgorod region the intensifying political competition in the late 1990s became expressed primarily in dirty politics, media wars, and public scandals involving regional elites. Within a few years public attitudes toward the regional government and regional elites deteriorated, and people retreated either into political apathy and absenteeism or protest voting, that is, supporting antisystem political actors or, even more radically, voting against all candidates. Political dynamics were very different in the noncompetitive Republic of Tatarstan, where elites avoided political fragmentation and the government maintained a higher degree of legitimacy using a "socially oriented" model of economic transformation. In this noncompetitive regime elections did not introduce the uncertainty and power struggle experienced in Nizhnii Novgorod. The dominant elite network had a greater influence over the election results through the control of public opinion, which was enabled by the government's control of the mass media, lower-level government officials, and the major economic elites in the region. The authorities did not have to resort to force, blatant manipulation, and dirty tactics to try to change voting outcomes. The public by and large supported the incumbent government and perceived the social and political situation in the republic as more stable than in other regions.

My investigation revealed that a crony capitalist institutional order might be present in both competitive and noncompetitive political systems. However, the degree of institutionalization or the degree to which it is taken for granted by the population differs depending on the political dynamics and, specifically, the presence of acute political competition. It is not simply the existence of informally colluding elite networks that is consequential for discrediting elites and the electoral mechanism but the fact that the public *expects* the political and the economic sphere to be dominated by such networks and that the public *believes* that private interests dominate the state. This perception that public authorities represent and promote the interests of particular informal networks instead of advancing public goals reflects the degree of instututionalization of these EPNs. The greater that perception is, the more institutionalized these EPNs and the crony system as a whole are.[35] Public apathy and the rejection of the entire political system, including some of its democratic elements, are consequently greater in systems where cronyism and corruption are perceived more acutely.

Why Tatarstan and Nizhnii Novgorod?

The choice of Tatarstan and Nizhnii Novgorod for this study was determined by several factors. The Russian Federation consists of units with differentiated status, and the main dividing line is between ethnically and nonethnically defined units. My earlier research on regional political competitiveness has found that ethnic republics in the 1990s tended to be less competitive than the rest of Russia's regions.[36] Evidently, the institutional structure of the Russian Federation played a substantial role in determining political outcomes. Based on this finding, selecting an ethnic republic and a nonethnic region was the best strategy for studying more closely the emergence of competitive and noncompetitive political regimes as well as the impact of competition on the political-economic realities of the Russian Federation. At the same time, I looked for regions that would be similar in terms of economic and social development and would have in common other structural characteristics such as territory and population size, geographic location, and economic diversification.

Tatarstan is one of the ethnic republics in the Russian Federation that has always attracted great attention from analysts and outside observers. Two main factors account for this. First, it is one of the more economically advanced regions, featuring developed oil-extracting, petrochemical, automobile, aircraft, and other industries that add to its political significance. Second, the Tatarstani elite has been a pioneer in advocating regional autonomy and genuine federalism in Russia, thus setting a path for other constituent units of the Russian Federation to follow.[37] Over the past fifteen years the Tatarstani elite has been able to construct one of the most stable and enduring noncompetitive political regimes in Russia; it is supported by the majority of the republic's population and recognized by the federal center as a party to be reckoned with. In fact, it could be seen as an ideal-type noncompetitive regime viewed as an example to be followed by Russia's other republics and regions. It appears possible to argue, therefore, that the main strategies undertaken by the republican elite with the purpose of consolidating their power base vis-à-vis the federal center and domestic sources of opposition represent not simply idiosyncratic factors that affected the evolution of relationships between Kazan, the capital of Tatarstan, and Moscow and the evolution of Tatarstan's political regime. Analyzing these strategies should help to uncover the micro-causal mechanisms of building noncompetitive political systems in other republics as well.

The Nizhnii Novgorod region (Nizhegorodskaia oblast) is a non-ethnically defined unit that has also been a visible part of the federation. I selected it for this study because it represents the closest to the ideal-type competitive political system characterized by the domination of several, easily identifiable EPNs. The political conflicts that played out in the region's capital city of Nizhnii Novgorod (known as Gor'kii until 1992) in the past decade and a half are representative of interelite clashes in other regions of Russia with competitive political systems. Therefore, the study of the emergence and the outcomes of competitive politics in this region could uncover the political dynamics in many other regions in Russia.

These two regions share important structural similarities, which makes it possible to represent this comparative case study as following the model of "most-similar" systems (table 0.1).[38] Both are heavily industrialized and economically diversified. Similar to Tatarstan, the Nizhnii Novgorod region has an extensive industrial potential, especially in the

TABLE 0.1. Republic of Tatarstan and Nizhnii Novgorod Region: Basic Facts

	Republic of Tatarstan	*Nizhnii Novgorod Region*
Territory (sq. km)	68,000	76,900
Population (1998)	3,774,000	3,697,000
Urban population (1998, %)	73.6	78.2
Ethnic breakdown (1989, %)	Tatars 48.5 Russians 43.3 Chuvash 3.7	Russians 94.6 Tatars 1.6 Mordvins 1.0 Ukrainians 0.9
Student population (Sept. 1, 1997, %)	198 per 10,000	182 per 10,000
Pensioner population (1997, %)	25.07	28.89
Proportion of people with higher education (%)	9.5	9.6
Number of telephones per 100 families	38.9 (cities), 13.6 (villages)	46.2 (cities), 14.3 (villages)
Average monthly personal income (July 1998, rubles)	686.3	627.4
Industrial production as % of all Russian production (Jan.–Aug. 1998)	2.81	2.4
Economic structure (1999, %)	Industry 40.2 Agriculture 9.2 Construction 11.0 Transport 6.8 Trade 7.8	Industry 36.6 Agriculture 6.0 Construction 8.5 Transport 12.5 Trade 11.6
Industrial structure (1999, %)	Electricity 27.4 Fuel industry 22.9 Ferrous metallurgy 0.4 Chemical and petro-chemical industry 20.4 Machine building 12.5 Forestry 1.4 Industrial construction materials 2.5 Textile 1.3 Food industry 8.3	Electricity 10.3 Fuel industry 2.7 Ferrous metallurgy 4.6 Nonferrous metallurgy 0.4 Chemical and petro-chemical industry 7.8 Machine building 51.9 Forestry 5.1 Industrial construction materials 2.0 Textile 1.6 Food industry 9.3

Source: Orttung 2000, 362–63, 537–38; *Rossiia Regionov* 2001.

fields of machine building and automobile production and in the petro-chemical sector. Both belong to a small group of donor regions in Russia that contribute more to the federal budget than they receive in transfers from the center.[39] They are similar in size and are geographically proximate. The choice of two economically strong regions was determined by the consideration that the existence of power decentralization and elite differentiation requires diversified economies. Competitive politics can hardly be maintained when structural preconditions are absent. Therefore, the puzzle to be explained is why some diversified economies end up with monolithic power structures while others take the path of a competitive polity. According to structural theories of power distribution, both of these regions could be expected to have competitive polities with differentiated elites.[40] Yet the variation in the political processes in each of them is drastic. Tatarstan is characterized by an authoritarian-style, monolithic polity with a unified elite integrated under a single EPN and an absence of any meaningful opposition. Nizhnii Novgorod has evolved in the 1990s into a fragmented polity with recurrent conflict among several EPNs. In addition, state-society relations and popular perceptions of regional elites and political institutions in these two regions differ dramatically. The residents of Nizhnii Novgorod grew increasingly frustrated with regional elites and competitive elections as they played out in the region. The Tatarstani elites, on the other hand, were able to maintain solid popular support for the government and used elections mostly as a mechanism for legitimizing the regime.

One important structural factor that differentiates these cases is related to the presence of oil in Tatarstan and its absence in the Nizhnii Novgorod region. This factor was very important in the context of economic transformation in the Russian regions. As I discuss in chapter 3 the Tatarstani elites used oil resources along with institutional privileges conferred by the Russian Federation as a major foundation for constructing a noncompetitive regime. The oil factor, however, is neither a necessary nor a sufficient condition for the diverging political outcomes in the two cases explored here. As exemplified by the political regime built by Mayor Yuri Luzhkov in Moscow, regional political elites in Russia had resources other than oil and ethnic federal status to construct a noncompetitive regime very similar to that in Tatarstan. These factors should therefore be viewed as structural and enabling rather than explanatory. The difference in political competitiveness levels and, especially, in how political competition played out during the electoral campaigns in the regions were in the end the driving force behind the changing popular perceptions of regional elites and political institutions.

Data and Measurement

Studying crony capitalism is not an easy task. It is a topic commonly reserved for investigative journalism. The biggest challenge is tracing cronyism and identifying EPNs, since by default these informal structures are hidden from public eyes. In my research, therefore, I relied on detailed case studies, combining eclectic methods for data gathering. The more competitive political environment in Nizhnii Novgorod proved better at producing data on informal networks. Unavoidably, well-publicized scandals in the competitive environment allowed for tracing patterns of relations and influence in the region. Competing media outlets produced a wealth of information that was used for this study, verified in interviews with regional experts and cross-checked using different media sources. The noncompetitive polity in Tatarstan is less penetrable because the conflicts are hidden, the opposition is co-opted or "exiled," and the media are tightly controlled. "Soaking and poking" in the republic over the period of many months and even years, reading regional periodicals and interviewing local journalists, experts, and business and government officials allowed for gathering the data on informal relations underlying the republican politics and the economy. These data revealed the cronyism embedded in the political-economic system and made it possible to discuss its political implications in both cases.

The data on voting results in both regions, on the other hand, are publicly available. I used the publications of the Central Electoral Commission of the Russian Federation to trace the results of regional elections. Data on public attitudes on the regional level were more difficult to find. In Nizhnii Novgorod I could rely on published research by local sociologists to investigate the developments in public attitudes and evaluations of regional authorities. In the more closed and controlled political environment of Tatarstan such publications were not readily available. Instead,

I had to use the results of sociological studies sponsored by various government agencies in combination with more informal surveys of public opinion conducted during electoral seasons. Data on regional perceptions of corruption in Russia were produced by a well-known Moscow-based think tank, INDEM, in conjunction with Transparency International.

Theoretical Contributions

This study, an attempt at theory-building, explains the dynamics of post-communist politics by illuminating the vulnerabilities of a politically competitive system in the context of crony capitalism. In a departure from earlier studies and theories, it is not elite centered. It incorporates into the analysis the role of elites and the masses and uses the concept of legitimacy as an important element in the survival of a political system. The main argument is nonlinear. It derives political change from the contradictions of various interacting parts of the system: formal democratic institutions and informal elite structures. In the end, the analysis of political regime transformation advanced in this study tries to integrate the role of the masses, elites, and institutions (both formal and informal), highlighting the role each element plays in effecting political change.

This study illuminates the limits of earlier approaches to explaining crony capitalism and informal institutions and advocates the use of historical institutionalism to understand the origins of postcommunist crony capitalism. The informal institutions that emerged in postcommunist Russia are not simply the legacy of corruption, or *blat,* prevalent under the Soviet system, and neither do they arise automatically in the absence of limited government. There are identifiable new incentive structures that emerged as a result of political and economic reforms and that conditioned the behavior of postcommunist elites confronted with new challenges and new opportunities. An understanding of crony capitalism that integrates this historical aspect allows for a more nuanced analysis of its different manifestations in different parts of the world and in different historical contexts.

This book advances the analysis of crony capitalism in other ways too. Most previous studies of crony capitalism have investigated its economic impact. The phenomenon itself, however, is clearly of both a political and an economic nature. The political implications of crony capitalism might be even more consequential than its economic effects. This study therefore focuses on the political implications of crony capitalism.

Finally, this book adds to conceptual innovation. Most arguments dealing with regime change assume the existence of separate political and economic spheres and the possibility of analyzing politics (the political) as an autonomous sphere. Economic factors enter the analysis at best as exogenous variables. This assumption often appears invalid in the postcommunist context and results in the proliferation of "shallow" explanations that do not take into account the more fundamental realities of life in this part of the world.[41] At least in the type of system that emerged in postcommunistt Russia, one must recognize the fusion of political and economic power and incorporate such an understanding in the analysis of political developments. If anything, this realization was probably the biggest motivating factor for the analysis advanced here.[42]

Outline of the Book

To address the issue of the implications of political competition in the context of crony capitalism, I divided my work into four tasks. The first task involved the analysis of crony capitalism, its nature and its emergence in postcommunist Russia. The first chapter therefore examines what crony capitalism is, reviews various approaches to explaining the origins of crony capitalism, and advocates historical institutionalism as the best approach to make sense of the postcommunist path to cronyism. Based on Russia's experience with postcommunist transformation, I argue that the process of privatization and the newly introduced electoral mechanism created incentives for political-economic collusion that was not checked by the institutions responsible for the rule of law. The first chapter also introduces the concept of informal economic-political networks as the main embodiment of crony capitalism.

The remaining tasks concerned political competition in the context of crony capitalism. In particular, I had to address the questions of who the main actors in political competition are, what the prevailing form of political competition is, and what the implications of political competition are. Chapters 2, 3, and 4 answer these questions. Chapters 2 and 3 extend the analysis of crony capitalism to the regional level in Russia. Based on the analysis of political and economic transformation in Nizhnii Novgorod and the Republic of Tatarstan, I examined two political models of crony capitalism: a fragmented, competitive system and a centralized, noncompetitive system. It emerges that the main actors competing for state resources in the regions are informal economic-political networks. I trace the emergence of main informal elite networks in these two regions and advance an explanation for their different political trajectories.

Chapter 4 focuses on how competition plays out in the regional elections and develops the main argument about the implications of political competition under crony capitalism. It combines two methods for doing that. First, based on the examination of electoral campaigns held in Nizhnii Novgorod and Tatarstan, I illustrate that competitive elections have the unintended effect of undermining the legitimacy of elites and the overall political order because the methods of political struggle rely on publicizing corruption and the use of other manipulative strategies aimed at shaping public opinion. Even the electoral process itself gets delegitimized as a mechanism for elite struggle rather than an institution for promoting public good.

Second, I analyze statistically one of the implications of this argument using the data from forty regions of Russia. Specifically, I test whether political competition is responsible for public perceptions of corruption in the regions while controlling for several other factors that might also influence perceptions of corruption. This analysis illustrates that public perceptions of corruption are indeed higher in more competitive regions.

Chapter 5 examines the evolution of political competition in postcommunist Russia. Consistent with the findings from the previous chapters, the competitive regime under Yeltsin proved unsustainable. The changes in public attitudes toward government and democracy and public perceptions of corruption provide strong support to the argument about the interaction between crony capitalism and political competition. The authoritarian turn under Putin is best comprehended as a logical response by the Russian political elite to the challenges that emerged under

Yeltsin's competitive crony system. Putin broke away from the vicious, destabilizing cycles of rival elites clashing over property and state power and undermining the legitimacy of state authorities and political institutions in the process of these clashes.

The sixth, concluding chapter draws policy implications from this study and situates the argument advanced in this book in the context of broader developments in the postcommunist region. I extend the analysis to other post-Soviet countries, positing the existence of two alternative scenarios of development after the collapse of communism. Those countries in Central Europe and the Baltic region that aligned themselves with the European Union are gradually breaking free from the logic of democratic perils under crony capitalism and evolving in the direction of functioning market economies and sustainable competitive systems. Belarus, on the other hand, after the initial confrontation with competitive crony capitalism, turned in a noncompetitive direction, erecting an authoritarian system based on controlling the economy, mass media, and security forces. Finally, Ukraine represents a special case of a country divided between East and West, between the European Union and Russia. Initially repeating the Russian path of development and facing the problems of competitive crony capitalism, Ukraine in 2004 advanced an alternative scenario of political developments that diverged from the Russian path. The Ukrainian Orange Revolution does not fit fully the pattern identified in this book that highlights an authoritarian solution to the problems of competitive cronyism. It rather draws attention to the role of other factors, national identity related and geopolitical, as crucial for understanding regime transformation. In this last chapter I also discuss the causes and assess the consequences of the Orange Revolution and the potential for Ukraine to overcome the logic of democratic perils under crony capitalism.

CHAPTER 1

Postcommunist Crony Capitalism

Its Nature and Origins

Most pervasive, least observed categories, [are] those which lie
closest to us and which for that very reason escape description.
— Isaiah Berlin, *Sense of Reality*

In summer 1996, after presidential elections that returned
Boris Yeltsin to power in Russia, the infamous oligarch Boris Berezovsky
proclaimed that half of Russia's gross domestic product was controlled
by seven bankers.[1] Following suit, many observers referred to Russia
of the mid-1990s using the informal label *"semibankirshchina"* (rule by
seven bankers).[2] This was the time when not only vast economic resources but also significant political resources fell under the control of
several big businessmen, including, most notably, Berezovsky himself,
who had developed close personal relationships with President Yeltsin
and his family.[3] Later, the term *Family* percolated into the press to refer
to a close-knit group around President Yeltsin that included members of
his administration, his younger daughter, Tatiana, as well as such businessmen as Berezovsky and Abramovich. The Family essentially ruled
Russia on a day-to-day basis, while its frail president only intervened
from time to time with sudden decisions, often regarding the personnel

changes in the government. While journalists sought the details of personal relationships between the main players inside and outside the Kremlin and traced the particular economic and political deals that were made or broken, World Bank analysts used the "state capture" model to investigate this phenomenon.[4] By now it has become common knowledge that from the mid-1990s until the late 1990s, the Russian state appeared to be ruled by a few, very powerful economic actors, the so-called oligarchs.

In this book I characterize the system that emerged in Russia in the 1990s as crony capitalism. The term *crony capitalism,* though not new, is of recent origin. Following the East Asian financial crisis of 1997 it has been used primarily to point out the virtues of American-style capitalism and criticize the East Asian economic model for allowing a close linkage between government and big business.[5] Stephen Haber, exploring Latin American politics and development, defined *crony capitalism* as a system "in which those close to the political authorities who make and enforce policies receive favors that have large economic value."[6] In such systems governments grant certain economic actors favors and entitlements that allow them to earn profits that are higher than those that would prevail under competitive markets or even, in some cases, monopoly rents. These entitlements might comprise tax breaks, cheap credits, and other forms of governmental protection from international and domestic competition. This definition, while very accurate, stresses the economic implications of the system. The important thing to keep in mind is that crony capitalism is neither solely political nor solely economic. Characterized by close ties between economic and political elites, it has significant implications for both spheres. Recent studies have identified variations in the degree to which crony capitalist arrangements can inhibit or promote economic growth and development.[7] Most observers, however, have focused on the economic effect of crony capitalism and have little to say about its political consequences.[8]

How is crony capitalism different from capitalism? Two pivotal differences are related to the rule of law and property rights. In his analysis of capitalism, Max Weber identified "calculable law" as one of the six main prerequisites for modern capitalism: "The capitalistic form of industrial organization, if it is to operate rationally, must be able to depend upon calculable adjudication and administration."[9] In this way Weber connected the rise of capitalism with the rise of the rational state based on modern bureaucracy and argued that modern capitalism can flourish only in the rational state.[10] In contrast, crony capitalist systems lack calculable adjudication and administration. The implementation of the law becomes arbitrary, unpredictable, and dependent on informal relations and factors other than universal rules.

In addition to "calculable law," advanced industrialized democracies—the birthplace of capitalism—have a long tradition of secure property rights. Underpinned by Lockean philosophy postulating that "government has no other end but the preservation of property rights,"[11] Western capitalism long promoted the sanctity of property rights. Private property is protected by a well-established system of rights and such political changes as the rotation of power do not have a direct impact on the owners of wealth and the existence of economic actors. Crony systems differ in that respect. Instead of rights, crony capitalism is based on privileges; the rights to property are weak and transitory. It is a system based on personal exchange, allowing limited economic entry and profit-making to a selected elite group in exchange for political support. It is a system that guarantees property rights to that specific group of selected economic actors. Crony capitalism differs therefore from capitalism in that it lacks secure property rights and "calculable" law applied equally to all social and economic actors.

Finally, the term *capitalism* normally connotes an economic system. Weber, for example, argues that "capitalism is present wherever the industrial provision for the needs of a human group is carried out by the method of enterprise."[12] Crony capitalism, on the other hand, is not merely an economic phenomenon. It is better viewed as an institutional order that encompasses both political and economic spheres and is defined by the type of institutional structures that order human interaction in a society.[13] These institutional structures are informal in nature. Political scientists frequently employ the concepts of clientelism, patronage networks, and corruption to refer to the types of social and political interaction that such informal institutions result in. I opted for the term *crony capitalism* to refer to the prevailing political-economic system in the post-Soviet region because it has been used successfully in other contexts without the negative prejudgments associated with the term *corruption*.

Indeed, crony capitalism is not unique to postcommunist states. It is to be found in Southeast Asia, in Latin America, and in Africa. The unifying features of these regional versions of crony capitalism are the absence of secure property rights and calculable law—the two key features of capitalism. The features that separate them originate in a different historical context and what may be referred to as cultural particularities that shape social, political, and economic interaction in respective societies. Different historical contexts give rise to different manifestations of cronyism. Russia's crony capitalism manifested itself most clearly in the sudden emergence of a group of super-rich businessmen, who were able to take advantage of specific state actions and policies and even wield enormous influence over government policy making. The Family under Yeltsin was only one of the informal elite groups, albeit at the very top of the state, that emerged in Russia. Similar informal elite alliances emerged at all other state levels and branches.[14]

The regional scene became an especially fertile ground for nurturing informal relations between regional authorities and business elites. Starting in the mid-1990s economic elites channeled massive resources into the regional electoral campaigns in support of specific candidates for gubernatorial posts.[15] In exchange, they expected a more favorable political and legal environment, easier access to regional parliaments, and, of course, informal means of lobbying their interests in the regions.[16] The public recognized and reacted to these developments, referring to elite groups that dominated the government as "clans." This term was also adopted by foreign observers and used, for example, by the U.S. diplomat Thomas Graham, who caused an uproar with his straightforward analysis of the Russian political scene published in *Nezavisimaia gazeta*.[17] Some Russian analysts referred to these emergent elite groups as a financial oligarchy,[18] another term that was widely used in Russia during the 1990s. Such high-ranking foreign officials as the managing director of the International Monetary Fund (IMF), Michel Camdessus, warned in the late 1990s about the pervasive crony capitalism afflicting the Russian state.[19]

The political implications of cronyism have been especially apparent in the countries undergoing democratization. While scholars of Latin America and Southeast Asia focused on whether and how crony capitalism explains an underperforming economy, scholars studying democratization processes explored the effect of crony capitalism on political outcomes. Frances Hagopian linked traditional elite networks in Brazil to democratic consolidation problems, while Kathleen Collins analyzed, in a postcommunist setting, how clan-based systems have undermined democratization in Central Asia.[20] Indeed, because the political economies of postcommunist states are frequently dominated by informal elite networks that undermine formal institutions, democratization, and the rule of law, the concept of crony capitalism appears especially useful for examining problems of democratization in these societies.

The examination of crony capitalism as it applies to the postcommunist region yields new theoretical findings driven by new puzzles from this part of the world. Postcommunist democratic transitions have moved the issue of the relationship between crony capitalism and democracy to the forefront. Are the two compatible? What is the impact of crony capitalism on democratic institutions and vice versa? Earlier theorists of crony capitalism suggested provocatively that electoral democracy is incompatible with crony arrangements based on close ties between political and economic elites.[21] New insitutionalist thinking has suggested that the electoral process would always give the disadvantaged elites an opportunity to mobilize and defend their interests.[22] Those who are not among the privileged elites could supposedly use elections to break such crony ties. The assumption underlying this argument—that of a monolithic state selecting one group of economic elites and upholding their rights while leaving the rest disadvantaged—is too restrictive, however. In the postcommunist context, for example, a more accurate representation would involve various groups *within* the state having their preferred economic elites. It is also not clear in this argument why those disadvantaged actors, who could mobilize and win elections, would not reestablish crony arrangements once in power, thus continuing the cycle of cronyism.

Other scholars have linked democracy, governance, and corruption and argued that a democratic institution such as political competition fosters good governance and prevents corruption.[23] When competition is clear, plausible, and vociferous and when it creates a credible threat of power transfer, it could be expected to promote greater government accountability and limit corruption.[24] This argument also envisioned political competition as undermining crony capitalism. In addition, several scholars of Latin American politics have ascertained that political competition has a positive impact on the rule of law and governance by promoting an independent judiciary,[25] strengthening legislatures, and reinforcing trends toward decentralization.[26]

The optimism embedded in these arguments with regard to the impact of competitive elections on governance and crony capitalism (either in the form of greater government accountability or less corruption) derives from the analysis of incentives facing the incumbent government that is confronting the threat of electoral replacement. This is indeed the core of the mainstream democratic theory postulating that competitive elections provide for government accountability because voters can punish unaccountable, corrupt governments by bringing the opposition to power. This influential argument does not always hold up to reality (at least in the short run). Lucan Way and Steven Levitsky have convincingly argued that political competition, or "pluralism by default," could sometimes be a result of state weakness and coexist with ineffective and fragmented governments, not revealing many beneficial consequences.[27] I extend this argument to show that in the short run political competition not only can coexist with ineffective and fragmented governments but also can have damaging effects in at least two realms: (1) discrediting of political elites and (2) undermining the electoral mechanism. As Russia's case demonstrates, these short-term destabilizing effects of political competition might be detrimental in nascent democracies.

Origins of Cronyism: Culture, State Requirements, or Individual Interests?

The body of literature dealing with the phenomenon of crony capitalism has usually relied on such concepts as corruption, clientelism, and informal institutions. Not surprisingly, among the arguments discussed below only one analytical perspective was developed to investigate the phenomenon identified as crony capitalism per se. Nonetheless, in the absence of alternative theorizing of crony capitalism per se, the explanations for the phenomenon can be aggregated around three approaches: cultural, new institutionalist, and historical institutionalist. I focus on a particular, postcommunist version of crony capitalism and advocate the use of the historical institutionalist perspective, drawing attention to the particular historical context of postcommunism and the issues underlying the main political conflicts in this context. The emergence of crony capitalism in postcommunist Russia is comprehended here as the result of interaction between the main political and economic reforms undertaken during the 1990s. The process of property redistribution unleashed by economic reforms created opportunities for enrichment as well as the need to protect newly created private property. Close ties to the state were a crucial resource for securing both aims. The causal arrow went in the opposite direction as well. The electoral mechanism of power transfer introduced as part of the democratization process produced the need for financial resources among politicians, who now had to run expensive election campaigns. Close ties to the wielders of economic resources were therefore important for political aspirants as well as for officeholders who wanted to stay in power. This potential coincidence of interests on the part of political and economic elites created the propensity for informal corroboration between certain individuals, frequently based on old personal connections, newly garnered personal ties, or even consciously built links.

In brief, the process of property redistribution and elections represented the key challenge as well as the main opportunity confronting the Russian state and the elites in this period. Facing these challenges and realizing these opportunities—the very essence of postcommunist politics in Russia—resulted in crony capitalism characterized by the domination of the newly emerged informal political-economic elite groupings. Below I review alternative explanations for the rise of crony capitalism, noting their strengths and analytical limitations, and advocate historical institutionalism by illustrating how privatization and elections created pressures for political-economic collusion. Then, I introduce the concept of economic-political networks, which I view as the main embodiment of crony capitalism in postcommunist Russia.

Cultural Theories

The cultural approach views cronyism and the importance of informal relations on different societal levels as a result of long-standing cultural patterns of behavior in a given society. Corruption and clientelism, based on personalized relationships, are thus culturally embedded practices. Alena Ledeneva's studies of informality in communist, precommunist, and postcommunist Russia use this cultural approach and explore the relevance of such premodern informal institutions as *krugovaia poruka* (collective responsibility) or Soviet-period *telephone justice* in present-day Russia.[28] Along similar lines, the modernization framework views informality and particularity as features of a traditional society that has not yet fully modernized or modernized in such a way as to preserve certain elements of the premodern order.[29]

A slightly different version of the cultural approach grounded in a more recent history attributes the predominance of informal rules in the postcommunist states to the legacy of the communist economy of shortages in which informality served as a crucial mechanism of adjustment to the rigidities of the formal system, which was characterized by top-down administrative control.[30] This "path-dependent" view of informality as a legacy of the communist system is very potent in terms of illuminating the lingering heritage of communism that has acquired the power of a cultural script and continues to influence the behavioral patterns in a society.[31] It would entail an expectation, however, that, given the radically different conditions of a market-oriented economy, such Soviet-acquired cultural legacies would slowly wither away. What was learned under the communist economic system would eventually be replaced by new lessons as people adapted to the new economic system. This expectation does not seem to bear out in Russia. If anything, the role of informality has expanded, which is reflected, among other things, in the growing levels of corruption.[32] Such persistence and even the growing relevance of cronyism point to the existence of present-day incentives conducive of such behavior.

There is an additional reason not to study elites and political regime transformation based solely on the cultural argument. Although a cultural argument might be warranted when considering the society at large, it fails to account for agency. Elite behavior is conventionally understood as strategic in that it is driven by political constraints, incentives, and opportunities. Even if culture ordinarily affects elite decision making by providing a normative scheme within which the decisions are taken, political actors are still most concerned with practical outcomes and react to the more immediate incentive structures. The "rule of informality" reflected in terms of the economic-political elite groups that emerged in the post-Soviet era is, therefore, better understood as an appropriate (rational) reaction to the historical opportunity structures confronting the elites. Reverting to culture to account for informality at the higher echelons of power means, in essence, letting the strategically acting elites off the hook.

New Institutionalism

The new institutionalist approach advanced by Haber, Maurer, and Razo suggested, provocatively, that crony capitalism is an alternative solution to the government commitment problem.[33] In advanced capitalist countries the problem of credible commitment to protecting property rights is resolved by setting up limited government that respects universal individual political and economic rights. In countries characterized by political instability, on the other hand, the commitment problem is resolved through informal arrangements between political authorities and economic elites. This happens, these analysts suggest, because limited government operating through sets of self-enforcing institutions that create multiple veto points in the decision structure of the government (system of checks and balances) is a very rare phenomenon.[34] Most governments are not limited by institutional arrangements, even if some institutions of checks and balances are formally in place. Instead, they rule arbitrarily and have discretion whether to follow the formal rules or not. However, such governments also face the commitment problem and need to guarantee the security of property rights to asset holders. In brief, crony capitalism is an alternative and very common solution to the commitment problem in countries where limited government is absent. There, the government guarantees security of property rights to a particular subset of property holders, thus making state guarantees particularistic rather than universal.

Haber's approach provides a solid starting point for thinking about crony capitalism and is specifically relevant for postcommunist states that faced the government commitment dilemma anew with the transition to a market economy. It does not address the issue of the origins of cronyism, however. As with any other problem, the existence of the commitment problem does not necessitate the emergence of its solution. Viewing the collusion between political and economic elites as a means for the government to solve the commitment problem in the absence of limited government draws attention away from the fact that the absence of limited government is directly reflected in the crony arrangements. In addition, how would new institutionalists explain the existence of some features of crony capitalism in Western countries, which have supposedly solved the government commitment problem through limited government? To the extent that some degree of cronyism is present in these countries,[35] it cannot be understood as a solution to the commitment problem; it must be treated as originating in different conditions. Such concerns notwithstanding, informal or crony arrangements do play a role in reassuring economic and political actors and reducing transaction costs for those inside such arrangements.[36] In recognizing that functional aspect of crony capitalism, the new institutionalist approach provides a more neutral view that is ordinarily condemned and helps us to understand the noncultural reasons for its prevalence in many parts of the world.

A different version of a new institutionalist approach was advanced through the theory of natural state and limited access orders. In an ambitious effort to explain why most nations failed to achieve sustained economic growth, North, Wallis, and Weingast attempted to integrate political and economic theory differentiating between three main types of social orders: the primitive, the natural state, and the open access.[37] The "natural state" and "limited access" orders introduced in that analysis closely correspond to the crony capitalism examined here. These terms refer to a system of privilege, characterized by personal exchange and limited political and economic entry. This theory views the natural state as a natural solution to the fundamental problem of providing social order. The natural state comes into being as a mechanism of state survival: rulers use economic rent to create credible commitments among elites to support the current regime and provide order, thereby creating political security and preventing disorder and violence.[38]

Natural state theory closely approximates Haber's theory of crony capitalism as a solution to the government commitment dilemma, though it takes a broader view of the benefits provided by limited access orders. The analytical challenges of natural state theory are also similar to the ones discussed with regard to Haber's approach. The recognition of certain functional effects of a system cannot be taken as a reason for the emergence and the existence of the system. North, Wallis, and Weingast view the natural state as an almost automatic response to the problem of social disorder.[39] Such a view of the natural state emerging "naturally" ignores the different political variants of crony capitalism, the construction of which is very far from being natural and automatic. As I discuss in the next two chapters, crony capitalism can be both competitive and noncompetitive, and this has large implications for political stability and order in the society. The second problematic assumption in the new institutionalist view of crony capitalism is that the state is a monolithic whole, expending privileges to a specific group of elites, the dominant coalition. There is no space for a more fragmented state, with different subsections having their preferred elite groups.

Finally, both of the neoinstitutionalist arguments operate at a high level of generalization that does not allow for distinguishing specific models or versions of crony capitalism or "limited access orders." In the analysis by North, Wallis, and Weingast (2009) crony capitalism and limited access orders refer to all systems that are not "open access orders" characterized by limited governments. They develop an elaborate explanation for how open access orders emerge; the limited access orders, on the other hand, are "natural" and do not require any special explanation. The category "limited access orders" therefore turns out to be residual, emerging by default. If one allows for different types of limited access orders, however, their emergence requires careful historical examination. In this study about the postcommunist brand of crony capitalism, therefore, I focus on the postcommunist political and economic context.

Historical Institutionalism

Historical institutionalists focus on the enduring effect of institutions and political patterns emerging in response to fundamental challenges confronting the key political actors and societies at specific points in history.[40] Accordingly, manifested in the rise of informal economic-political networks, crony capitalism in Russia is intimately linked to the unique challenges and opportunities confronting the Russian state and its elites in the period following the collapse of the previous political and economic system. The most crucial challenges and opportunities of postcommunism derived from the new mechanisms of redistribution of power and property and were therefore closely linked to the process of privatization and the electoral method of power transfer.

Privatization that ensued from the dismantling of the socialist economic system represented a critical juncture in postcommunist Russia, underpinning central political struggles and conditioning political and economic outcomes.[41] In effect, it opened avenues for the demonopolization of key resources and, thereby, for the decentralization of power, which was reflected in the emergence of autonomous elites. The existence of autonomous elites, with their independent resource bases, cleared the way for oligarchic struggles for political power, since only by being represented in the government could these newly emerging elites ensure the safety of their ownership or obtain additional ownership. Privatization occurred in the absence of institutions guaranteeing safety of property rights. The concept of private property itself was foreign for entire generations that grew up under communism. In this context only direct links to the state or, sometimes, the mafia that controlled means of violence along with the state provided the new owners with certain guarantees of their possessions.

The electoral institution introduced as the basis of the postcommunist political system introduced additional incentives for politicians to collude with economic elites. Top state officials needed to obtain political and financial support to run expensive electoral campaigns. In this situation, having resourceful allies controlling financial assets was of primary importance for political victory. Not to be discounted is the motive of personal enrichment, which was quickly turning into a new norm in the context of emerging capitalism. Additional cash infusions and favors afforded for securing the backing of regional elites were all part and parcel of cronyism in this new political and economic context. In brief, I argue that this mutual coincidence of political and economic interests in the pursuit of power and wealth in the transforming society lies at the origins of crony capitalist arrangements in Russia.

This explanation brings to the center of attention the individual incentives of political and economic agents that emerged in a particular institutional context of transformation. As such, it aims at accounting both for structures that opened opportunities and raised constraints and for the agency operating within those structures. It is not an entirely new effort. Venelin Ganev called for the investigation of "historically constituted opportunity structures" that shape strategic behavior of the elites and, reversing the Tillyan model of state building, analyzed the rise of postcommunist crony capitalism in the framework of the new "dominant elite project," referring to it as "extraction from the state."[42] In his framework struggle over property becomes the defining moment of postcommunism.[43] The approach to crony capitalism developed here allows for broadening this view and considering the struggle over property and the struggle over power as two equally important and interacting dynamics that defined postcommunism.

Struggle for Property in Postcommunist Russia

The privatization process in Russia was of the systemic type intended to "reshape the entire society by fundamentally altering economic and political institutions and by transforming economic and political interests."[44] Systemic privatization involves restructuring of the institutional arrangements of the society with the aim of shifting the mechanisms of social control "from overt bureaucratic and political structures to the less accountable and more subtle forces of the market."[45] The process of privatization in the postcommunist world was thus part and parcel of the overall radical political shift away from communism; it represented the "dominant elite project" of the times.[46] Its political significance, that is, creating new interests for advocating a new political order, far outweighed its radical economic impact (at least for such policy makers as Anatoly Chubais, father of the mass privatization program in Russia).[47]

In its spontaneous version privatization started under Gorbachev, several years before the official program of mass privatization conducted by the Russian government during 1992–94. The large-scale redistribution of state property did not end there, however; property reform continued, and in 1995–96 some of the best pieces of state property ended up in the hands of a few well-connected bankers. Even the lavish "loans-for-shares" deal did not bring privatization to an end. Contrary to expectations that ownership patterns would stabilize, the struggle over property continued in different but always intense forms in the late 1990s and in the new era under President Putin.

Different explanations have been offered by scholars to explain the absence of stable property rights and the continuing struggle over property in Russia. David Woodruff blamed it on the perceived illegitimacy of privatization, which precluded any kind of accommodation between the stakeholders in state enterprises and potential shareholders, thus opening the Pandora's box of future contestations of property rights.[48] Indeed, Russia's privatization was referred to by some analysts as "piratization."[49] Andrew Barnes analyzed the actions of the main actors fighting over property as responding to new incentives and constraints and thus as a rational response to increasing opportunities.[50] Whatever the ultimate answer to this grand puzzle of secure property rights in postcommunist Russia is, I explore here only some of its implications. One clear implication is the perpetuation of crony capitalism and the informal elite networks dominating the political and economic sphere because, just like privatization, the struggle over property does not occur without state agents. Political power or connections to state institutions—courts, lawmaking, police—serve as a resource and an instrument of promoting someone's economic interests. Therefore, the continuing struggle over property has also promoted close ties between big business representatives and government officials. These ties were necessary to ensure continuing ownership of the assets as well as acquisition of new assets.

The most visible early outcome of privatization in the mid-1990s—the rise of the oligarchs, exceptionally rich and powerful businessmen with close connections to the state—has been described in detail by others.[51] The oligarchs wielded enormous influence in politics during the Yeltsin era. Since then, however, their role in politics has changed.[52] The balance of power has shifted in favor of the state. At the same time, the deep and intense interconnection of the political and economic spheres, especially with regard to property redistribution and the pattern of preferential treatment accorded to selected economic actors, is still present. Crony capitalism, therefore, can still be viewed as the foundation of the political-economic order that emerged in Russia.

Elections and Political Stakes in Russia

Struggle over property is central to the postcommunist era. But a view of the political economy that focuses solely on property misrepresents the dynamics of social interaction by overemphasizing the greedy and material-wealth-oriented aspects of the human character. As noted by Aristotle, man is by nature a political animal: *homo politicus* and not only *homo economicus*. The pursuit of power is as central to human endeavors as the pursuit of wealth. The opportunities and constraints provided by the new institution (elections) installed for the pursuit of power represented the political dimension promoting crony capitalism under postcommunism. As a central and, in fact, indispensable institution of democracy, elections have acquired an unassailable reputation and are assumed to be valuable on their own. A more careful exploration of the democratic theory literature, however, warns against such simplistic assessments by pointing to a host of other conditions and environmental variables that need to be present in order to ensure democracy. The hard lesson learned by many countries of the Third Wave of democratization is that elections are only one of many instruments used to organize a political system.[53] Like any instrument, it is neither good nor bad in itself. Much depends on how and with what aims it is used. As posited by a Russian legislator, "elections and representation are two different institutions."[54] Indeed, in the Russian circumstances competitive elections "did not produce an effective and accountable democracy."[55] To the contrary, competitive elections not only coexisted with the corrupt system but also, as argued by other observers of Russian politics, induced elite strategies that contributed to the failure of democracy.[56]

One significant reason that promoted corruption was the need for electoral resources. In established democracies, political parties play a central role in the provision of electoral resources. In Russia, however, in the years that followed the introduction of a multiparty system, political parties failed to monopolize political space. Those who ran for political office rarely turned to political parties. Instead, they turned to financial-industrial groups or created political machines that became electoral substitutes for political parties in providing the candidates the resources necessary to win.[57] In brief, the electoral mechanism of power transfer created an additional logic prompting the formation of informal elite groups. To the extent that electoral campaigns depended on financial resources that party organizations could not provide, political aspirants turned exclusively to the wealthy. The owners of economic resources, in turn, had their own formidable reasons to play politics. As discussed above, the struggle over property did not end with the official privatization programs of the 1990s. State institutions were determining the rules of the game that governed the struggle over property; these rules created motives and opportunities for continuing the process of property redistribution.[58] The economic players therefore benefited enormously from their close connections to the state both in terms of acquiring new resources and privileges and in terms of keeping the ones they had.

One of the most critical effects of the instability of property rights was on the intensity of political competition. The continuing struggle over property enhanced the stakes involved in electoral victories because the forces controlling the state influenced access to property. The high stakes involved in who controls the state therefore gravely intensified political competition, conditioning the methods of campaigning and raising the financial requirements of elections. Due to the overwhelming predominance of the executive branch of power in Russia's political system, political competition was especially acute in presidential and gubernatorial elections. Both on the national and the subnational level, the costs of electoral campaigns in Russia soared through the 1990s.[59] A new, multimillion-dollar market of political consultants emerged, along with numerous think tanks and institutes. A plethora of methods and techniques used in electoral campaigns under the label "political technologies" became increasingly elaborate. Negative PR and dirty tricks became a norm not only at national but also at regional elections. The high stakes were reflected not only in the costliness of campaigns and the elaborate methods created to compete in the elections. In extreme cases, elections could involve violence, murders, provocations, jail terms, and other threats deriving from the potential transfer of power.

In short, the change of government under crony capitalism is not a mere change of leadership but also a change of rules, access to resources, and practically an overthrow of an existing regime of political and economic arrangements. The forms of and the effects from political competition under such a system therefore differ dramatically from the forms and effects of competition in "open-access orders," that is, established democracies, with secure property rights and the rule of law.

Cliques, Clans, and EPNs

I view the Russian political scene as populated by informal elite networks,[60] but this does not mean that presidents, governors, political parties, parliaments, or even individual politicians and businessmen do not matter and should be excluded from analysis. The analysis of Russian political transformation taking into account these institutions as well as taking a more individualist approach to studying the dynamics of Russian politics has already enriched our understanding of postcommunist Russia.[61] The consequences of a polity dominated by informal elite networks, on the other hand, have been mostly debated by journalists;[62] they have rarely been subjected to a serious scholarly inquiry, except in the studies of Central Asian political transformation.[63] Incorporating the existence of such economic-political groupings into the analysis of political transformation in Russia is long overdue. In a polity dominated by such elite networks, political pluralism is manifested in power competition among these EPNs.[64]

The role of informal personal networks has been mostly underestimated by scholars studying the new Russian state. This omission is surprising, given earlier studies that focused on the informal underpinnings of the Soviet state.[65] Informal networks have played an essential role in the early years of Soviet state building and regime formation and influenced the dynamics of the Soviet state's collapse.[66] Their emergence and influence in the Soviet system has been attributed to the specific politico-administrative circumstances and the general conditions of life "which encouraged everyone to rely heavily on personal connections and mutual favors for their daily bread, security, and any luxuries that were going."[67] These circumstances have, of course, changed after the collapse of the Soviet system, but politics dominated by informal elite networks has emerged as a crucial characteristic of postcommunist Russia. These informal structures are well recognized on the level of popular perceptions. Since the infamous 1995 loans-for-shares program that promoted Yeltsin's reelection and led to the redistribution of some of the most attractive pieces of state property within a small circle of well-connected entrepreneurs, the terms *oligarch* and *clan* have found their inalienable place in the popular vernacular. A more careful and systematic conceptualization and analysis of the origins and functioning of these structures, as well as the development of theories about their impact on political transformation, remains an intellectual priority for scholars of postcommunism.

What exactly constitutes an EPN? It is an informal institutional arrangement through which different elite groups compete for power and wealth. These networks represent a crucial informal power resource and a route "along which resources are exchanged, information is obtained, and collaborative actions are planned."[68] As opposed to Soviet patronage networks, which served mainly as means of elite recruitment and were confined to the political sphere,[69] postcommunist EPNs emerged in the process of the transformation of property relationships and became the means of acquiring and maintaining private economic wealth. The close ties between government officials and business representatives embodied in the EPNs led some analysts to compare Russia's new system with the feudal system.[70] This analogy appears too far-fetched: the differences in political organization and in the social and economic institutions of postcommunism are much greater than their similarities to feudal institutions. A more contemporary notion of crony capitalism aptly captures the essence of the system characterized by fusion of the economic and political spheres.

These elite networks operate in society but compete for access to state resources and rule making. More precisely, they straddle both the private and public arenas. If a network lacks a close connection to the state, it aims at developing that connection and getting access to the state. In most cases the networks already have state links. Is there really a need for creating this new concept of EPNs instead of simply relying on already existing terms describing postcommunist elite groups or those derived from the literature concerned with crony capitalism? The existing theorizing on crony capitalism has not yet generated many new concepts. While the context of East Asian crony capitalism produced such established terms as *chaebols* (in South Korea) and *keiretsu* (in Japan) to refer to large corporate conglomerates that have close ties to the government, investigation of cronyism in Latin America, for example, has not resulted in any particular label for colluding politicians and businessmen.[71] With chaebols and keiretsu being too context-specific to be applied to the Russian context, framing the discussion in terms of collusive elite behavior detracts from the systemic character of such groups' operation within a transforming polity. A reference to a specific concept, such as economic-political networks, elaborated in regard to these groups, allows for recognizing the institutionalization of cronyism and highlights the idea that power is fungible.

How do we know an EPN when we see one? An EPN is a group of elite members—politicians and businessmen—linked through special relationships of mutual support. These groups began forming under Gorbachev's reforms, developed and reformed during the subsequent large-scale transformation of property relationships under Yeltsin. Personal relations and networks played a key role in the success of the first wave of entrepreneurs in the period 1988–91.[72] The role of connections and access to state resources had increased in the next wave, as the *nomenklatura* (the upper level Soviet bureaucracy) joined young *kooperativshchiki* (small entrepreneurs, managers of cooperatives) in the pursuit of wealth and property, in the course of which the old practice of *blat* was replaced with higher-level and better-organized corruption.[73] A speedy privatization process spearheaded by the Russian state starting in 1992 resulted in the sudden and rapid emergence of a small number of super-rich individuals. Close ties to state officials or even direct control of various state ministries was vital for such sudden enrichment.

The accumulation of wealth in private hands was only the first step. The new owners needed to secure their rights. And close ties to the state were vital for keeping property. Not everyone in Russian society supported privatization and especially the way it was accomplished. By the mid-1990s most of the Russian public perceived privatization as illegitimate and corrupt. Chubais, one of the architects of the voucher program in Russia, became one of the least trusted and most hated political figures in the country. The new owners were therefore deeply interested in who controlled the state. This interest was not one-sided. The power transfer in new Russia was governed by the electoral process. The operation of elections as the key institution for selecting public officials necessitated a search for allies and financial support to fund electoral campaigns. The links between the state officials administering property redistribution and the businessmen who took advantage of this process were therefore a likely outcome of the environment characterized by the new rules: elections and privatization. Hence the EPNs manifested the dual match of interests and the synergy among the politicians desiring reelection and the economic actors seeking property and its protection. They served as the main vehicle for the advancement of group members' interests.

The ties among the key actors in the network can have a different history and a different degree of intensity, depending on the degree of personal trust among the network's members. The most cohesive networks are based on family relationships; then an EPN resembles a kinship-based clan.[74] The next factor contributing to a network's cohesion and longevity is friendship. EPNs can be made up of long-term friends, colleagues, and associates with well-developed personal ties. Regional or geographic association among individuals is another factor that contributes to evoking trust and, in turn, to a more cohesive EPN. The least cohesive and most short-lived EPNs are based on a commonality of interest at a particular moment in time. These are networks driven by short-term political or economic expediency and are likely to quickly break up with the evolving context.

There is an internal evolutionary logic to EPNs' development. Just as politicians are generally driven by power motives and businesspeople are profit maximizers, these informal groups are characterized by some kind of "will to domination" or a hegemonic drive. This expansionary tendency is essential for the advancement of the interests of network members because the acquisition of power requires financial resources and access to and protection of wealth is impossible without state support. In this regard it appears useful to apply Mann's analysis of the basis of social power and his distinction between political, military, economic, and ideological bases of power.[75] Similar categories appear in Giddens's distinction of four types of power institutions: symbolic orders/modes of discourse, economic institutions, law/modes of sanction/repression, and political institutions.[76] EPNs reveal the tendency to expand or at least seek expansion in all four spheres. The EPN that has accumulated a certain amount of power resources would struggle for obtaining the resources that it does not yet possess. The dominating (hegemonic) EPN would have access to administrative resources (thus representatives in government structures), financial basis (capital in the form of banks and profitable enterprises), media sources (as an ideological resource), and security forces, which in 1990s Russia often took the form of protection rackets (the so-called roof, or *krysha*).[77] The actual networks might lack some of the aforementioned components, but they reveal the tendency to acquire them because they are confronted by other networks seeking expansion and are therefore at risk of being outcompeted.

Based on informal, personal relations, EPNs are not public institutions. Therefore, their identification is complicated. The networks' existence is most clearly revealed during competitive electoral campaigns, which lead to publicizing compromising materials about informal links and relationships, illegal deeds, and corruption. Although making such information public is itself driven by the logic of political struggle and the information is therefore far from trustworthy, certain assessments as to "who pays for whom," or which economic actors finance the electoral campaigns of specific politicians, can be made. The second venue for identification is the sphere of property redistribution ("who gets what") and, more generally, the sphere of economic policies, which reveal whose interests and property are protected, who gets tax breaks and other governmental favors. Finally, criminal cases initiated against and targeting specific individuals accused of corruption and other misdeeds can also be highly revealing of interelite rivalries and clashing interests.

Informal, personalized policy making in Russia started at the very top, at the level of the first Russian president, but did not end at the higher echelons of federal politics.[78] Political developments in Russia's hinterland reveal similar impotence of the formal institutions of democracy and their subversion by informal elite structures. While the national-level EPNs in Russia are relatively well known, having received much attention in the press in the 1990s (when the media was relatively free), the identification of regional networks requires more local expertise. The biggest advantage of studying crony capitalism on the regional level, however, is the fact that it allows for analyzing and distinguishing between the two political forms of cronyism: competitive and noncompetitive. While most regions in Russia have been a battlefield for multiple EPNs (similar to

Russia's national model during the 1990s), a few regions have been able to avoid fragmentation and maintain the predominance of a single EPN, in which major economic and political resources are concentrated. These regions developed a noncompetitive, monopolistic variety of crony capitalism. The implications of this difference are explored in chapter 4; in the next two chapters I illustrate the emergence of these two forms of cronyism.

Why Networks?

Why should we pay attention to informal networks as opposed to individuals or formal political groups such as political parties? After all, there are identifiable key politicians and political parties operating in Russia and its regions. What do we gain by interpreting the political landscape as structured by informal elite networks? There are two main advantages to this strategy. First, it brings us closer to the public's view of political life. The Russian public tends to view the top echelons of power, as well as the middle and lower echelons of the Russian state, as populated by self-serving clans rather than individual politicians. While in some situations scholars might benefit from taking an outsider look and advance an interpretation based on a lens different from the one used by lay observers, an incorporation of what is perceived as common understanding or common knowledge seems essential for scholars trying to make sense of specific sociopolitical dynamics that involve the issues of legitimacy and voter attitudes. After all, to a large extent legitimacy is in the eyes of the beholder, and voter attitudes and behavior are rooted in and motivated by how ordinary people interpret events. Putting oneself in their shoes might therefore be necessary if one is to give a meaningful explanation of the public behavior and attitudes. Understanding and incorporating such a view therefore helps in deciphering more accurately the roots of uneasy state-society relations in Russia and comprehending political attitudes on the mass level.

Second, informal networks seem to be the most relevant and accurate representation of institutional structures that matter in Russia. Such formal political institutions as political parties, for example, which commonly play a key role in the political life of democratic states, were not the most important institutions in the Russian political system. The economic-political networks challenged the relevance of political parties in Russia by, in essence, substituting them.[79] No wonder, then, that neither the first nor the second president of Russia identified clearly with a specific political party, preferring to remain above parties. The role of political parties was undermined even further under Putin as the Kremlin strategists muscled out oppositional parties from the political scene and created new political parties controlled from the Kremlin.[80] Parties are better viewed now as an instrument in the hands of the political establishment rather than as independent players in politics.

The choice between the other two alternatives—individuals or elite groups—as the main competing actors is even more challenging. A recent study by Regina Smyth, for example, suggests that individual candidates' electoral strategies matter for the ultimate success of democratic consolidation in Russia, thus promoting the merits of an individual-based analysis of transformation outcomes.[81] Furthermore, elite networks are not limited to postcommunist countries. Even in advanced Western democracies politicians have election teams, advisers, and consultants as well as wealthy donors and financial contributors. Even in the West there are those economic groups that benefit more from the victory and specific policies promised by one or another candidate. Therefore, competing *groups* of interest are present everywhere, not only in Russia. The reality of crony capitalism in Russia, however, makes things different. The interest vested in associating with a politician in the West is different from what such an association might allow for in a crony system.

This difference can be best illuminated if we look at the issue of property rights. As noted earlier, capitalist systems in advanced industrialized democracies rely on secure property rights, whereas crony capitalist systems are based on privileges. Rights to property in crony systems are weak and transitory. This attribute of crony capitalism increases dramatically the stakes involved in association with a politician. In a crony system links to the state are essential for the very existence of economic actors and for preserving or obtaining property. For those in elite networks it is often a matter of survival rather than merely some material advantage. Therefore, the competition for state power is unrestrained in such systems and, in places with limited economic resources, can result in violence, even murder. Personal links and informal support become the most important channels for advancing the political and economic interests of specific elite members. The informal networks and competition among them therefore become the key determining factor of major political and economic outcomes in such systems. The concept of networks allows for capturing this reality and incorporating it in the analysis of political change.

CHAPTER 2

Fragmented Cronyism

The Case of Nizhnii Novgorod

Scholarly exploration of Russia's regional politics thrived during the 1990s. Driven by the process of decentralization under Yeltsin, it developed into a field of its own, producing numerous studies of patterns in regional development in Russia.[1] Many analysts of regional politics in Russia view the local scene as an arena characterized by the operation of competing groups of political and economic elites.[2] I share this interpretation and explore these informal elites groupings, or EPNs, that represent the most important actors and the embodiment of crony capitalism in the regions. This chapter takes a first step in the exploration of different political forms of crony capitalism. Based on the analysis of political and economic transformation in Nizhnii Novgorod, I trace the emergence of main informal elites networks in this region and examine the emergence of a fragmented, competitive model of cronyism. In chapter 3 I examine the case of the Republic of Tatarstan to uncover the origins of a centralized, noncompetitive model of cronyism.

The emergence of a politically fragmented crony capitalist system in Nizhnii Novgorod had roots in institutional and economic policy. It was propelled, on the one hand, by a rapid privatization and a set of liberal economic reforms under the region's first governor, Boris Nemtsov, that resulted in the creation of autonomous economic actors. The political fragmentation in Nizhnii[3] was also encouraged by the existence of an autonomous municipal branch that under certain circumstances could become a political challenge to the regional authorities. In the broader Russian regional context Nizhnii Novgorod's fragmented system appears to be a typical case.

"Local Heroes" Turning into Local Cronies? The Rise of Competing Networks in Nizhnii Novgorod

Located about 250 miles east of Moscow, Nizhnii Novgorod has always been one of the more visible regions in Russia, frequently discussed in the national press (in more positive terms in the early 1990s and progressively more negatively in the late 1990s). The region's road to fame started with the November 1991 appointment by Yeltsin of a new governor, the young physicist and ecological activist Boris Nemtsov, who became one of the most famous and popular Russian governors in the early 1990s as well as the nucleus of the first visible economic-political network in the region. Nemtsov's governorship, which lasted from 1991 to 1997, laid the foundation for the ensuing political fragmentation in the region, in terms of creating both economically autonomous actors and personal discords and rivalries that played out dramatically after Nemtsov left the region.

Nizhnii under Nemtsov

Nemtsov came to power as a political outsider after the collapse of the Communist Party in the aftermath of the August 1991 putsch (for biographical information, see Appendix 1). As across all Russia and the Soviet Union before August 1991, the main line of political opposition in the region was "democrats versus partocrats."[4] After August 1991 the "partocrats" lost their direct influence on the political scene, while the *obkom* (regional committee of the Communist Party that used to be the main political actor) simply disappeared as an autonomous actor. In this context Nemtsov was able to negotiate with the regional Soviet (council of people's deputies) and find a compromise solution, which allowed him to win the nomination for the governorship. There were other strong candidates, in particular, the democrat Igor Petiashin, whose nomination was supported by most democrats in the regional Soviet.[5] However, Nemtsov was backed by the majority in the regional Soviet, including former communists and influential enterprise directors.[6] In addition, Nemtsov enjoyed the strong support of the Russian president, Boris Yeltsin, who appointed him in August 1991 to serve as presidential representative in the region.[7] After he became governor in November 1991, Nemtsov combined these two positions.

Despite the fact that Nemtsov came to power as a result of bargaining with the regional Soviet,[8] the regime did not evolve as an "elite settlement" but revealed a strong tendency toward monocentrism.[9] The basis of Nemtsov's authority as a governor lay, ultimately, not in the compromise he reached with regional elites but in the support he had from the Russian president, who appointed him to this position.[10] It appeared initially that Nemtsov supported regional enterprises and the regional economy, at least indirectly, through his active policies aimed at improving the regional image abroad using his personal appeal among foreign leaders and the support he had on the highest level in Moscow. During the early 1990s Nizhnii Novgorod oblast attracted much attention from international organizations and various foreign companies, which resulted in numerous foreign investment projects.[11] To address the problems of the defense sector, Nemtsov created a conversion fund to help finance the process of shifting production from defense to consumer goods.[12] Also, under his leadership, the region witnessed the revival of the famous trade fair Nizhegorodskaia Yarmarka, which attracted attention from other regions in Russia and from other countries. Overall, however, Nemtsov's economic policies were driven more by a market-oriented ideology than pragmatism and local interests. He never perceived the directors of large regional enterprises as an organic support base for his regime and never attempted to maintain their position in the regional economy.

The role of these regional enterprise directors in the politics and economics of the region was crucial in the Soviet period. Nizhnii Novgorod is a highly industrialized region, with approximately 30 to 40 percent of its workforce in the defense sector in the early 1990s.[13] The civil sector of the economy included among other entities a large automobile combine, the Gor'kii Automobile Factory (GAZ); significant chemical industry in the town of Dzerzhinsk; and an oil-processing plant, called Norsi, in

Kstovo. All these industries, which in Soviet times were under the jurisdiction of Union ministries, had enormous political clout by virtue of the socioeconomic role they played in the lives of hundreds of thousands of citizens (not to mention the role of defense industries in state security).[14] Being an outsider to the regional government, Nemtsov did not have any preexisting support among these key regional players. His economic policies, in turn, only foreclosed any potential for building an alliance with "red directors." Driven by the ideology of liberal reform and the pursuit of state withdrawal from the economy—in accord with Yeltsin's national policies—he undermined the power of this group and failed to secure their support.

According to a regional expert, relations between Nemtsov and the directors could be described as one of "guarded neutrality," amounting to "diplomatic recognition" but not mutual support and cooperation.[15] The red directors had to consent to his leadership, which had been imposed by the Russian president. Despite their reluctant acceptance, they never joined the ranks of his active supporters.[16] This was not surprising. The red directors were the product of the Soviet system, socialized and accustomed to working in very different political and economic conditions, whereas Nemtsov represented the new generation of reformist democrats. More important, Nemtsov's policies went directly against the interests of the enterprise managers. Nemtsov supported a radical transformation of the economy and strongly promoted privatization on all levels. As a member of the Highest Economic Council of Russia's Supreme Council, he even participated in the writing of the privatization law.[17] The enterprise managers sought to maintain control over their firms, but Nemtsov was opposed to the insider privatization that became a widespread practice in other regions.

One of the first incidents that revealed the absence of strategic partnership and cooperation between the regional administration and the management of large regional enterprises involved a conflict between Nemtsov and the director general of GAZ, Boris Vidiaev. Nemtsov did not agree with GAZ management's development and privatization strategies. Management wanted control over 50 percent of the company's stock, but Nemtsov supported another scheme, according to which the shares had to be sold openly to outsiders. Furthermore, Nemtsov wanted to change from producing luxury Volga cars to small vans, whereas Vidiaev insisted on maintaining production the way it was.[18] Fighting for control over the enterprise, Vidiaev used the funds intended for the development of a new product to buy the company's shares.[19] Furthermore, both sides became involved in information warfare, with each party trying to mobilize public support.[20] Ultimately, Nemtsov won. He lobbied the central government to create an independent commission to investigate the GAZ situation. The commission concluded that the enterprise's management indeed misused the federal funds allocated to the company. Following the investigation, Vidiaev was replaced as director general of the company by Nikolai Pugin, a former Soviet Union minister of the automobile industry and the former director general of GAZ.[21] Due to his enormous popularity among the workers, Vidiaev was allowed to remain as chair of the board of directors; however, this was a formal position without any real influence.[22]

A similarly radical approach was pursued by Nemtsov in the agricultural sector. His liberalizing policies in the rural areas resulted in marginalization of the managers of state and collective farms. In his encouragement of rapid privatization of regional enterprises and farmlands, Nemtsov, like most of Russia's liberal reformers, probably expected that privatization would result in a creation of a middle class that would have a vested interest in maintaining the political regime in its democratic form. This was the primary ideological argument for the rapid process of privatization that swept through Russia.[23] Alas, in Nizhnii Novgorod the main result was the enactment of short-term enrichment schemes by the new owners, which resulted in insolvency of many of the privatized enterprises.

Lessons from Rapid Privatization

The rapid privatization undertaken in Nizhnii resulted in disastrous outcomes for the regional economy. A telling example is the effect on the chemical enterprises in Dzerzhinsk. The town of Dzerzhinsk is located only forty kilometers from the regional capital; it is the site of a major chemical complex that consists of eight plants, including Orgsteklo, Korund, Zaria, and Kaprolaktam. In June 1994, during privatization, Orgsteklo and Korund, which were experiencing financial problems, came under the control of a Moscow-based financial-industrial group, Ruskhim.[24] The transfer of the federal packages of company stocks to Ruskhim was done with the condition that Ruskhim would invest U.S. $154 million in the development of these companies. This condition, however, was never met. Ruskhim's management of these companies caused a major crisis involving the working collectives of these companies, the municipal authorities of Dzerzhinsk, and, ultimately, Nizhnii Novgorod's regional authorities. It appeared that instead of developing the companies and leading them out of their precarious financial condition, Ruskhim simply used them for short-term enrichment. The companies' products were sold through trading houses monopolized by Ruskhim, with the profits accumulated in bank accounts in Moscow while the companies were drowning in a heightening financial crisis.[25] The losses were externalized on other regional companies such as the joint-stock company Norsi, one of the main suppliers of Kaprolaktam.[26] By the end of 1996, when wages had not been paid to the workers at these enterprises for more than ten months, Aleksandr Romanov, mayor of Dzerzhinsk, started an information campaign against Ruskhim.[27] Later, in early 1997, the regional authorities also became involved. Nemtsov (who was soon to leave for Moscow) admitted that transferring control of these companies to Ruskhim had been a major mistake on the part of the regional administration.[28]

The transfer of these companies to Ruskhim's management and the absence of a coordinating body that would control their operation resulted in two major negative consequences. First, it allowed for a new owner to strip the companies of their value. Second, it broke the ties between the interdependent chemical plants of the entire Dzerzhinsk complex. It soon became evident that the new owners were not interested in the long-term well-being and profitability of these enterprises. Although the arrival of Ruskhim in Dzerzhinsk appears to have been orchestrated from Moscow rather than driven by the regional government, Nemtsov supported the privatization of the chemical plants. It went along with his policies of economic liberalization and of lifting state controls over the economy. He did not comprehend the continuing importance of state interference in certain strategic sectors of the regional economy and underestimated the problems of contract enforcement in Russia's emerging market economy. His energetic pursuit of rapid economic liberalization in all sectors of the economy was therefore sometimes damaging for the long-term interests of the regional economy.[29]

Several regional privatization deals with foreign companies also turned out to be short-term profit-extracting projects. One such deal was even apparently based on illegal decisions by the regional governor as well as officials of Russia's State Committee for Administration of State Property.[30] The Balakhninskii paper combine (renamed Volga) was privatized in fall 1994 and sold to HIT, a subsidiary of the German Herlitz company. The 1999 investigation of this privatization deal by Russia's Accounting Chamber revealed numerous flaws. Most conspicuously, the charter capital of the company was seriously undervalued by omitting earlier investments in modern equipment. The charter capital was evaluated to be around $189,000, while the investment in the new equipment amounted to $110 million (a difference of over 500 times). In addition, the auction organized for selling this company involved only one bidder—the ultimate winner. No other bidders were allowed to participate. Some other tricks uncovered by the Accounting Chamber included a scheme that allowed the buyer to quickly release new shares with the aim of obtaining the controlling stake in the enterprise. These new shares were purchased by the International Financial Corporation (IFC), CS First Boston, and several German banks that became Volga's shareholders and issued a credit of $75 million for further reconstruction of the enterprise.[31] This deal was initially advertised as one of the successful foreign investment projects in Russia. It turned out, however, that paper production was only profitable in 1995. When prices started dropping in late 1995, the company ran into financial problems. It emerged later that HIT possessed exclusive rights to trade the company's production and set very low prices that did not even cover production costs. At the same time, transport and storage services were overpriced. Ultimately, in 1997, HIT withdrew from the company, leaving it without capital, without clients, and with the deadline approaching for returning the credits received from the IFC and the German banks. The creditors agreed to settle on the amount of $50 million. They blocked $22 million in the company's bank accounts, and the company was left to look for the remaining $28 million. At that point the regional government did not want to make this investment, considering the project to be too risky.[32] Hence the company faced bankruptcy.[33]

A new investor was eventually found, but the new owners were burdened with the old debt to the creditors for several more years.[34]

The regional economic elite was strongly discontented with the results of privatization in Nizhnii Novgorod and blamed Nemtsov for the negative economic outcomes in many of the privatized enterprises. In the words of one of the representatives of the regional elite, "In Soviet times the [Balakhninskii] paper combine worked very effectively. . . . An American firm with the help of Nemtsov and his friends was able to buy off the control stock of the company. The Americans started to suck out the last drops from the combine and the combine crumbled. The German firm later bought it off from the Americans."[35]

The discord within the elites was intense. In their view, privatization did not take into account the interests of the regional economy but benefited transnational corporations. In particular, privatization touched strategically important companies such as the glass-making company in the town of Bor, Borskii stekol'nyi zavod.[36] In 1997 it fell under the control of a consortium of foreign investors led by a Belgian company, Glaverbel. As one of the representatives of the regional elite complained, "Now a Belgian firm is an actual owner of the enterprise. Her [the Belgian firm's] interests are neither oriented toward Russia nor toward the Nizhnii Novgorod region. Perhaps they plan to produce cheap products and compete on the world markets. Perhaps they plan not to produce at all . . . these cheap products," thus threatening the well-being of GAZ and other regional enterprises that might lose a traditional supplier.[37] Whether or not these fears were justified, it is clear that Nemtsov's policies of privatization, which opened the region up to outsiders, did not benefit the regional elites and contributed to their fracturing.

Nemtsov's radical liberal policies were also directed toward reforming the agricultural sector. The infamous project ZerNO (*zemel'naia reforma nizhegorodskoi oblasti*), designed with the help of the IFC and Gretchen Wilson of CS First Boston bank during 1992–94, required splitting up the collective and state farms and forming private farming plots.[38] In the course of implementing the reform 2,096,000 hectares were privatized (from the total of 2,712,000 hectares available).[39] However, the results of this project were fairly disappointing (some critics would even claim that the results were devastating for the region's agricultural sector). The main effect of the reform was that almost 15 percent of the arable land in the region was simply abandoned; starting to cultivate this land again would require much more resources than would be necessary if it had been kept productive.[40] Furthermore, not only did the intended rise in productivity not happen; Nizhnii Novgorod's agricultural yield decreased during the 1990s (see table 2.1). Although the number of private farms grew much faster and higher in Nizhnii Novgorod (when compared to Tatarstan, for example), the yield indicators in Tatarstan were invariably better than in Nizhnii Novgorod. In fact, the divergence between the two regions in terms of agricultural indicators increased, with Nizhnii Novgorod lagging further behind in the late 1990s while starting out with better indicators (see table 2.1). The reasons for this drop in agricultural production in Nizhnii Novgorod were directly linked to the reform advanced by Nemtsov. The early success of a few private farms was explained by significant government subsidies to new farms.[41] As the project was expanded and the subsidies decreased, the private farms turned out to be less profitable than the farms that were not reorganized.[42] Without the necessary infrastructure available for the development of private farming, including access to financial credits and agricultural equipment suitable for small-scale farming, the shift away from collective farming was doomed to failure. These necessary prerequisites were not in place in the early 1990s and are, arguably, absent even now.[43]

The above discussion points to two important features of policy making under Nemtsov. First, Nemtsov was driven by ideological rather than pragmatic concerns in his aggressive promotion of privatization. As a strong supporter of a market-driven economy, Nemtsov actively promoted liberal economic reforms in the Nizhnii Novgorod region and opened the region up to foreign investors and capital. Second, judging from an analysis of specific privatization deals, especially those involving foreign investors, there may have been collusion between the regional government (and especially Nemtsov himself), federal officials, and specific foreign investors. The overall results of privatization in industry and agriculture were fairly bleak. In the second half of the 1990s the region faced growing financial, social, and political problems and fell from its leading position among Russia's regions (at least, in terms of visibility, as the pioneer of market reforms) to become an average region with a

TABLE 2.1. Selected Agricultural Indicators, Republic of Tatarstan (RT) and Nizhnii Novgorod Region (NN), 1991–2001

		1991	1992	1993	1994	1995	1996	1997	1998	1999	2000	2001
Number of private farms	RT			583			780	849	1078	1370	1631	1,637
	NN			2502			3,637	3,625	3,546	3,340	3,251	3,155
Cultivated land area*	RT	3,390.6	3,414.2	3,394.7	3,339.2	3,337.7	3,337.4	3,263.2	3,132.7	3,037.9	2,991.4	
	NN	2,055.5	1,993.2	1,987.4	1,948.6	1,781.8	1,716.4	1,691.2	1,663.4	1,608.1	1,552.9	1,494.6
Yields on grains**	RT	13.2	21.1	21.2	24.3	21.3	30.2	41	19.3	22.3	28.6	
	NN	16	19.1	15.2	16.9	12.9	16.2	18.1	12.4	11	16.3	
Agricultural production***	RT	7	68.6	622	2,695	7,941	11,877	12,626	10,930	21,442	31,049	
	NN	5.8	55	401	1,540	3,919	5,225	5,699	5,869	12,836	15,212	

* in thousands hectares

** in 100 kilograms from a hectare of land

*** in billion rubles until 1998

depressed economy and petty interelite political bickering. By 2001 the
Nizhnii Novgorod region neared bankruptcy.[44] To deal with the financial
crisis, the new governor, Khodyrev, had to sign an agreement with the federal Ministry of Finance, which amounted, essentially, to surrendering
control over the financial flows within the region.[45]

Nemtsov's EPN

If there was a particular group in the economy that could be considered
Nemtsov's power base, it was members of the financial-entrepreneurial
class. The regional administration under Nemtsov developed close ties
to the newly emerging commercial structures in the region, as noted by
regional analysts early in Nemtsov's tenure.[46] Among Nemtsov's closest
associates and friends, who could be seen as the key members of the informal group dominating the region, were Boris Brevnov, chair of Nizhegorodskii Bankirskii Dom (NBD bank); Sergei Kirienko, chair of Garantiia bank; Vladimir Bessarab, chair of Nizhegorodskaia Yarmarka;
Andrei Zaderniuk, a well-known expert in the energy sector; Vladimir
Sedov, a businessman; and Andrei Kliment'ev, a businessman and Nemtsov's erstwhile friend. Nemtsov also had the personal loyalty of Evgenii
Krestianinov, speaker of the regional legislature, who, through his control of the legislative body, secured support for Nemtsov's policies and
initiatives.

These individuals received systematic support and privileges from
the Nemtsov-led regional government. Brevnov's NBD bank was founded
based on the conversion fund, which was created by pooling money from
the state and regional defense enterprises.[47] The bank was also involved
in other projects initiated by the regional administration, including projects in the energy sector.[48] Kirienko's Garantiia bank worked closely with
the regional department of Russia's Pension Fund. Later, in 1996, Kirienko
became president of the Norsi oil company. Nemtsov's clientele clearly
revealed themselves when he suddenly moved to Moscow in March 1997
to assume the post of Russia's deputy prime minister. His closest associates
followed him. Brevnov became deputy chairman of Russia's utility monopoly, United Energy System of Russia (RAO EES). Krestianinov, who at
that point was Nizhnii Novgorod's presidential representative, became
head of Nemtsov's secretariat. Zaderniuk became chair of the Federal

Energy Commission.[49] Kirienko became minister of fuel and energy. In addition, Igor Maskaev, Sergei Mitin, Pavel Chichagov, and Andrei Kotiusov followed Nemtsov to Moscow and got various positions in the federal bureaucracy. This phenomenon of "followership" is by itself a clear indicator of the importance of personal relationships for career opportunities in Russia. It operates on a much larger scale than equivalent processes in Western democracies and is similar to the Soviet-era phenomenon of "tailism" *(khvostizm),* which involved an official promoted to a job in Moscow bringing with him a "tail" of his cronies from his previous location.

Nemtsov's relationships with Andrei Kliment'ev deserve special attention as they have had the most lasting impact on the regional political system. Nemtsov's childhood friend, Kliment'ev became a famous entrepreneur in Nizhnii Novgorod at the time of Nemtsov's governorship.[50] He opened two supermarkets in the center of the city (Nizhegorodskii and Evropa) and a nightclub called Rocco, and was a co-owner of the Navashinskii shipbuilding plant, Oka.[51] These acquisitions could not have been made without active support from the governor. Having considerable influence over Nemtsov, Kliment'ev became an important figure on the regional political scene. His friendship with Nemtsov certainly guaranteed that Kliment'ev would have the green light for his initiatives. Asked during an interview about his interaction with regional authorities, he replied, "I play tennis with them."[52] Kliment'ev sometimes behaved arrogantly, even in the presence of Nemtsov.[53] The two friends' paths diverged in 1995, when Nemtsov accused Kliment'ev of mismanaging the credit that was given to him from the federal budget for renovating Oka. A criminal investigation into Kliment'ev's activities was opened in 1995.[54] He was convicted and sentenced to prison but was released from prison in 1997 because he had served his sentence while under investigation. It is hard to determine the true reasons for the conflict between Nemtsov and Kliment'ev, except for noting that it originated in the vicissitudes of their personal relationships. Kliment'ev tried to fight back when freed in 1997 and, in turn, accused Nemtsov of wrongdoing. In response, Nemtsov initiated another round of criminal proceedings charging Kliment'ev with libel. In the end, Kliment'ev was arrested (following his victory in the March 1998 mayoral elections) and sentenced to six years in prison.[55] Although Nemtsov won this fight, at least formally, it could also be seen by the public as his personal loss. After all, the $18 million in state funds that were given to Kliment'ev were guaranteed, in the first place, by Nemtsov's regional administration. Kliment'ev had access to these financial resources only because of his close personal connection to Nemtsov.

To conclude, Nemtsov's domination on the political scene did not lead to the establishing of a stable and long-lasting political regime. He was never able to create a strong governing coalition by linking and balancing various regional interests and taking into account strategically important economic and political actors in the region. Instead of building up the links to and among the region's most powerful interests, he relied on his personal friends and, among various economic interests, privileged financial capital as his support base. The interests of managers of regional industrial enterprises, especially in the process of privatization, were either ignored or opposed. While Nemtsov's personal domination kept the polity relatively stable and cohesive during his time in office (with the exception of several conflicts discussed below), the latent fragmentation of the regional political structure manifested itself immediately after his departure to Moscow in March 1997.

The Post-Nemtsov Era and the New Political Structure

When Nemtsov left for Moscow, the political system established during his governorship quickly lost its balance as the question of succession emerged. Ivan Skliarov, Nemtsov's former deputy who was elected mayor of the region's capital city of Nizhnii Novgorod in 1995, was perceived as his natural successor; Nemtsov's most recent deputy and protégé, Yurii Lebedev, was seen as an alternative candidate. Nemtsov himself did not openly support either of the candidates. It was only at the end of the electoral campaign that he publicly supported Skliarov while promising Lebedev the post of the presidential representative. The problem of succession was ultimately resolved, but the opposition between the new governor, Skliarov, and Lebedev (later, the mayor of the capital city) became the defining point for the regional political regime under Skliarov.

The post-Nemtsov era in the Nizhnii Novgorod region was characterized by increasing fragmentation of the political system, with several

EPNs coming into existence and engaging in permanent rivalry. Skliarov had been a good choice for deputy governor (1991–95) and enjoyed a successful term as mayor of the region's capital (he won the race against a very popular politician, Dmitrii Bedniakov, in the 1995 mayoral elections). When he became governor most actors and especially the industrial enterprise managers supported his candidacy.[56] As a former party secretary, he held a worldview similar to that of the red directors; he was not as flashy as Nemtsov and was perceived to be a good manager *(khoziaistvennik)*. However, although he was a good manager on the city level, Skliarov turned out to be mediocre at dealing with regional affairs. His management of the Eurobonds issued by the region is one of the most revealing examples in this regard.[57] The money was used to pay salaries and to fund several ecology-related projects that had no prospects for a financial return.[58] It was not surprising, therefore, that by late 1999 the region came very close to defaulting on its debts.[59] By the new gubernatorial elections in 2001, the region was in deep financial crisis. To be fair, it was not all Skliarov's fault, and Nizhnii Novgorod was not the only region in Russia in financial crisis during the late 1990s. The Russian economy as a whole faced an acute financial crisis in August 1998, when Russia defaulted on its debts and devalued its currency.[60] Also, major privatization deals that resulted in the stripping of assets of formerly productive enterprises had been signed under Nemtsov. When Skliarov became governor, he essentially lacked any means to control the economy, but, as head of the regional executive branch, he was seen as the one who was responsible for regional economic conditions. Nonetheless, Skliarov was a very weak politician who was neither able to create a strong governing coalition nor rule by charisma as Nemtsov did before him. It is hard to point out a coherent network of reciprocal relationships associated with Skliarov.[61] In fact, his closest associates, such as his deputy Ol'ga Savinova, a family friend, and the chief of his election team in 1997 and his deputy afterward, Boris Dukhan, left him. His 2001 gubernatorial campaign was managed by people who did not have much to do with his governorship.[62] Not surprisingly, when Sergei Kirienko, the new presidential envoy, entered the regional political scene in May 2000 Skliarov had no choice but to attempt to join forces with him.

Skliarov's main political opponent, Lebedev, was also not very successful in developing a stable political-economic network. He did attract strong allies, such as Dmitrii Savel'ev, who owned vast media resources. That partnership, however, was more a matter of political expediency than the product of a long-term personal relationship. Lebedev is often perceived as similar to Skliarov: a good manager, rather simple,[63] appealing mostly to older people and pensioners. During 1994–97 he was a presidential representative in the region and by 1997 was already very critical of Skliarov's leadership.[64] When Lebedev became mayor in 1998 and thus acquired popular legitimacy, the opposition between these two politicians took on a new turn, as Lebedev fought to establish the autonomy of the local government in the city of Nizhnii Novgorod and frequently stepped on the toes of the regional administration.[65] This conflict continued until the end of Skliarov's governorship, culminating in the 2001 elections, when Lebedev attempted to run for governor against the incumbent Skliarov.[66]

The Rise of Kirienko's EPN and Continuing Fragmentation in Nizhnii Novgorod

The period from 1997 to 2000 featured two main political poles in the regional politics: the governor and the mayor. This bipolar structure was transformed with the entry of a new powerful actor on the regional political scene. Soon after his victory in the presidential elections of March 2000, Vladimir Putin initiated federal reforms that involved dividing the country into seven federal districts *(okrugs)* and sending presidential envoys to each district. The envoys were given formidable tasks related to building the new "power vertical" and bringing the regions under tighter control of the center.[67] They were hand-picked by Putin from among trusted individuals (many from security organs) and given the rank of federal minister and included in the staff of the presidential administration. Nizhnii Novgorod became the capital of the Volga Federal District, and in May 2000 the city welcomed the return of Sergei Kirienko as a presidential envoy to the newly created Volga okrug.[68] For Kirienko it was practically a return home since he started his career in Nizhnii and moved to Moscow not long after Nemtsov's departure in 1997. Relying on his new official post and his former personal ties in the region, Kirienko built what became the most developed and visible power network in the region.

Although for a long time Kirienko's name was linked with Nemtsov's network, in 1998 when Kirienko was appointed Russia's prime minister, he surpassed Nemtsov on the career ladder. Since then their paths have diverged, and their interests have often clashed.[69] While in Moscow Kirienko maintained close ties to the region and was actively involved in the projects for restructuring the petrochemical industry concentrated in the city of Dzerzhinsk.[70] Therefore, when he returned to Nizhnii in 2000 he quickly reestablished himself, gathering a team of his longtime personal friends and colleagues from his previous work in Krasnoe Sormovo, the Garantiia bank, the Norsi oil company, and the Fuel and Energy Ministry. The people closest to Kirienko—Sergei Obozov, Liubov' Glebova, Sergei Novikov, and Viktor Ratnikov—have all had an extended history of working with him.[71]

Kirienko's network reveals very dynamic and expansionary qualities that allow us to treat it as an archetypal EPN driven toward all-encompassing control not only in the region but also beyond its boundaries (table 2.2). It possesses broad administrative resources derived from the placement of its core member within the presidential administration.[72] The incumbent governor Skliarov attempted to tap into these resources when faced with reelection in 2001. Kirienko's support came at a very high price. In spring 2001, under pressure from Kirienko, the regional legislature created a new institution of regional government that paralleled the regional administration. This new structure was expected to take over the day-to-day administration of regional affairs. It was to be headed by Sergei Obozov, Kirienko's closest associate, and it meant that, were Skliarov to become governor again, he would have been a governor without power. Kirienko's network would have attained complete control over regional affairs. The expansionary tendencies of Kirienko's EPN are also seen in the attempts to place Kirienko's allies in other important positions of power. After the overwhelming victory of the Union of Rightist Forces (SPS), Kirienko's party, in the Oblast Legislative Assembly elections in March 2002, Evgenii Liulin, Kirienko's personal friend, was elected speaker. Kirienko determined many of the Volga District's appointments to the Federation Council, with several of the new senators coming from his staff. Mordovia delegated Kirienko's former deputy for economic issues, German Petrov; Komi-Permyak delegated former

TABLE 2.2. Main EPNs in the Nizhnii Novgorod Region by 2001

	Political Pillar	Economic Pillar	Ideological Pillar
Kirienko	Presidential envoy	Nizhnovenergo, Kaprolaktam, Norsi Oil	MK v Nizhnem, Delo, Sem' piatnits, Leninskaia smena, and the Dialog television company
Savel'ev	Ran for governor	Interests in the oil industry (former president of Transneft', Norsi, Lukoil-Ufa, and Lukoil-NN)	Novoe delo, Leninskaia smena plius,Gorod i Gorozhane, Novaia gazeta v Nizhnem, Volga and TNT-Nizhnii Novgorod TV channels; STS TV company; Volga media advertising agency; IF-region information agency
Bulavinov	State Duma deputy Ran for mayor in 2002 and won	N/A	Seti-NN TV channel
Kliment'ev	Ran for governor and mayor	Supermarkets Nizhegorodskii and Evropa, nightclub Rocco, shipbuilding plant Oka	N/A

Chief Federal Inspector Vladimir Solomonov;[73] Ulianovsk chose former Ulianovsk Chief Federal Inspector Valerii Sychev; Yamal Nenets selected former deputy envoy Aleksandr Evstifeev; and Marii El appointed Kirienko's ally, Aleskandr Torshin.[74]

Kirienko's personal connections and activities in Nizhnii Novgorod allowed him to exert influence not only in cadre policy but also over wide economic resources in the region, especially in the energy sector and the chemical industry. Nizhnii Novgorod's main energy company, Nizhnovenergo, was headed by Kirienko's friend Aleksei Sannikov, who was appointed to that position in summer 1998, when Kirienko was Russia's prime minister. This personal connection with Nizhnovenergo gave Kirienko a powerful tool for pressuring the energy-dependent enterprises in the region and specifically the plants making up the petrochemical complex in Dzerzhinsk.[75] This was the period in Russia when bankruptcy law was widely used for property redistribution; therefore, having influence over the key creditor, such as the regional utility company, provided Kirienko with a powerful stick.[76] In addition, Vadim Vorob'ev, Lukoil Volga region director, was also Kirienko's friend and ally. With such connections, Kirienko's economic influence went beyond the confines of the Nizhnii Novgorod region. He played a direct role in the creation of a new joint Volga energy company called Middle Volga Interregional Energy Management Company (SMUEK) and Volga Hydroelectric Cascade, uniting all the Volga's hydroelectric stations.[77] Furthermore, Kirienko's closest associate, Leonid Sukhoterin, was sent to Kirov oblast to become a deputy director of the regional electricity company Kirovenergo.[78]

In addition to a solid administrative and economic basis, Kirienko's EPN had wide access to the media. Leonid Sukhoterin, a member of Kirienko's team,[79] was often described as the Volga region's Boris Berezovsky (*privolzhskii Berezovskii*).[80] His media holdings included the *MK v Nizhnem, Delo, Sem' piatnits,* and *Leninskaia smena* newspapers and the Dialog television company. Kirienko also influenced the editorial policy of the daily newspaper *Nizhegorodskii rabochii.*[81] Kirienko had also attempted to control the media in other regions of the Volga District. His efforts in Udmurtiia, for example, eventually brought him into conflict with the republic's President Aleksandr Volkov.[82] Despite this influence over vast media resources in Nizhnii Novgorod, Kirienko faced a tough challenge from another media magnate in the region and one of his strongest political opponents, Dmitrii Savel'ev.

Savel'ev's EPN

For most of the 1990s Savel'ev had been Kirienko's ally. In 1994–97 Savel'ev worked in the regional oil sector, directing the branches of Lukoil: Lukoil-Ufa and Lukoil-NN. When Kirienko left for Moscow as part of Nemtsov's team, he appointed Savel'ev to his former position as the head of Norsi Oil. Also, at Kirienko's initiative Savel'ev was appointed in 1998 the president of Russia's oil pipeline monopoly, Transneft'. Savel'ev was removed from his position at Transneft' the following year and, as it became apparent later, redirected his ambitions to the political scene in

Nizhnii Novgorod. By the 2001 gubernatorial elections in the region, Savel'ev had created a political coalition with Lebedev. The implementation of his far-reaching agenda of capturing the governorship (either by supporting Lebedev's candidacy or running for governor himself) involved construction of a vast media empire. Savel'ev's media holdings included two influential TV channels, TNT-Nizhnii Novgorod and Volga, the radio station Nizhegorodskaia volna, the information agency IF-region, the Volga-media advertising agency, and several newspapers, including *Novoe delo, Leninskaia smena plius, Gorod i gorozhane,* and *Novaia gazeta v Nizhnem.* He also controlled 50 percent of another TV station, STS, which allowed him to select its director general. As discussed in chapter 4, these media resources were employed to the fullest during the electoral campaigns in 2001 and 2002, and Savel'ev became known as a key producer of electoral dirty tricks in Nizhnii Novgorod. By 2003, however, Kirienko had gradually stripped Savel'ev of the most important media resources. Thus Savel'ev's cofounders of the Volga TV channel were pressured to transfer their 49 percent of shares to the regional branch of Lukoil, headed by Vorob'ev, Kirienko's close associate.[83] Savel'ev also lost his appointee, the director general of STS.[84] The personnel change at STS was also apparently orchestrated by Kirienko's team.

The gubernatorial elections in 2001 clearly demonstrated the regional political structure. The main battle occurred between two major EPNs, that of Kirienko allied with the incumbent governor Skliarov and that of Savel'ev allied with Mayor Lebedev and one antisystem candidate, the infamous Kliment'ev who was released from prison in fall 2000.[85] The 2002 mayoral elections in the capital of the Nizhnii Novgorod region revealed once again the region's main political rivalries and featured the same political forces that have been clashing in the region over the past several years, although the degree of fragmentation has increased since the last gubernatorial elections. Analysis of the specific electoral campaigns and their outcomes is the subject of chapter 4. Here, it suffices to note that the political situation that developed in the Nizhnii Novgorod region by the late 1990s characterizes, to a larger or smaller extent, most other regions of the Russian Federation and the whole of Russia in the 1990s as well. The rushed economic demonopolization that occurred in the absence of a state capable of enforcing the rule of law resulted in the rise of rival economic-political elite networks, with each network struggling for more power and economic resources and employing all means possible in pursuit of their expansionary goals.

Theoretical and Conceptual Observations

The Roots of Political Competition in Nizhnii Novgorod: Fragmentation by Default

The Nizhnii Novgorod region experienced political transformation that was typical for many regions of Russia and can be compared to the 1990s political scenario that played out in Russia at large. The political transition from the Communist-led system ended with the appointment of a democrat, Nemtsov, as governor in 1991. Yeltsin's political ally, Nemtsov eagerly promoted liberal economic reforms and opened up the region to foreign investors and businesses. Essentially a political outsider when he was brought to power, Nemtsov relied on the newly forming commercial interests in the region rather than building a political base that would include the existing elites, especially the influential enterprise managers. In contrast, Nemtsov undermined the influence of the red directors by opening up privatization deals to outsiders. While political cohesion in the region was maintained by the weight of Nemtsov's charismatic personality and his close links to Russia's president, his economic policies resulted in the creation of structural preconditions for political fragmentation and, specifically, the rise of economically autonomous regional actors. Regional political institutions—the electoral mechanism of power transfer as well as the existence of local self-government—represented the other crucial structural prerequisites for political contestation. With these elements in place, the fragmentation of political space in Nizhnii Novgorod began as soon as Nemtsov left for Moscow and only intensified in the following years. It seems fair to argue that political competition emerged in Nizhnii Novgorod by default, in the absence of institutional foundations of a centralized political regime and a strong leader that could unite various regional actors.

The fragmented and politically competitive model of cronyism depicted in this chapter is one that prevailed in most other regions of the

Russian Federation. This model was propelled by Russia-wide economic liberalization and privatization that resulted in the emergence of autonomous economic resources mobilized by competing political factions and the institutional characteristics of regional politics. Many regions in Russia witnessed intense confrontations between the holders of the two most important executive positions in the regional and local government, that of the governor and the mayor. The reasons for such conflicts were fairly obvious. After the August 1995 law on local self-government, elections conferred on the mayor the legitimacy that allowed him to engage in the struggle for resources in transforming the economy. The dominant position of the governor was endangered, especially in regions with a high degree of economic concentration in the capital city. The importance of both posts was also manifested in the fact that in many regions of Russia powerful economic actors clashed in their choice of the governor or the mayor. Regional political rivalries were both promoted by and manifested in the competition for gubernatorial and mayoral seats.

Types of Regional Networks: Friends and Co-believers versus Strategic Allies

The investigation of key networks in Nizhnii Novgorod in this chapter allows for making some observations on the types of informal elite networks that can form in Russia as well as the type of resources they operate with. The Nizhnii Novgorod region gave rise to two different types of EPNs. The most prominent network, associated with Kirienko, was based on long-term relationships rooted in the workplace, friendship, and collaboration. An active and enthusiastic youth leader, Kirienko created a strong basis of personal ties in Nizhnii, his hometown, where he started his career. When he left for Moscow in 1998 he did not abandon those ties. He actively participated in advancing and nurturing his relationships, so that when he returned to Nizhnii Novgorod as a presidential envoy in 2000 he was able to quickly reassemble a team of close friends and associates who shared his goals and advanced his policies. This network has the capacity to expand if its leaders are well placed and can affect appointment decisions. This EPN is like a club of selected, like-minded believers owing allegiance to its leader.[86]

The second type of network that operated in Nizhnii was based on a short-term political alliance of actors who perceived that their immediate interests would be served by such association. Lebedev and Savel'ev brought their respective resources together to fight for the gubernatorial seat in 2001 and the mayoral seat in 2002. But the alliance disintegrated after the elections. This was a transient network since it was only short-term interests that brought these actors together. It can be compared to a faction or a political coalition, with minimal influence of personal ties.

The operation of these networks revealed the types of resources that were important for pursuing the interests of network members. On the more transparent side, each network relied on a combination of administrative, economic, and media resources. Indeed, political competition, manifested primarily in the electoral competition (discussed in detail in chapter 4), would not have been possible without autonomous economic resources and access to the media. Even more important was access to administrative resources, which gave political actors an additional capacity to mobilize votes and, under certain circumstances, even change the rules of the game. Administrative resources are provided by the access to and control of state power. These can include coercive capacities and personnel, financial, and material resources that incumbent politicians or political parties have access to by virtue of controlling a state office. These resources were widely used for promotion of individual and group interests of EPNs and in violation of legal norms and responsibilities governing the exercise of public office. It is also important to note, however, that economic activity in Russia's early capitalism could not survive without security underpinnings (the so-called roof) designed to protect business from racketeers.[87] Therefore, it is plausible to suggest that each network competing for power and resources relies on some kind of "roof," whether connected to the state or to private security services. Such security bases of these informal elite groupings are the hardest to gauge. With certain exceptions, there are no visible private armies one can point to, and most links to security services (whether state or private) are hidden. This issue is therefore discussed here as something that plausibly exists but without specific evidence pointing to it.

Finally, the networks differed with regard to state penetration or the extent to which they were able to integrate themselves into the official power structure. Kirienko's network enjoyed the closest connection to the state: as a member of the presidential administration apparatus Kirienko himself had privileged access to the central state. Skliarov, drawn into his network, controlled the executive branch of the regional state. The Lebedev-Savel'ev network, on the other hand, could rely only on the municipal branch of power. Savel'ev's earlier work as the head of the Transneft' monopoly, of course, could have given him informal connections to the federal ministries. These connections, however, did not openly manifest themselves in the regional power struggle.

CHAPTER 3

Centralized Cronyism

The Case of Tatarstan

The centralized model of cronyism is a less common phenomenon among the Russian regions. It did not emerge merely by default in
the context of the economic and political liberalization that characterized Russia of the early 1990s. The noncompetitive, integrated systems
required methodical, careful construction that involved, on the one hand,
blocking the conditions that promoted political fragmentation and, on
the other, creating an institutional, economic, and ideological basis for a
monocentric regime. This case study of political consolidation and the
emergence of a noncompetitive crony system in Tatarstan focuses on the
special political and economic conditions that proved relatively exceptional in the context of Russia. Still, Tatarstan's was not a unique system.
As noted by various analysts, Russia's ethnic republics generally tended to
develop less competitive political systems than the rest of the regions.[1]
Bashkortostan, for example, undertook in the 1990s a political trajectory
very similar to that of Tatarstan.[2] In this chapter I address both the more
common and exceptional features of the case of Tatarstan that allowed
its government to construct a centralized crony system.

Building Hegemonic Cronyism in Tatarstan

Federal Structure

In contrast to the fragmenting political scene in Nizhnii Novgorod, Tatarstan's ruling elite gradually monopolized the republic's political machinery

as well as its economic resources. These developments became possible as a result of the evolution of federal relations in the early 1990s as well as Tatarstan's special negotiations with the federal center. The Russian Federation is a complex entity that in the 1990s consisted of eighty-nine units (regions) with differentiated status.[3] Ethnically defined entities (21 republics, 10 autonomous okrugs, and 1 autonomous oblast) are supposed to represent "homelands" for ethnic minorities and were named after the ethnic group they represented.[4] Nonethnically defined oblasts (49) and *krai* (6) represent administrative-territorial units mostly dominated by the Russian population. In addition, two cities, Moscow and St. Petersburg, are separate federal units.[5] Article 5 of the 1993 Constitution of the Russian Federation recognizes all the constituent units as "equal subjects" of the federation; however, the regions are differentiated according to their status, also defined in the Constitution. The twenty-one ethnically defined republics, Tatarstan among them, are the highest-ranking units, designated as states *(gosudarstvo)*. They have the right to establish their state languages (Article 68) and design their own governmental structure; they also have the powers of independent legislation and taxation. The ethnic republics presumably allow for political self-determination of their titular populations. Thus Tatarstan has proclaimed both Russian and Tatar as its official languages. The republic has its own president, state symbols, and a constitution that was adopted in November 1992 (for details on the ethnic composition of Tatarstan, see table 3.1).

The autonomous okrug and autonomous oblast are lower-ranking ethnic units. Their status in the federal structure is not very clear. On the one hand, they are recognized as equal constituent units within the federation; on the other hand, they are usually located within larger territorial units, "forming part" of krais, as described in the Constitution (Article 66.4), and in some respects subordinated to them. The 1993 Constitution states that the relations between krais and okrugs must be regulated by federal law or bilateral treaties (Article 66); however, federal law regulating these relationships still does not exist.[6] Overall, in the delimitation of authority between the center and these units, they are similar to oblasts and krais, the nonethnic regions of Russia. Oblasts and krais are territorially defined administrative units in the federation. They are not considered states and lack the symbolic attributes of statehood

TABLE 3.1. Ethnic Composition, Republic of Tatarstan

	1989 (%)	*2002 (%)*
Tatars	48.5	52.9
Russians	43.3	39.5
Chuvash	3.7	3.3
Others	4.6	4.2

enjoyed by the ethnic republics (such as a constitution and president); instead, each has a regional charter *(ustav)* and a governor as its chief executive.

The asymmetry of the Russian Federation is an institutional legacy of the Soviet Union that was adopted in modified form by the 1993 Constitution. The asymmetry is not solely formal. Republic status, for example, allowed the authorities of these constituent units to follow the steps undertaken by Union Republics of the Soviet Union during 1990–91. Mimicking Yeltsin's actions, leaders of the autonomous republics of the Russian Federation (then a part of the Soviet Union) declared sovereignty, pronounced the supremacy of republican laws over federal laws, and introduced the elected post of republican president.[7] The Federal Treaty signed in March 1992 gave the republics control over their governmental institutions. However, Tatarstan along with Chechnya did not sign the treaty, demanding instead special provisions for the republic's status in Russia. Based on its Declaration of Sovereignty, adopted in August 1990, and the March 1992 referendum that confirmed the republic's sovereignty by 61.4 percent, the Tatarstani government adopted a new republican constitution and maintained a tough stand vis-à-vis Moscow.[8] Eventually, in February 1994, the issue of the republic's status was resolved in a bilateral treaty between Tatarstan and the Russian Federation.[9] This treaty was the first one of its sort but by no means unique; forty-six similar treaties were later signed by other regions of Russia. The treaty allowed Tatarstan a great degree of institutional and economic autonomy and, in essence, untied the hands of the republican government, enabling it to control the republic without interference from the center. The treaty also boosted the reputation of the president of Tatarstan, Mintimer Shai-miev, who was seen as a skillful negotiator and a shrewd politician (for biographical information on Shaimiev, see Appendix 1).[10]

In short, one of the important structural preconditions that allowed the republican government to build a noncompetitive political system involved special federal status of ethnic republics within the Russian Fed-eration, along with an even more privileged position that the Republic of Tatarstan was able to obtain for itself through bargaining with the fed-eral center.

Institutional Foundations of the Regime

Constructing a sustainable noncompetitive regime in Tatarstan required, first, an institutional engineering aimed at the centralization of adminis-trative resources and the construction of an electoral machine that would ensure the perpetuation of the regime. One important institutional fea-ture that distinguishes Tatarstan from many other regions in Russia is the president's right to appoint and remove the heads of local administration, effectively extending state power to the local level. Local self-government institutions in Tatarstan exist only at the lowest settlement level, that is, villages and small towns, whereas in most other regions local self-government is present at the city level. This institutional arrangement plays an important role in the republican political system. On the one hand, the appointment system for local chief executives secures their loy-alty to the president of Tatarstan. On the other hand, the rules required the local chiefs to run in the elections to the republican parliament and city or district representative bodies. Tatarstani officials have often claimed that participation in parliamentary elections by local chief executives is aimed at ensuring public support for the appointed officials and, there-fore, represents a democratic feature of the political system.[11] However, Kimitaka Matsuzato has argued convincingly that this is a way that "meso-elites" demonstrate their ability to mobilize votes for the president and thus represents an important element of the republican electoral machine. The meso-elites, Matsuzato argues, act as "intermediary brokers between the central authorities and local communities."[12] They were given exten-sive powers and were expected to ensure votes for the president. In addition, this system of local government resulted in a specific composition of the republican legislature that included all the district chiefs, who were entirely dependent on the president for their appointments. As a result, the republican president killed two birds with one stone; he secured control over the parliament and ensured the loyalty of appointees capable of mobilizing popular votes during the elections.

This institutional peculiarity of extending state power to the local level is not specific to the Tatarstani political system. Other ethnic republics had similar procedures.[13] This institutional feature had important practical implications: it enabled the republican elites to avoid intraelite factionalization rising from the independent local government. The mayor/governor split, which has been a prominent source of political opposition in non–ethnically defined Russian regions, was a rare occurrence in republican politics.[14]

Although it prevented the public schisms that can occur in systems with elected local governments, the appointment-based system had its own weaknesses. In Tatarstan, for example, the president's power to appoint regional chiefs gave extensive political influence to the head of his apparatus in charge of personnel appointments. The most significant political challenge to the authority of President Shaimiev in the period from 1992 to 2002 was associated with Khaliaf Nizamov, head of the presidential administration at that time. During the elections of the speaker of the parliament during the May 1998 session of the State Council, Nizamov was suspected of organizing opposition to the presidential decision to elect Prime Minister Farid Mukhametshin as speaker. A group of deputies, including several chiefs of district administrations, voted for another candidate, Rafgat Altynbaev, the very promising mayor of Naberezhnye Chelny, the second largest city in Tatarstan. This incident was considered a revolt *(bunt glav)* on the part of district chiefs, and it was followed by extensive purges.[15] Nizamov himself, Minister of Interior Iskander Galimov, and several chiefs of district administrations were removed from their positions. Altynbaev left for Moscow soon after the incident but was still considered by some oppositional elites in Tatarstan the main challenger to Shaimiev in the republican presidential elections of 2001.[16] This episode revealed the key vulnerability of the system relying on personal appointments—the power wielded by the person who is in charge of the personnel policy. In this case, Nizamov, chief of the presidential apparatus, highly trusted by the president, and in charge of all key political appointments, secured such a degree of influence that he was able to conspire (if too recklessly) against the presidential decision. Not surprisingly, the next appointee to this position was much less ambitious.[17]

Nevertheless, Shaimiev's control over the district chief appointments as well as executive control over the legislature were crucial ingredients of the republican political regime. By themselves, though, these institutional mechanisms of political control would not have been sufficient for regime survival. Ultimately, the maintenance of political domination rested on the availability of economic resources. In the absence of an economic foundation, the republican elites could have easily become dependent on either the federal center or other actors for financial transfers, becoming vulnerable to manipulation from external forces and more prone to intraelite splits. The presence of a strong economic basis was an important precondition for the maintenance of unity and political domination by the ruling elite as well as a certain degree of independence from the federal center. This is in fact the key factor that distinguishes successful monocentric regimes from those that collapsed during the 1990s.[18]

Economic Foundations of the Regime

The process of regionalization during the early 1990s in Russia had an impact on all the regions but benefited the ethnic republics the most.[19] Using their privileged status within the federation and taking advantage of the weak federal center, the republics attained autonomy not only in terms of institution building but also in terms of their economic assets. In their declarations of sovereignty, the republics unilaterally asserted control over their main economic resources (and most important, over their natural resources). The Federal Treaty confirmed these assertions and secured those rights.[20] Later, the bilateral negotiations between certain republics and Moscow delineated the ownership of the largest economic enterprises located within the republics.[21] The Republic of Tatarstan was at the forefront of this process. By the end of the 1980s the government of Tatarstan possessed only 2 percent of the industrial enterprises located in its territory.[22] On the other hand, 80 percent of republican industries were controlled by the Union ministries and 18 percent by the Russian Federation ministries.[23] The assertion of control over economic resources started with the Declaration of Sovereignty, which stated that "the land, natural and other resources belong to the people of Tatarstan."[24] Further, in August 1991, the newly elected president of Tatarstan signed a decree according to which all the enterprises located in republican territory were transferred to the jurisdiction of the Republic of Tatarstan.[25] All enterprises were required to reregister.[26] The government also decided to license all activities related to the exploitation of natural resources.[27] According to some local estimates, by 1994 the government of Tatarstan obtained control of about 65 percent of the enterprises located within the region.[28]

This seizure of economic assets occurred throughout the territory of the disintegrating Soviet state and was specifically promoted within Russia by the example of the actions undertaken by the authorities of the Russian Federation itself. However, the distinctiveness of Tatarstan (along with several other economically strong republics such as Bashkortostan) is revealed in the fact that Tatarstani elites were able to maintain the political and economic control seized in the early 1990s. The special path taken by the republican elites in the process of economic demonopolization is an important element that enabled the stability and longevity of the regime. Tatarstan pursued its own privatization program through which the government supplemented the Russian privatization vouchers with additional individual privatization vouchers (IPVs) distributed among the population of Tatarstan. More important, the government introduced a three-year moratorium on the sales of privatized enterprises' stocks. This measure was designed to avoid the quick sale of underpriced enterprises, as happened throughout Russia when some of the most valuable enterprises were sold out for absurdly low prices. By 1999 around 1,100 republican enterprises were privatized, with the government controlling the "golden share" in more than 390 joint-stock companies.[29] Even after the three-year moratorium ended, the government controlled the golden share in all the biggest enterprises, which gave it veto power over any decision and direct control of the appointments of management. A few large enterprises that were not controlled by the state were still very close to official authorities at various levels.[30]

The early economic strategies of the Tatarstani government (1991–94) are best viewed as an attempt to maintain control of the republic's economy and enhance the legitimacy of republican authorities. Contrary to the federal market-oriented reforms initiated by the Gaidar government,[31] the republican elites promoted a "soft entry into market" approach that involved preserving subsidies in various industries and agriculture, maintaining some level of control over prices, and delaying the process of privatization.[32] Tatarstan's model of economic development was marketed by the republican authorities as an alternative path to economic transformation that aimed to mitigate the social cost of reforms. Some observers referred to it as state capitalism; others labeled it "mintimerism" (after President Mintimer Shaimiev).[33] This model fit quite well in the context of the late 1990s, when the economic and political discourse in Russia started to shift in favor of recognizing the benefits of state regulation. Not surprisingly, the republic's image was transformed from "an island of communism," as it was called in the early 1990s, into "an island of pragmatism" in the second half of the 1990s.[34]

Throughout the decade the government played an important role in protecting the industries in critical situations. Protectionist measures included tax breaks and lower energy costs for major enterprises and the agricultural sector, as well as support of less profitable enterprises through the redistribution of resources from the more profitable sectors (cross-subsidization). The government linked all the major enterprises that were interdependent in a chain of mutually beneficial prices. Thus an obligation was imposed on Tatneft' to deliver oil at lower than market price to the petrochemical enterprise Nizhnekamskneftekhim, which, in turn, would deliver lower-than-market-priced rubber to the neighboring Nizhne-kamskshina tire plant.[35] This strategy created favorable conditions for the republican enterprises that otherwise would have faced severe financial difficulties. At the same time, most important republican companies benefited from lowered tax obligations. To encourage technological innovation the government offered tax benefits to Tatneft' and a few smaller companies for extracting oil from depleted oil wells. The truck maker KamAZ received benefits on its property tax.[36]

Securing of low energy costs for republican enterprises required republican control over the energy system. Until the late 1990s Tatarstan's main utility company, Tatenergo, operated as an entirely government-owned enterprise.[37] Its restructuring into a government-controlled joint-stock company started in 1999. However, the actual reorganization was accomplished only in 2002, when the company was divided into three separate entities (based on the functional division of power generation and power transmission), with shares distributed among major republican enterprises such as Tatneft', Nizhnekamskneftekhim, and Kazanorgsintez and with the government maintaining the golden share.[38]

Governmental support was crucial when lobbying the federal authorities. On several occasions the republican government had to intervene and negotiate with the federal institutions that threatened some republican enterprises with bankruptcy. In 1996, for example, Tatneft' appeared at the top of the federal bankruptcy department's list of the enterprises that owed the federal government large amounts of money and, therefore, were in line for bankruptcy procedures.[39] It turned out that the actual debt was not very significant. Tatneft' management argued that the federal agencies did not take into account previous agreements according to which Tatneft' had the right to count its deliveries to the agricultural sector *(tovarnyi kredit)* as part of its federal taxes.[40] However, the issue was resolved only with the intervention of the republican authorities. Similar problems emerged in 1998, when Tatneft' once again seemed to owe substantial federal taxes.[41] Further, the republican government practically saved KamAZ from bankruptcy by paying its federal taxes (elaborated below). In brief, these measures allowed the republic's government to avoid the bankruptcy of major industrial enterprises as well as maintain agricultural production at a stable level.

To focus its efforts, the government chose priority sectors in the republican economy. Oil and petrochemical industries constitute the cornerstone of the economy, providing for over 90 percent of republican exports. Their development therefore has been considered of utmost priority. The oil-extracting sector, represented mainly by Tatneft', has been the economic backbone of the republic. Tatneft' became a joint stock company in 1994 but, along with other big corporatized enterprises in the republic, remained under firm governmental control. The government owns 31 percent of the company's shares and therefore has veto power.[42] The company's board of directors includes top government officials.[43] As of this writing, Rustam Minnikhanov, Tatarstan's current president and former prime minister, serves as the chair of the Tatneft' board of directors. Tatneft' accounts for about 40 percent of the republican budget and has an important role in supporting government investment initiatives as well as maintaining significant social obligations.[44] According to republican officials, Tatneft' pays more taxes per ton of oil than any other oil company in Russia.[45] In the past few years Tatneft' has been considered the basis of the republic's vertical integration process and has become one of the primary bases for capital accumulation. In the course of 2000–2001 Tatneft' obtained the government-controlled shares of Nizhnekamskshina, the technical carbon plant in Nizhnekamsk, and the Minnibaevskii gas-processing plant and in 2002 created the holding company Tatneft'-Neftekhim.[46] These deals included investment and other obligations from Tatneft' that were to ensure a stable resource supply to the plants as well as financing for their modernization. In Nizhnekamskshina, for example, Tatneft' promised to invest 1.2 billion rubles by 2003.[47] Furthermore, Tatneft' was temporarily expanding not only into sectors related to its production chain but also into sectors beyond its specialization. In 2001 the government transferred to Tatneft' 78 percent of the shares of Tatinkom-T, then the largest republican cellular phone operator.[48] A few years later, though, Tatneft' seemed to have shifted its strategy to focus on the sectors that the company specialized in. Thus Tatinkom-T was sold in September 2003 to OAO Sviazinvest. In addition to its control of Zenit Bank in Moscow and Devon Credit Bank in Almet'evsk, Tatneft' in 2001 acquired a blocking stake in the largest republican bank, Ak Bars.[49]

The degree of governmental control over Tatneft' profits was revealed in the 1997 court case between Tatneft' and the oil-trading company Suvar. Suvar (also controlled by the government) traded with oil extracted by Tatneft'. By early 1997 Suvar owed Tatneft' over $25 million and did not pay back the sum, claiming that it was acting in conformity with the republican Cabinet of Ministers, which controls how much oil is extracted, when and whom to sell it to, and what to do with the profits.[50] Therefore, in the end, this was a conflict not between Tatneft' and Suvar but between Tatneft', which wanted more autonomy from the government, and the government, which was making decisions about what to do with the company's profits. The incident ended with the replacement of Tatneft''s director general, Rinat Galeev, by the more pliant Shafagat Takhautdinov, thus demonstrating who the ultimate boss *(kho-ziain)* was.

The republican government has been aware of the fact that oil reserves in Tatarstan territory are being gradually exhausted. The biggest oil field, Romashkinskoe, has been in production since the 1950s and is about 80 percent depleted. To make better use of republican oil resources, therefore, the government worked out special policies to promote oil extraction from less profitable oil wells. In 1998, for instance, the government provided about 900 million rubles in tax breaks to smaller companies extracting oil from such wells. Additional oil extraction from such wells reached 7.2 million tons, and the republican budget gained 1.3 billion rubles while providing 11,000 additional jobs.[51]

The automobile industry is second on the list of priorities of the republican government. This sector faced enormous challenges in the 1990s across Russia. The problems Tatarstan faced in this sector can be best illustrated with the case of KamAZ. This plant was damaged by a big fire in 1993 and had been in crisis during the 1990s, representing a financial liability to the government, as well as a hub of corruption.[52] In 1996 KamAZ was included in the federal government's list of companies that had failed to pay their taxes and faced bankruptcy. The Tatarstani government prevented the bankruptcy by agreeing to pay the company's 51-billion-ruble ($9 million) tax debt. The first deputy prime minister, Ravil Muratov, was made chair of the plant's board of directors; he became actively involved in resolving the problems faced by this truck maker.[53] In summer 1999 Muratov was replaced as chair by Russian economics minister Andrei Shapoval'iants, revealing that the republic did not have sufficient resources to revive the plant.[54]

The economic situation of KamAZ stabilized only in the 2000s following the restructuring efforts of its new director general, Sergei Kogogin, appointed in 2002.[55] The federal authorities that by then controlled a large stake in KamAZ were closely involved in the restructuring of the company's debts. With Putin's new strategy of creating national champions—large state corporations in strategic sectors of the economy—KamAZ was absorbed into the state-owned Rostekhnologii (Russian Technologies Corporation).[56] Although the government of Tatarstan has lost its control over the company, as long as KamAZ is successful, the republican government can take credit for its success.

Enormous lobbying efforts and financial resources of the republican government were also directed at preserving and developing the aviation industry and, specifically, licensing and promoting the newly designed airliner Tu-214. Through protectionist and developmental policies, the government was able to maintain the productive capacities of the main republican aircraft plants, including Kazan Aviation Enterprise (KAPO) and the KVZ helicopter plant, although both have a long way to go to become competitive in the world market.[57] The republican authorities have systematically lobbied the federal government to buy domestically made aircraft rather than Boeings and Airbuses.[58] Considerable efforts were also spent on developing leasing schemes for Tu-214.[59]

Similar to KamAZ, both of these companies became part of the state-owned corporations controlled by the federal center: in 2007 Rosoboron-export acquired the controlling stake in the KVZ helicopter plant, and in 2009 KAPO was integrated into the newly created United Aircraft Corporation (OAK).[60] The companies' incorporation into federally controlled national champions was supposed to bring new investments and government procurements; the long-term impact remains to be seen, however.

The agricultural sector receives governmental subsidies as well as support at the level of legislative initiatives.[61] Thus Tatarstan was one of the first regions in Russia to adopt a land code in April 1998 that allows for buying and selling land.[62] The results of governmental policies in the agricultural sphere are relatively impressive in the context of the increasingly depopulated rural areas of many other Russian regions. Government officials have declared that the republic is self-sufficient in terms of most basic food products; rural infrastructure is developing,[63] and land is cultivated and remains productive rather than being abandoned as in many other regions. It has to be noted, however, that the achievements in this sector have been realized at the price of preserving in the 1990s many features of the communist system in terms of how state and collective farms function as well as redistributing profits from the oil sector to agriculture in the form of subsidies. This policy of promoting and supporting the agricultural sector in the republic was initiated and promoted by President Shaimiev. It represented in essence a system of patronage that in the end earned Shaimiev widespread support not only from the rural population but also from urban residents, who benefited from regulated, lower prices on food products. The economic costs of this policy were recognized by the republican government but deemed justified.[64]

To gain access to additional resources, the government monopolized alcohol production and distribution in the republic. In 1996 the state-controlled company Tatspirtprom was given exclusive rights over alcohol distribution within the republic.[65] Furthermore, in a fairly aggressive attempt to access the alcohol market outside the republic, the government set the lowest prices for alcohol in Russia (the Russian minimum price was set at a higher level).[66] Interestingly, such measures were later implemented by the federal government as well.[67]

The measures designed to secure control of republican economic assets included policies preventing the entrance of outside capital into the republic. The chairman of Tatarstan's National Bank, Evgenii Bogachev, had openly called Moscow-based banks "vacuums" that suck money out of the regions and transfer it to Moscow.[68] Therefore, the government limited the opportunities of banks from outside the region to open their branches in Tatarstan. Among those that were able to open their branches were Mezhkombank, Rossiiskii kredit, and Inkombank; but these banks closed their offices in Tatarstan after the 1998 ruble devaluation. More outsiders have negotiated their expansion into the republic in recent years: Alfa Bank opened its branch in Kazan in 2003,[69] and the Bank of Moscow, in 2006. Moscow-based Zenit occupies a special position in the republic: it was founded by Tatneft' to serve company interests. The main republican banks are Ak Bars, Tatfondbank, and Kazanskii, and none of these banks is free from governmental control. Ak Bars is the main republican bank serving the government;[70] in 2001 Tatneft' acquired a controlling share of this bank, thus fusing the political and economic spheres in the republic even further.

All these measures aimed at enhancing the government's control over the republic's economic and financial resources allowed republican authorities to undertake forward-looking policies that went beyond simply protecting the existing industries and maintaining current levels of production. The government undertook the project of constructing an oil-processing plant in Nizhnekamsk, thus trying to avoid dependence on oil extraction and export of crude oil and instead exporting higher value-added oil-based products. The construction of the Nizhnekamsk oil-processing plant (NPZ) required a huge investment that was initially undertaken by Tatneft', Nizhnekamskneftekhim, and TAIF, later joined by a Korean consortium, LG.[71] The government has initiated other large-scale investments in republican infrastructure. The rural population has benefited from the program for full gasification of the republic.[72] The construction of a bridge across the Kama River has helped optimize transportation routes beyond as well as within the republic.[73] The government has also initiated costly construction of a metro system in the republic's capital, Kazan.

Several other socially oriented projects promoted by the republican government indicate the elites' concern for the legitimacy of the authorities and the political regime. The government devised special social assistance programs targeting the most disadvantaged groups in the society. This program was initiated and implemented much before similar actions were undertaken by the Russian government. Also, the residents of Kazan have greatly benefited from the Dilapidated Residential Houses Liquidation Program (*vetkhoe zhil'e*). This project, implemented since 1996, has provided for free new housing for the residents of very old buildings due for demolition.[74] Though the special tax invented for the purposes of this project and levied on republican businesses was greatly resisted and eventually brought to court and declared illegal, the public benefit of this project as well as its political benefit for legitimizing the authorities can hardly be denied.[75]

The transformational path undertaken by Tatarstan in the economic sphere has been marketed within Russia and to the outside world as "the model of Tatarstan."[76] The list of Tatarstan's advertised achievements include economic growth starting in 1995,[77] steadily rising volumes of industrial production,[78] housing construction, and, of course, the long-term investment projects initiated and successfully implemented by the republican government (table 3.2). Tatarstan's successes have received external validation as the republic has consistently ranked among the top ten Russian regions in investment attractiveness, with the peak of foreign investment in 1997–98.[79] In short, Tatarstan's political centralization went hand in hand with economic protectionism and state control over the key economic sectors. Economic elites—formerly "red directors"—were in

TABLE 3.2. Selected Socioeconomic Indicators, Republic of Tatarstan (RT) and Nizhnii Novgorod Region (NN), 1991–2001

		1991	1992	1993	1994	1995	1996	1997	1998	1999	2000	2001
Population (1000s)	RT	3,684										3,777
	NN	3,781										3,633
Income monthly, per capita*	RT	.403	2.93	37	153	394	546	691	760	1,294	1,779	1,779
	NN	.423	3.1	39	164	382	532	654	721	1,134	1,562	1,561
Gross regional product (GRP)	RT					37,829.5	57,642	64,605.7	70,967.9	12,3671.8		
	NN					35,172.3	42,559.4	51,145.9	51,687.3	83,456.2		
Investments in main capital stock**	RT											42,743
	NN											14,656
Industrial production volumes***	RT	31.7	521	3266	9,687	31,761	44,184	49,948	59,568	97,605	191,300	
	NN	34.7	542	4,023	11,193	29,631	34,978	41,512	43,437	74,331	106,984	
No. of privatized objects	RT			42	179	265	134	151	86	128	104	
	NN			1290	510	203	73	82	59	41	31	
No. of small businesses****	RT					18.2	15.8	16.4	15.6	17.2	16.1	
	NN					11.4	14.1	14.9	13.9	15.8	13.6	
Housing construction*****	RT	1,576	1,453	1,296	1,227	1,327	1,387	1,407	1,467	1,504	1,503	
	NN	968	969	1,065	912	737	644	563	537	574	577	

* in thousands of rubles until 1998
** in millions of rubles
*** in billions of rubles until 1998
**** in thousands
***** in thousands of square meters

effect incorporated into the political elite. Not only were they state appointees, but they were also expected to run for the republican legislature.

The Tatar Version of Cronyism

The importance of informal relationships and networks in Tatarstan has been noted by numerous observers.[80] Some authors have even raised that issue as a special feature of the republican political regime, explaining it either by ethnic or rural background of its leaders, more traditionally oriented than in other regions.[81] Commenting on informal networks in Tatarstan a British scholar noted, "Elite networks have an all-pervading role in the economy. They operate across the FSE [former Soviet enterprise] networks and the interactions of state power."[82] Reflecting on his work experience in Kazan, a foreign businessman noted, "The most important thing is to have connections. Influence in the government is essential. Influence, not money, is the problem."[83]

While the importance of connections and influence is not restricted to Tatarstan only,[84] the crony capitalist system in this republic indeed has its own distinctiveness associated with the nature of its monocentric political system. In the words of one member of the republican economic elite, "In the Republic of Tatarstan all is managed from one center. . . . Sometimes even small questions are decided only by the president of Tatarstan. In Tatarstan, nothing is done without Shaimiev's consent."[85] The political domination of the president manifested itself in economic transformation as well. The emergence of crony capitalism in Tatarstan can be seen in the case of Tatar-American Investments and Finances (TAIF), the most significant new business structure in the republic during the 1990s. While Russia's cronyism was reflected in, among other things, the emergence of oligarchs, in Tatarstan there were no oligarchs—unless the TAIF "empire" is viewed as the Tatar version of an oligarchy.

TAIF was established as a public joint stock company, involving private, state, and foreign capital.[86] Over a period of several years TAIF expanded at an unprecedented rate and became a diversified holding company composed of over forty subsidiary firms. Investment is one of the most important aspects of TAIF's activities. The subsidiary TAIF-INVEST was established in 1997 to work with big corporate clients as well as with individual portfolios. TAIF owns large shares of major Tatarstan enterprises, including Tatneft' and Kazanorgsintez and such national entities as Sberbank and Lukoil.[87] Tatarstan's petrochemical industry represented another important direction for TAIF's expansion. The company started by investing in and renting oil-processing equipment from Nizhnekamskneftekhim. It later joined one of the most ambitious republican projects, the construction of a new oil-processing plant in Nizhnekamsk (NNPZ), only to take it away from its largest investors and stakeholders, Tatneft' and Nizhnekamskneftekhim. By the end of 2005 TAIF was the primary owner of NNPZ.[88] This purchase undermined Tatneft''s reputation to a certain extent. The oil company was the biggest investor in this oil-processing plant and, after selling its shares to TAIF, immediately initiated a construction of a new oil-processing plant.[89] TAIF's grand expansion into the petrochemical industry continued, and in 2005 it secured a controlling interest in Kazanorgsintez, the biggest producer of polyethylene in Russia.[90] Then, even more strikingly, in 2006 the company obtained control over Nizhnekamskneftekhim after the republican-controlled holding company Sviazinvestneftekhim entrusted TAIF with almost 30 percent of Nizhnekamskneftekhim's shares for five years.[91] Of course, this remarkable expansion of a privately owned company into the most strategic sectors of the republican economy was not accidental; it could not have happened without the republican government's active participation.

Telecommunications was another profitable sector that TAIF came to dominate in Tatarstan for several years. In 1998 the joint stock company TAIF-Telecom was established and started to introduce in Tatarstan the GSM-900 cellular system. Santel, a subsidiary of TAIF-Telecom, had over fifty thousand clients and was considered one of the largest regional cell phone companies in Russia.[92] Furthermore, in 2000 TAIF created a new telecom company, IntelSet (Intellectual Nets), which was expected to provide its clients with the most advanced multimedia services, including IP connection, cable TV, video-conferencing, and fast-speed Internet connection. In 1998 the government almost sold to TAIF its telecommunication company, Tatincom-T.[93] However, the deal was halted on the grounds that it was illegal; it was initiated with no regard for the republican laws on privatizing state-owned enterprises.[94] TAIF's expansion into the telecommunication sector was accompanied by attempts to monopolize this rapidly developing industry. In fact, the republican state committee of communications (Goskomsviazi) was sued for illegal demands in regard to licensing of telecommunication companies (some of which were denied licenses in favor of TAIF).[95]

TAIF is also heavily involved in construction.[96] Its construction-related subsidiaries include Meta-TAIF (created in 1996 to participate in the republican program of liquidating dilapidated housing), TAIF-ST (created in 1999 for construction of a cultural-entertainment center and other buildings), MT-Servis, and TAIF-Art, which is involved in the reconstruction of the buildings in the capital's historic center, among other projects.[97] As soon as the buildings are constructed, another subsidiary of TAIF, IntelSet, establishes telecommunications in them,[98] revealing once again the monopolistic nature of the economic activities in the republic.

In the words of Albert Shigabutdinov, director general of the company, TAIF is involved in just about everything. It provides security services, insurance, trade, air transportation, and consulting services on customs issues. It appears that TAIF represents a weblike business structure that is expanding in every profitable sector of the economy. As Shigabutdinov stated, "We find open niches in the service industry and create firms that fill those niches."[99] In terms of its potential for expansion, TAIF has no rivals in Tatarstan. With an annual capital turnover of over $1 billion, the company is comparable to the biggest Russian enterprises.[100] Yet, in contrast to the infamous Russian oligarchs, TAIF and its owners are not very well known. TAIF's expansion was so rapid, overwhelming, and hidden that even republican residents are not always aware of the extensiveness of its reach. What allowed this company to expand so dramatically? The answer is simple: government connections. TAIF is directly linked to the first president of Tatarstan through his son, who occupies a key position in the company.[101] Not surprisingly, it has enjoyed direct entitlements and favorable policies from the government. From 1996, based on a resolution of the Cabinet of Ministers, TAIF has had privileged access to oil (one million tons of oil were sold to this company at below-market prices) and considerable tax breaks, including profit taxes and the republican portion of VAT.[102] It might not have been an accident, then, that the only person who advised against this resolution on privileged access to oil, Dmitrii Nagumanov, then minister of finance, was soon replaced by Rustam Minnikhanov (current president of Tatarstan). In addition to signing the resolution, Minnikhanov removed the specification of the time period during which TAIF would have access to oil.[103]

Radik Shaimiev, son of Mintimir Shaimiev and a key individual controlling TAIF, is also one of the owners of Nira Export, a trading company created in 1992 and still operating in Tatarstan. Nira Export is involved in oil exports and receives privileged access to oil at below-market prices.[104] Another son of the first president, Airat Shaimiev, was the director general of the joint stock company Road Services (Dorozhnyi servis) and in 2008 continued as head of its replacement company Tatavtodor, which controls all the state resources associated with road construction in Tatarstan. Tatarstan's electric utility company Tatenergo is headed by Mintimer Shaimiev's nephew, Il'shat Fardiev, who was often spoken of as the designated successor of the president.[105] He is also a member of the board of directors of Ak Bars bank.[106] The son-in-law of the president's sister is the director general of Nizhnekamskshina, the big tire-making plant that became part of Tatneft''s holdings in 2000. There are other personal ties linking the government and the business elite: Tatarstan's former prime minister, Rustam Minnikhanov; Shaimiev's two sons; and the minister of internal affairs, Asgat Safarov, all have the same hobby, car racing.[107] It would be unrealistic to consider their political and business careers entirely isolated from their close social interaction. In short, the prevalence of familial links (especially to the first president of Tatarstan) is very noticeable in the republic. The importance of these links was highlighted, ironically, in an attempt to extort money from local chiefs by means of proposals for nonexistent leasing projects for agricultural trucks and equipment in which one of the con men claimed to be the president's son.[108] Before the crooks were caught, they successfully defrauded at least six chiefs of regional administration in Tatarstan.

TAIF's expansion illuminates one important aspect of the political-economic system that emerged in the republic during the 1990s. While some of the most significant economic assets have been kept under state control, with state officials serving on the boards of directors and the directors of major enterprises being appointed by the president, the opportunities for private enrichment and economic expansion were open to the selected few individuals who have close (in this case familial) links to the highest state authorities.

TABLE 3.3. Main EPNs in the Republic of Tatarstan by 2001

	Political	*Economic*	*Ideological*
Shaimiev	President	Tatneft',	TV channel
	Prime minister	TAIF	Respublika Tatarstan
Iskhakov	Mayor	Edelveis group,	TV channel Efir,
		Krasnyi Vostok	*Kazanskie Vedomosti*
			Vecherniaia Kazan

Other, smaller business structures also potentially represented the economic foundation for alternative EPNs in Tatarstan (table 3.3). One such business group consisted of the industrial and trading group Edelveis, which included a successful chain of supermarkets in Kazan and other cities in Tatarstan, the successful and expanding beer company Krasnyi Vostok, and a number of smaller firms in the dairy industry.[109] This group, led by the Khairullin brothers, was closely associated with the former mayor of Kazan, Kamil Iskhakov. In fact, the city owned the blocking share of Krasnyi Vostok and has been invited to participate in other business initiatives related to this group.[110] The group also had media outlets such as the TV channel Efir and the newspaper *Kazanskie Vedomosti*. This network, however, did not fully realize its potential in Tatarstan. The main reason for its relative political passivity was the absence of an independent political basis in the context of political centralization characterizing the republican political system. The post of the mayor of Kazan was the position appointed by the president; Iskhakov, therefore, lacked any independent political power and could not undertake serious political activities that would challenge the president. Any threatening independent move would have resulted in his removal.

In the context of federal reforms undertaken by Putin in his first presidential term, the issues of local self-governance in Russia have gained temporary prominence, and local governments, especially the mayors of big cities, were considered allies of federal authorities in the stand-off with supposedly overly independent regional governments.[111] The shift toward mayoral elections in Kazan seemed imminent and threatened to change the political landscape in Tatarstan. These expectations did not reach fruition, however. A new federal law on local self-governance was adopted in 2003,[112] and the president of Tatarstan promised to implement it by 2006.[113] Indeed, new municipal formations were created in 2006, including Kazan municipality. The mayoral elections have still not been held however. After Iskhakov, Kazan's first mayor, left the republic for a high-level federal job in 2005,[114] the mayor was determined by the Kazan city council rather than citywide elections.[115] Adhering closely to Shaimiev's plan, the city council elected Il'sur Metshin, former chief of the Nizhnekamsk region, as the mayor of Kazan. The alternative EPN that could have rivaled the dominant president-controlled elite network thus never emerged.

If Kamil Iskhakov had been an elected mayor of Kazan, then the EPN he controlled would have been armed with necessary political, economic, and media resources. However, such a scenario did not come to pass, and Iskhakov's EPN existed only in an embryonic form.

The types of EPNs that Tatarstani transformation gave rise to were very different from the networks that emerged in Nizhnii Novgorod. During the 1990s Tatarstan witnessed the rise of a broad-based dominant elite network that involved the top political elite on the republican level, the mid-level political elite on the regional level, and the economic elite represented by the directors of key republican enterprises. This broad coalition was formed intentionally by the top republican leadership, which aimed to create a centralized pyramid of power in the republic. This process involved co-optation and integration of diverse political and economic interests under the same political umbrella, as well as removal of potential political rivals from positions of political prominence. Such an EPN can be referred to as a catchall, hegemonic EPN.

Also, as noted earlier, Tatarstani crony capitalism has a strong familial, kinship element. The most successful new business structure in the republic involved a direct family member of the republican president. The dramatic expansion of this business enterprise could not have occurred without direct or indirect governmental assistance. It should be emphasized that this business enterprise does not constitute the cornerstone of the republican political and economic system. The real cornerstone, Tatneft', is still controlled by the government of Tatarstan. TAIF is a successful business venture that is a side product of capitalist development in the context of political centralization. Therefore, it is difficult to equate the overall political-economic system with a clan-based or patrimonial arrangement. It is rather a political machine that has a strong economic foundation with a monopolized economy open to selected few companies.

The "Chicken and Egg" Problem: Political Incentives and Economic Transformation

The discussion of political and economic transformation in Tatarstan presented in this chapter raises two questions about the extent to which the strategies chosen by the republican elites to maintain political and economic dominance were interrelated. To what extent was the non-competitive political regime constructed in the republic crucial for its path toward economic transformation? And to what extent were the economic policies themselves crucial to creating and maintaining political control in the republic? A "slip of the tongue" on the part of the republican president is illuminating in this regard. In an interview published in *Izvestiia*, commenting on Putin's federal reforms and on his efforts to strengthen the vertical of power, Shaimiev said:

> Everything that we have achieved in the republic—from implementing our own privatization program and maintaining state control over oil industry to saving the agriculture—was possible only because we had strong power. I cannot imagine, for example, how it is possible to work if the financial flows are nontransparent. And until recently the federal financial flows were controlled not by the Russian president but by oligarchs.[116]

On the one hand, Shaimiev noted the importance of "strong power" for maintaining control over the economy, thus revealing the importance of politics for the implementation of economic reforms. On the other hand, he hinted that control over financial flows underlies all the achievements in Tatarstan. Hence the interrelationship of the political structure and the economy in Tatarstan is two-sided: the attainment of control over the major economic resources allowed for integrating the political system, which, in turn, allowed for the controlled process of economic transformation aimed at maintaining the political regime. To the extent that there are new significant economic actors that emerged in the process of transformation, it is a single business group that dominates the economic scene.

Although economic transformation in Tatarstan did not result in restructuring and modernization of the economy, it was successful in terms of creating the social conditions for the republican elites' political survival and ensuring the legitimacy of the regime. The major resource-generating sectors in the economy remained under the control of the government, thus preventing the emergence of independent economic elites that could engage in competition for political power. The major new business structure that emerged during the 1990s has a family connection to the top republican leadership. Most important, by maintaining control of key economic entities, the government was able to devise a distribution system within the republic that allowed for keeping the major enterprises going, thus avoiding bankruptcy and securing employment for thousands of people. In the absence of such redistribution schemes that rechannel resources from more profitable oil extraction to "value-destroying"[117] agriculture, as well as subsidizing other manufacturing sectors, many of the industries that have persevered would have collapsed, leaving thousands of unemployed people—a recipe for social instability and even interethnic tensions. Hence through their economic policies the authorities were able to maintain social stability and the legitimacy of the regime.

By themselves, the special institutional arrangements underpinning the system of political domination in Tatarstan would not have been able to prop up the regime in the long term. Without the social stability and political integration generated in the republic through a system of redistribution that allowed for maintaining production levels and employment, the federal center would have been more prone to intervene and attempt to replace the too-independent-minded leadership by influencing elections.[118] In fact, an attempt to test the ground for such an action was made prior to the March 2001 presidential elections in the republic. A public survey sponsored by the federal center was conducted with the aim of determining the extent of popular support for the government.[119] It appears that the presidential administration in Moscow was indeed considering the likelihood of success of promoting an alternative candidate to replace Shaimiev.[120] However, having found considerable support for the current leadership, plans to replace Shaimiev were dismissed in favor of negotiating with him. Thus the transformation strategies undertaken by the republican elites were successful also in the sense of creating the conditions for regime survival. It is in this sense that economic transformation was conditioned by political imperatives and, specifically, by the need to maintain a political monopoly. The economic sphere in Tatarstan was in effect used for a political purpose.

In Nizhnii Novgorod the transformation strategy was very different. The process of economic liberalization and fast-paced privatization under Nemtsov was motivated by a strong ideological preference for promoting a market-oriented economy. Conducted in the context of an underdeveloped institutional and legal environment, alas, this strategy did not produce the expected result of economic growth and modernization but was very costly socially and politically. An open fragmentation of Nizhnii's political regime after 1997 and an ensuing political rivalry, on the one hand, and growing popular disappointment with regional authorities, on the other, revealed the limits of Nemtsov's liberal policies that ignored the interests of key economic players in the region. Numerous privatization projects resulted in asset-stripping and bankruptcy of major regional enterprises. Therefore, most of the 1990s in Nizhnii were characterized by increasing deterioration of the regional industry and agriculture (see tables 3.2 and 2.1 for a comparison of the dynamics of industrial and agricultural development in Nizhnii Novgorod and Tatarstan). Instead of improving the regional tax base as a result of expected economic growth following economic liberalization, the regional government simply lost control over financial flows and lacked other mechanisms to control the regional economy as the resources flowed into the hands of a more diverse group of actors.

In short, while neither strategy (that of Tatarstan or Nizhnii Novgorod) could be claimed to be economically successful, the socially oriented strategy pursued by the Tatarstani government was evidently more successful politically. To what extent was oil a factor crucial in determining this success? After all, as an oil-producing region the Republic of Tatarstan had access to financial resources from oil exports. Could not oil rents have provided the republican government with advantages not available to Nizhnii Novgorod? Are the legitimacy of and popular support for the Tatarstani government better explained by the availability of resources from oil exports?

Industries linked to the fuel and energy sector as well as metal production fared better than other industries in the transition period in Russia.[121] Consequently, regions lacking a natural resource extraction sector experienced greater industrial decline in the first years of the transition than regions that could rely on natural resources.[122] Undoubtedly oil was extremely important for the political success of Tatarstan. The government-controlled Tatneft' has been a crucial element in Tatarstan's political and economic system and is rightly seen as a power base of the republican ruling elite. The presence of oil served as a structural precondition for the success of the transformation strategy undertaken by the republican elites. And it is oil resources that differentiate Tatarstan from the neighboring region of Ulyanovsk, where a similar strategy of "delayed" economic reforms ended with the collapse of the political regime led by Yuri Goryachev.[123] Oil revenues in Tatarstan allowed for constructing the wealth-sharing schemes that not only sustained the major sectors of the Tatarstani economy but also, more important, unified the republican elites, which might not have been possible without the availability of that wealth in the first place. But the strategy chosen by the government was important as well. The presence of oil in the republic is not by itself a sufficient explanation for the differing political and social dynamics in two regions. A counterfactual is helpful here.

How would the presence of oil in Nizhnii Novgorod have changed the region's political trajectory? I would argue that the trajectory would not have been radically different, given Nemtsov's liberalization and privatization policies driven by ideological zeal rather than pragmatic concerns of maintaining elite and mass support for the regime. If oil had been available in Nizhnii, then the situation there would have resembled that in the Komi region, where the regional oil conglomerate Komineft' was stripped of its assets by the numerous joint ventures formed with Western partners.[124] This scenario seems more likely in Nizhnii given the notorious cases of asset-stripping at several major regional enterprises. Another analogy could be drawn between Nizhnii Novgorod and Yeltsin's Russia, even if these are different types of political units. Like Nemtsov, Yeltsin pursued a strategy of economic liberalization and rapid privatization, so by 1996 most of Russia's oil resources ended up in private hands and were used for private enrichment rather than subsidizing other economic sectors that were less profitable and sustaining support for the political regime. In short, oil was important in Tatarstan as a resource that made it possible to successfully incorporate major elites into the political system and thus served as a precondition to the politically unified and nonfragmented elite. When in private hands, oil resources enable political competition and could create a challenge to the regime.[125] Not surprisingly, Putin has been eager to consolidate state control over the oil industry in Russia, as I discuss in later chapters.

Another important structural difference between Tatarstan and Nizhnii Novgorod is the ethnic factor. The Tatarstani elites had the additional resource of nationalism, which was not available to the elites in Nizhnii Novgorod. Throughout the 1990s Shaimiev presented himself as a defender of the national interests of Tatarstan vis-à-vis the federal center, without antagonizing the Russian population in the republic. He was able to carve out considerable autonomy for the republic and thus had greater leeway in terms of decision making, including greater control over regional economic resources. Does this factor explain a higher degree of stability and popular support for the regime in Tatarstan?

The ethnic factor has to also be pointed out as an important structural precondition for a different political trajectory of Tatarstan. Its status as an ethnic republic, as noted above, undoubtedly made a significant difference for political outcomes in Russia's regions.[126] In particular, it allowed for greater autonomy in regional institution building, which regional elites took advantage of. Similar to the oil factor, however, ethnic status is more potent in explaining the origins of noncompetitive regimes among Russia's regions than their transformational dynamics and political success.[127] Ethnicity was not the decisive factor that determined Tatarstan's political trajectory. Other, nonethnic regions in Russia have built political regimes similar to that in Tatarstan. The political system built by Yuri Luzhkov in Moscow, for example, is based on institutional, ideological, and economic foundations similar to those discussed in the case of Tatarstan.[128] Luzhkov's system, often noted for its cronyism, had also demonstrated significant durability and a considerable level of support from Moscow residents. Other notorious cases of nonethnic regions that evolved in an authoritarian direction are the Orel and Kemerovo regions.[129] The long-term governors of these regions, Yegor Stroev and Aman Tuleev, respectively, have also enjoyed popular support in the absence of regional democracy and political competition. In short, the ethnic factor did not predetermine the political fortunes of Tatarstan but rather served as an enabling, structural factor.

CHAPTER 4

Regional Lessons of Electoral Competition

Nie wird soviel gelogen wie nach einer Jagd, im Krieg und vor Wahlen. [People never lie so much as after a hunt, during a war, or before an election.]

—Otto von Bismarck

Political Competition, Elections, and Democracy

One of the lessons offered by the collapse of the Soviet Union is that a political system based on an empty ideological shell without real content and popular legitimacy is doomed to become destabilized. Accordingly, a political system claiming to be democratic and accountable to the people but in reality serving the interests of the few—exemplified by Russia—might also seem to be doomed to delegitimization and political instability. But destabilization of the system does not occur automatically. Even with an empty democratic shell covering the undemocratic content of the crony system, political elites have various resources for manipulating and shaping public opinion: controlling the media and administrative resources, playing the nationalist card, and creating images of external enemies so as to divert public attention from domestic problems, among others. The real destabilization occurs when the government is not able to instill faith in the system and influence public opinion in favor of the establishment. In this chapter I focus on how political competition played out during electoral campaigns undermines the legitimacy of the system by revealing the real cronyism and corruption of political elites as well as publicizing fabricated corruption stories.

The analytic link between crony capitalism and political stability was first established by the new institutionalists. Haber's theory of crony capitalism, discussed in chapter 1, postulated that the absence of limited government and self-enforcing institutions is commonly associated with conditions of political instability. New institutionalists in fact argue that crony capitalist systems originate in unstable polities and represent "the only exit" from political instability.[1] "In an unstable polity it is impossible, by definition, to create self-enforcing institutions," Haber and colleagues argued.[2] Hence, to promote growth and resolve the commitment problem the government promotes crony arrangements whereby it ensures property rights to a selected group of economic actors. This link between political instability and cronyism places all the crony systems into one category in terms of political stability. While on an analytic level this might be justifiable, in practice some crony systems have a much greater degree of stability than others. Several decades of Suharto rule in Indonesia, for example, were fairly stable, whereas neighboring Thailand, also a crony capitalist system, underwent numerous coups and suffered from much political instability during the same time. The regional examples of cronyism in Russia are also characterized by varying degrees of political stability. Nizhnii Novgorod oblast became increasingly fragmented and destabilized after Nemtsov's departure to Moscow, whereas Tatarstani authorities built a remarkably stable, noncompetitive political regime.

A comparison of crony capitalist systems with different degrees of stability and an exploration of reasons for the differing political scenarios draw attention to the role played by political competition. The argument developed in this chapter allows for reversing the neoinstitutionalist claim that cronyism is an "exit" from political instability. It appears from this case study that instead of instability "causing" cronyism, cronyism itself causes instability when revealed through the workings of political competition and the electoral mechanism. When functioning as an actual mechanism of power transfer, competitive elections have the unintended effect of uncovering the predatory nature of crony elites and thus undermining the legitimacy of the overall political-economic order crafted by a self-serving ruling class. Involved in an intense fight for state office, political candidates and their supporters resort to manipulative techniques and dirty tricks, which, in the end, discredit not only their opponents and themselves personally but also the state and political institutions in general. Political institutions are delegitimized as means adapted by predatory elites for their ends. Paradoxically, instead of undermining crony capitalism (as new institutionalists expect), the electoral process itself gets delegitimized, along with the overall political-economic system that is perceived as corrupt. In such circumstances, political competition played out in public through competitive elections cannot be sustained without endangering the very existence of the overall system.

Earlier studies of political corruption in transition countries have noted that the public perception of corruption "is not always the result of genuine endogenous factors,"[3] and therefore perceptions of corruption do not necessarily correspond to the actual degree of corruption. The case study explored here suggests that these perceptions can be linked, in part, to the degree of political competitiveness in the system that plays out in such a way as to create an image of corrupt rivaling elites. I illustrate this idea by focusing first on political conflicts in each region and, specifically, how the electoral campaigns played out in the competitive system in Nizhnii Novgorod and the noncompetitive system of Tatarstan. I then illustrate this point using a statistical study of political competition levels and perceptions of corruption in forty Russian regions.

Political Competition and Elections under Crony Capitalism: Development of the Negative Scenario

To summarize the evidence from the outset, after Nemtsov's departure from the region Nizhnii Novgorod experienced progressive political fragmentation and intensifying competition that revealed itself primarily in the elections for its two main executive posts, governor and mayor. Elections became more heated, scandalous, and marred by a variety of dirty tricks, while the level of public apathy and protest against the regime progressively increased. In political struggle, candidates used various kinds of electoral tricks, including political provocation, massive negative campaigning, and compromising materials (often fabricated) against the competitors. With each successive election, these methods became more brazen and elaborate, so that by 2001 Nizhnii Novgorod was one of the most infamous showcases for new "political technologies"[4] and "black PR" used during the elections in Russia's regions.[5] The public reaction to these elections was decreased voter participation, a larger number of people voting against all the candidates, rising attitudes of distrust and disaffection with regional elites, and emerging signs of disillusionment with regional and local elections.

In the noncompetitive environment of the Republic of Tatarstan, on the other hand, interelite fragmentation, though sometimes present, did not play out during the elections. The regime dealt with such fragmentation undercover, avoiding public spillover. The strength and flexibility of the regime was reflected in its ability to accommodate or expel potential opposition forces, so that no force that could challenge the establishment would be able to consolidate during the 1990s. Well-controlled elections held in the republic avoided the scandals characterizing the elections in Nizhnii Novgorod. Held in a very calm, Soviet-style manner, they were used as a legitimation tool for the republican authorities. Attitudes toward the government remained favorable, and there were fewer protest votes.

Nizhnii under Nemtsov: Dominant Actor Politics under Informal Rules

The weakening of the newly introduced formal democratic institutions in Nizhnii Novgorod started under its first governor, Boris Nemtsov. Although he appeared to be one of the most democratic and reform-minded governors in Russia, Nemtsov's political style was nondemocratic and revealed the predominance of informal relationships in the region. This "rule of informality" can be clearly seen in the character of resolution of the main political conflicts of Nemtsov's era and, especially, the way in which they were resolved. The first serious conflict in the upper echelons of power in the region occurred in early 1994 and involved a controversy between the governor and the mayor of Nizhnii.

Mayor Bedniakov's growing influence as a result of a successful small-scale privatization that started in 1992 brought these two actors face to face. This happened as Bedniakov attempted to hold a referendum on the draft city charter at the same time as the mayoral elections. The charter conferred wide prerogatives on the local government, freeing the municipal authorities from state supervision. It appeared that Bedniakov, who had been a member of Nemtsov's team, became more autonomous and formed a potential alternative to the regional administration power center. To prevent actual consolidation of a new power center, Nemtsov promoted another candidate, Evgenii Krestianinov, who was personally loyal to him. When right before the election it became clear that Krestianinov would lose, he withdrew and the election was canceled because there were no other candidates.[6] This disingenuous trick on the part of Governor Nemtsov to get rid of his opponent was one of the first incidents that undermined his democratic image; regional commentators noted that it demonstrated Nemtsov's disregard for the popular will in the region.

This governor/mayor divide became a common source of regional intraelite fragmentation throughout Russia,[7] though how the conflict was dealt with differed. In Nizhnii Novgorod the conflict between Nemtsov and Bedniakov was resolved with help from the Russian president. Using his close connection to Yeltsin, Nemtsov lobbied for the removal of Bedniakov from his position. Nemtsov's efforts resulted in Yeltsin's decree dismissing Bedniakov from his post "for a single violation of his professional duties."[8] Nemtsov practically used Yeltsin as a "roof" to protect himself from a perceived challenger and, in doing that, revealed his political weakness. An appeal to Yeltsin in that situation amounted to resorting to force and manipulation rather than facing the challenger publicly.

The other two noteworthy conflicts of Nemtsov's period in Nizhnii Novgorod involved the governor and GAZ director Boris Vidiaev and his onetime friend Andrei Kliment'ev (see chapter 2). Although Nemtsov won in both confrontations, proving his dominant stance in regional politics, these victories (just as the first one) did not add to the consolidation of the political system and strengthening of democratic institutions in the region. All these conflicts involved actors that were well known and popular in the region. They were heavily publicized and, for the most part, interpreted as cases of personal confrontations and struggles for power rather than attempts to promote regional, institutional, or state interests.[9] They strengthened Nemtsov's personal power but had a negative impact on formal political institutions in the region. The 1994 mayoral elections, for example, manifested very clearly to the public that it is not sovereign in making its choices. The electoral process was manipulated to avoid the victory of the popular opponent. The electoral laws were used for the benefit of *Nemtsov's* vision of who should become mayor.

Despite problematic mayoral elections in 1994, the first gubernatorial elections, held on December 17, 1995,[10] demonstrated strong support for Nemtsov. At that time the incumbent governor ran in tandem with Skliarov, who was seeking reelection as mayor of Nizhnii Novgorod.[11] Their main strategy consisted of numerous meetings with the electorate. It was very effective and easy to implement because Nemtsov, as governor, had access to administrative resources and could rely on the district chiefs as well as on the public enterprise directors to organize the meetings. Absent administrative resources that could match the governor's, Nemtsov's main contender, Viacheslav Rasteriaev (an entrepreneur, head of the joint-stock company Nizhegorodskii Dom), depended on the support of the regional branch of the Communist Party (CPRF). This support allowed him to organize meetings with the electorate, especially in districts where support for Nemtsov was lower than average.[12] Rasteriaev's campaign got a boost from two major scandals that erupted shortly before the elections. One of the scandals was related to the bankruptcy of the Nizhegorodskii kredit bank, which Rasteriaev had cofounded. The bankruptcy was promoted by Nemtsov himself, and his involvement in this process was widely interpreted in the media as an attempt to weaken his political opponent.[13] Rasteriaev's team had also engaged in negative campaigning, accusing the regional administration of the misuse of funds from the sale of five hundred Volga cars intended for the agricultural sector.[14] Although the former procurator confirmed this information, it came too late during the campaign for Rasteriaev to reap the benefits. In the end, Nemtsov won in the first round, securing 58 percent of the vote, while Rasteriaev received 26 percent.[15]

In brief, despite the dominance of informal rules and relations and forceful methods of resolving conflicts, Nemtsov maintained his political stature and public support until his departure in 1997. He effectively eliminated potential challengers and pursued his radical policies, which eventually proved disastrous. But the public in large part trusted him. During 1992–97 the public's level of trust in Nemtsov remained stable, rising from 39 percent in 1992 to 55 percent in 1995 and 53 percent in 1997.[16] Much of the regional political evolution in Nizhnii Novgorod that occurred after Nemtsov was driven by his legacy, although the political context and structure changed dramatically. In a way Nemtsov set the stage for what was to come after him, and many of the regional conflicts, political actors, and economic scenarios can be traced to his time in office.

The 1997 Electoral Campaign: The Puzzle Solved Prior to the Elections

The second gubernatorial election in the region occurred after Nemtsov's departure for Moscow in 1997.[17] Nemtsov left considerable uncertainty behind when he refused to express a clear preference for either of the two potential heirs to his position. On the one hand, there was Lebedev, an energetic deputy governor who was not well known to the public but possessed administrative resources derived from serving as acting governor after Nemtsov left. On the other hand, Skliarov, mayor of Nizhnii Novgorod, was a well-known and respected politician who earned the support of the residents of the capital during his term as city manager. Skliarov was also supported by many of the enterprise managers in the region. In the end, it came down to the date of the election: Skliarov would benefit from an earlier date, whereas Lebedev saw benefit in a later date. When the regional legislature set the earliest date possible, favoring Skliarov's agenda, Deputy Governor Lebedev decided to withdraw from the race. Thus Skliarov's strongest opponent backed away from the competition, mooting any potential political intrigue. Not surprisingly, these elections are treated in regional political history as the most boring and uneventful. No negative campaigning, black PR, or dirty tricks were used during this campaign. It should be noted, however, that already in this election Skliarov demonstrated a lack of political skill and savvy. Despite overwhelming support from the most powerful regional interests (including enterprise directors as well as the regional intellectual and cul-

TABLE 4.1. Participation and Protest Vote in the Nizhnii Novgorod Region

	Turnout (%)	Against All (%)
1994 mayoral elections	Not held	Not held
1995 gubernatorial elections	63	5.3
1997 gubernatorial elections	40.1	2.9
Runoffs	48.9	3.5
1998 mayoral elections (March, results annulled)	51.1	4.5
1998 mayoral elections (September)	37.2	10.1
Runoffs (October)	36.1	12.8
2001 gubernatorial elections	37.3	8.2
Runoffs	37.7	10.4
2002 mayoral elections	29	30.4
Runoffs	36.6	29

tural elites), he had to go through two rounds of elections and won, ultimately, with a relatively small margin.[18]

Although public opinion surveys held prior to the elections revealed a high degree of interest and involvement on the part of the population,[19] the actual turnout was lower than expected and lower than that in the 1995 gubernatorial elections. Even in the second round, which attracted more voters than the first, turnout was lower than in the 1995 election (table 4.1). According to most observers, the relatively low turnout resulted from the absence of political intrigue. Apparently, some people simply decided not to bother going to the polls because they perceived Skliarov was the definite winner. Unexpectedly, though, the first round of elections resulted in a thin margin—3 percent—separating the two candidates, revealing that Skliarov's political opponents were more successful in mobilizing the voters. Consequently, more attention was paid to mobilizing voters for the second round, and the distance between the two candidates increased by approximately the same amount as the increase in the turnout, about 10 percent.

These elections in Nizhnii Novgorod adhered most closely to true democracy. Skliarov's main opponent, Gennadii Khodyrev, representing the Communists, was able to galvanize voters based primarily on criticism of Nemtsov's radical policies and reforms. His success in becoming a real challenge to the political establishment represented by Skliarov demonstrated that the elections could be a real tool for change in the region. As was appropriately noted by some regional observers, this election contributed to increasing the weight and the meaningfulness of elections in the regional political process.[20] Indeed, the general attitudes toward the elections at this point were very favorable. Alas, this situation would not last.

The 1998 Political Season: Stolen Elections

The political situation in the region changed dramatically with the 1998 mayoral elections in the capital city of Nizhnii Novgorod. The results of this election, held in March 1998, were akin to an explosion or an earthquake rocking the seemingly quiet political scene. Nemtsov's erstwhile friend and protégé, the infamous entrepreneur Kliment'ev, earlier charged with embezzlement, won the race. The two candidates representing the party in power, Bedniakov (former mayor, supported by Nemtsov) and Gorin (acting mayor), lost to the candidate accused of misappropriating funds and even convicted in 1982 of swindling.[21] Nobody expected such an outcome. Opinion polls conducted several months before the election did reveal some increase in support for Kliment'ev, but Gorin and Bedniakov had received considerably higher support.[22] Kliment'ev's campaign was very similar to Bedniakov's in that both candidates promised more money, care, and support to the electorate.[23] The major difference was that Kliment'ev also initiated a counterattack on Nemtsov, accusing him of bribery.[24] This was a response to Nemtsov's earlier accusations.

Kliment'ev's victory was a shattering embarrassment for the authorities. Both the regional and the federal authorities lost with the defeat of their candidates. The victory went to Nemtsov's personal enemy with a questionable past and, allegedly, a criminal present. The reaction was swift. The regional electoral commission immediately declared the results of the election invalid. The Central Electoral Commission voided the results, claiming that all the candidates had broken regional and federal electoral laws.[25] The federal authorities also responded by firing Lebedev, then the presidential envoy to the region; reprimanding Skliarov, the governor; and arresting Kliment'ev at the court hearings on the issue of the Navashinskii credit embezzlement.[26]

This incident represented a turning point in popular attitudes in Nizhnii Novgorod. Before this election people expressed trust for the authorities, with regional authorities scoring consistently better than the federal branches of power. The invalidation of the results of this election represented a "theft" conducted by the state; it reflected the hypocrisy of the electoral process and the alleged choice people had in who governs them. It appeared that people had a space only for a "proper" choice; if that choice was unsuitable for the political establishment, it was quickly annulled. Democracy seemed to be a game played by the elites. This was already the second time authorities in Nizhnii Novgorod, aided by the federal government, resorted to arbitrary political manipulation to avoid the "damaging" consequences of the elections. Popular faith in elections as an institution still remained high at this time. Public opinion polls conducted in May 1998 demonstrated that over half of respondents wanted a new election and opposed the idea of having their mayor appointed, even if it was by presidential decree.[27]

The next election was scheduled for September 27, 1998. Kliment'ev did not participate in the new race for the mayoral seat. He went to jail after the Supreme Court affirmed the decision of the regional court in regard to the embezzlement charges. The fall election involved intense competition and played out in two rounds.[28] From the original pool of twenty-two individuals who wanted to participate in the race, ten were registered by the regional electoral commission as official candidates. Most regional experts expected that the main competition would be among three candidates: Lebedev, Bedniakov, and Semago.[29] Governor Skliarov supported Bedniakov, hoping for a mayor who would share his political and economic agenda and recognize his political dominance.[30] In the end, the two top candidates, Lebedev and Bedniakov, went to the second round, held on October 12, 1998. Over 10 percent of the population voted against all the candidates, and the turnout was about 37 percent.

The second round turned into open information warfare between the two finalists, featuring mutual accusations in wrongdoing and the like.[31] Bedniakov's campaign was especially aggressive and aimed at compromising his opponent.[32] The major regional media aligned with different candidates: the Seti-NN TV company supported Lebedev; Volga and NNTV supported Bedniakov.[33] Lebedev won, and that resolved the mayoral issue in the regional capital. The entire 1998 electoral season, however, raised questions and doubts among the "traumatized" population about the worthiness of the electoral process. As one regional analyst asked, "Was the switch between the former mayor [Skliarov] and the former acting governor [Lebedev] worth such political turbulence, trouble, and anxiety that unfolded in the region after Nemtsov's departure and took a year and a half to complete?"[34] Even with such assessments, the 1998 electoral season in Nizhnii Novgorod was only a prelude to the mayhem that unfolded during the gubernatorial and mayoral electoral campaigns in 2001–2.

The 2001 Gubernatorial Elections: A Battle of Political Technologies

The gubernatorial election in July 2001 manifested further intensification of elite in-fighting in the region. It became exceptional in the degree of usage and types of political technologies and black PR employed to mobilize voters. If 1997–98 was a transition period between Nemtsov's era in the region and what was to come after, the 2001 election revealed the main fault lines of the new political structure. The new system consolidated along the two political poles. One pole, led by the EPN associated with Kirienko, represented both federal and regional authorities. As a presidential envoy to the Volga Federal District, Kirienko represented the federal center and, in this election, supported the reelection of the incumbent governor, Skliarov. The other pole was driven by the alliance between Savel'ev's EPN and the mayor, Lebedev, and was therefore associated with the city authorities. The resources controlled by these EPNs were estimated in chapter 2. They combined administrative, financial, and media resources all of which were employed in the fierce struggle for the gubernatorial seat.

Incumbent Governor Skliarov and Mayor Lebedev were the candidates from these two major political centers. However, Lebedev was disqualified from the race by the regional electoral commission for using administrative resources to gather signatures to support his candidacy. Savel'ev replaced him as the candidate representing this alliance. Three other candidates—the infamous antisystem candidate Kliment'ev,[35] State Duma deputy Bulavinov, and Khodyrev—entered the race for the gubernatorial seat without clear association with the authorities. However, they possessed considerable resources. Bulavinov, director of Seti-NN, had extensive influence over media outlets. In addition, he was a State Duma deputy and therefore a recognizable figure in the region. Kliment'ev, a populist and a successful businessman, controlled his own economic resources, and he could now claim that he was a victim of the authorities. Only Khodyrev, a former obkom first secretary, did not have visible financial or media resources in the region, but as a communist he could appeal to the nostalgia for the past and the stability associated with the Soviet period. In brief, the political setting prior to the 2001 elections in Nizhnii Novgorod was very complex. If anything, the degree of uncertainty was so high before the election that any predictions about the winner were implausible.

This election was characterized by an extraordinary level of negative campaigning and was perceived as one of the dirtiest regional campaigns in Russia. All the top contenders became tainted by scandal. Kliment'ev was the central target for negative campaigning originating from the party in power represented by Kirienko's EPN.[36] Numerous city billboards linked Kliment'ev to homosexuals, prostitutes, and gangsters. Later these billboard characters moved onto TV screens, discrediting Kliment'ev further. Threatening signs that appeared on the city's walls and fences before the elections were attributed to Kliment'ev.[37] Kliment'ev himself did not have access to mass media and had to rely on public meetings and his populist tactics of appearing as the only "people's advocate" in the pool of corrupt and self-interested elites struggling for power.

Another contender, Savel'ev, who owned some of the largest media holdings in the region and controlled most of the city's exterior advertising, organized his own lavish and scandal-driven campaign. In fact, his was the most expensive campaign of all the candidates; it involved various tricks to manipulate public opinion.[38] In March 2001 one of his TV channels, TNT, showed a two-year-old video clip in which Kirienko voiced negative opinions about Skliarov. Several days later Savel'ev's media sources announced the disappearance of the journalist who had provided this video clip, Gennadii Grigor'ev, hinting at the possibility that the disappearance was organized by some "prominent politicians" who did not like the clip. Grigor'ev was later found in a hotel owned by Savel'ev and guarded by TNT's security forces, revealing that the whole incident was a political provocation.[39] Another story, that a journalist who wrote anti-Skliarov and anti-Kirienko articles had been the victim of political persecution, in fact was a more banal story of drunken fighting. Kirienko and Skliarov were the major targets of Savel'ev's media sources throughout the campaign. Various newspapers exposed Kirienko's links with the Church of Scientology. They also systematically reminded readers about the August 1998 default initiated by Kirienko, who was prime minister at that time, and discussed his attempts to control the regional government by creating a parallel regional administration headed by Sergei Obozov, his close associate.

Bulavinov was also the target of political provocation and negative campaigning originating in media sources controlled by Savel'ev. A number of false letters were sent out to the public (with the forged signature of Bulavinov) soliciting contributions to Bulavinov's campaign and "explaining" to voters that Bulavinov had made a deal to allow nuclear waste into the region on very favorable conditions. Furthermore, some newspapers published bogus statements attributed to Bulavinov about legalizing prostitution and certain "light" drugs, as well as allowing nuclear waste to be buried in the region. In addition, Bulavinov was accused of secretly supporting the Catholic Church, which was not viewed favorably by the region's majority Orthodox population.

In the context of numerous scandals and political provocations, the most ordinary, even boring political campaign was associated with Khodyrev. He avoided negative campaigning and relied on such standard methods as distributing leaflets and meeting with voters.[40] He was not perceived as the campaign favorite, and therefore none of the other candidates paid much attention to him or tried to ruin his image. The outcomes of this election were unanticipated,[41] as well as revealing (table 4.2). Ironically, the victory went to Khodyrev, the candidate who spent the least amount on negative campaigning and who was an outsider (during most of the 1990s Khodyrev worked for the federal government in Moscow). Khodyrev's victory clearly indicated the high level of distrust toward local actors, whose familiar faces were buried by then in the piles of compromising material that appeared in the media. The gap between the two strongest contenders, Khodyrev and Skliarov, in the first round was only

TABLE 4.2. Gubernatorial Elections in the Nizhnii Novgorod Region

December 1995	June 29, 1997 (Round I)		July 15, 2001 (Round II)	
Nemtsov 58.1%	Skliarov	40.95%	Khodyrev	24.4%
Rasteriaev 26.0%	Khodyrev	37.84%	Skliarov	20.8%
Maslov 6.1%	Bulavinov	8.15%	Bulavinov	19.9%
Sokolov 2.3%	Zvereva	6.88%	Savel'ev	12.6%
Against all 5.2%	Speranskii	1.05%	Kliment'ev	10.6%
	Against all	2.91%	Against all	8.2%
	July 13, 1997 (Round II)		July 29, 2001 (Round II)	
	Skliarov	52.04%	Khodyrev	59.8%
	Khodyrev	42.15%	Skliarov	29.3%
			Against all	10.4%

4 percent. In the second round, the proportion of those who voted for Khodyrev was twice that for Skliarov (59.8 vs. 29.3 percent). This contrast was even higher in the capital (66 vs. 16.6 percent), indicating that Nizhnii Novgorod underwent the largest share of political technology treatment and demonstrated the strongest resistance to it.[42] Turnout rates were low in both rounds, 37.3 percent and 37.7 percent, respectively. The number of people voting against all candidates increased from 8.2 percent in the first round to 10.4 percent in the second.

2002 Mayoral Elections: Who Can Turn on the Water?

The mayoral elections, held in September 2002, revealed, once again, the region's main political rivalries and featured the same political forces that had been clashing in the region for several years. The degree of fragmentation even increased as the new governor entered the political scene. Thirteen candidates ran, including three people—Bulavinov, Dikin,[43] and Sentiurin[44]—associated with the party in power,[45] Lebedev, the incumbent mayor, and Kliment'ev, who was making another attempt to acquire an official seat. The list of main contenders for the gubernatorial seat became complicated with the appearance of their "doubles." Several weeks before the election the public witnessed the entry into the campaign of new candidates whose names were the same as some of the key contenders: a man named Dikin and a man named Bulavinov. These unknown individuals popped up from nowhere, having changed their names (and their passports) just days before registration. This was a new political technology of candidate cloning designed to confuse voters and steal votes from competitors. The "clones" did not engage in campaigning; what really mattered was simply the presence of the same name twice on the ballot.[46] In addition, this campaign featured the panoply of dirty tricks used in previous campaigns: newspaper articles and leaflets falsely attributed to particular candidates, fake "documentaries" discrediting the main candidate, and even a novel about the main political figures in the region under slightly changed names that was distributed free to the public.[47]

In addition to these dirty tricks, the political warfare involved the manipulation of the public goods provision issue. During both the gubernatorial elections of summer 2001 and the mayoral elections of fall 2002, the city population suffered from hot water switch-offs. Political bickering over who was responsible and how to solve the problem became an essential part of these two electoral campaigns. In summer 2002 the entire city was left without hot water, and some parts of the city had to endure without cold water. These circumstances resulted from the regional utility company's decision to stop the supply of energy to the municipal utility companies Teploenergo and Vodokanal because of nonpayment.[48] The problem was widely discussed in the media and turned into another information war—mainly between Lebedev's allies and Kirienko's EPN, which wanted to see Lebedev go. Each side blamed the other: the municipal authorities blamed the regional administration; the regional administration pointed back to the mayor.

How was this problem seen by the city's residents? Since Nizhnovenergo, the regional utility company, was part of Kirienko's EPN, the decision to turn off the electricity supply to the municipal water supplier during the electoral campaign was suspected to be a politically motivated step directed against Lebedev and aimed at discrediting him.[49] In the course of the summer, all the key regional political actors tried to gain political capital from resolving this problem, which ultimately required federal interference.[50] Contrary to the aspirations of political elites, however, following endless contradictory media reports, the issue was ultimately linked in public eyes to the interelite political clashes rather than to problems with the municipal budget and nonpayment.[51] Such politicization of the issues related to provision of basic utilities contributed to further institutionalization of cronyism in the region as the public became a witness to elite priorities of power maximization rather than the expected state provision of public goods.

Several weeks before the election the authorities faced a very unpleasant situation. The two political outsiders, Lebedev and Kliment'ev, showed the highest rates of public support. As some polls demonstrated, Kliment'ev's support was rapidly rising. Threatened by the possibility of these two candidates facing each other in the second round, Kirienko convinced Dikin and Sentiurin to withdraw from the race and give their support to the single candidate of the party in power, Bulavinov. Furthermore, at the last minute Kliment'ev's registration as a candidate was canceled, on the grounds that he had not followed some of the campaign rules.[52] Some newspaper reports discussed at length possible fabrications involved in making a case against Kliment'ev's candidacy.[53] This was nothing new for the public, which had already had abundant opportunity during the 1990s to learn about the ways of dealing with "undesired" candidates.

The final ballot had the names of twelve candidates.[54] The main struggle was between the incumbent mayor and Bulavinov. In the end, Bulavinov won by a thin margin (see table 4.3).[55] However, in this election both frontrunners competed against another serious candidate, "against all."[56] The continuous fighting and negative campaigning led 30.4 percent of voters in the first round and 29.4 percent in the runoff to vote "against all." And participation dropped: only 29 percent in the first round and 36.6 percent in the runoff. An incident that occurred after the elections discredited the final results even further. The night after the runoff election, ostensibly responding to a complaint by Bulavinov, the regional court "arrested" the ballots, claiming to introduce additional security measures for their safety.[57] The ballots were taken under guard, and the election committees were not allowed to count the ballots that night. The next day Bulavinov withdrew his complaint and the counting resumed. The

TABLE 4.3. Mayoral Elections in Nizhnii Novgorod

March 27, 1994	December 1995	March 29, 1998	"Repeat" Elections September 27, 1998 (Round I)	September 15, 2002 (Round II)
Annulled	Skliarov 59.58%	Bedniakov 24.29%	Lebedev 33.82%	Bulavinov 31.4%
	Bedniakov 27.5%	Gorin 31.32%	Bedniakov 25.1%	Lebedev 30.85%
	Chechevichkin 3.48%	Kirienko 3.87%	Semago 21.51%	Against all 30.35%
	Kamal'dinov 0.88%	Kliment'ev 33.67%	Bulanov 4.32%	Bogdanov 1.94%
	Against all 5.49%	Kurdiumov 0.30%	Sedov 1.44%	The remaining
		Against all 4.50%	Against all 10.12%	9 candidates got
			Five other candidates	less than 1% of
			got less than 1% of	the vote
			the vote	

			October 11, 1998 (Round II)	September 29, 2002 (Round II)
			Lebedev 44%	Bulavinov 35.57%
			Bedniakov 41%	Lebedev 34.93%
			Against all 12.8%	Against all 29.4%

damage to the elections, however, could not be undone. This interference from the court was widely interpreted as an attempt by the regional administration to take control of counting the ballots.[58]

The 2001 gubernatorial and 2002 mayoral elections in Nizhnii Novgorod revealed clearly the impact of constant and unhindered political competition, as it was expressed in electoral campaigns, on the long-term survivability of the political system. The chain of compromised election campaigns starting in 1994 brought about a systemic political crisis reflected in utter discrediting of official authorities and delegitimization of political elites. The level of trust toward the regional and local government and the entire regional political system dropped significantly, as was reflected in public opinion polls, meager participation in the elections, and, most revealing, in the record number of those voting "against all" (see tables 4.1 and 4.4). The two mayoral elections in 1998 made especially visible the negative public reaction to attempts to control the electoral re-

TABLE 4.4. Public Assessment of Regional Authorities in the Nizhnii Novgorod Region

	Positive (%)			Negative (%)		
	1997	1998	2001	1997	1998	2001
Governor	40	45	17	20	20	46
Mayor	30	35	12	16	22	38

Sources: Nizhnii Novgorod: Vybory mera, 8; Politicheskaia kul'tura i politicheskoe povedenie nizhegorodskikh izbiratelei, 8.

sults by the authorities. After the "inconvenient" results of the March elections were annulled, voter turnout in September dropped by almost 13 percent, while the protest vote "against all" increased by more than 5 percent (see table 4.1). Similarly, voter turnout remained low during the 2001 gubernatorial elections and fell even lower in the 2002 mayoral elections, while the vote "against all" increased dramatically in the last mayoral elections.[59] Public assessments of regional and local authorities also took a dramatically negative turn between 1998 and 2001 (table 4.4).

Arguably, the greatest harm to the legitimacy of state authorities was inflicted when the provision of public goods was perceived to be affected by the short-term electoral concerns of the competing elites. Such a situation played out dramatically in the 2002 mayoral elections but also characterized the 2001 gubernatorial elections and was even present during the elections to Nizhnii Novgorod's regional legislature in 2000.[60] A crisis of legitimacy and trust in the entire political system was inevitable when the vital issue of water provision in the city became the subject of political bickering and point scoring for rival politicians. Indeed, the pattern of competitive and dirty elections in the region contributed to the spread of public skepticism about the electoral process itself. Local sociologists observed a growing number of people disappointed in the elections, questioning their necessity and effectiveness.[61] It was quite symbolic that at a public press conference in 2002, a journalist from Nizhnii Novgorod suggested to Putin that regional-level elections be canceled and that governors be appointed rather than elected.[62] Ironically, this idea was implemented by Putin not long thereafter.[63]

Voting in the Absence of Alternatives: The Development of a Positive Scenario

The Republic of Tatarstan has held three presidential elections since 1991.[64] The first elections were held along with the first presidential elections in Russia on June 12, 1991. The political scene was still in flux at that point, though evolving toward a tripolar system, with the authorities representing the remnants of the old system and with popular opposition— represented by nationalists and democrats—gaining force.[65] However, the authorities were able to monopolize the electoral process. In April 1991 the republic's Supreme Soviet, controlled by the communist establishment,[66] adopted a draconian law on election of the president of the Tatar Soviet Socialist Republic. Those wishing to register as candidates were required to collect the signatures of at least 2 percent of all the voters within two weeks (May 14–27, 1991). This was impossible in the absence of solid administrative support. The lack of such organizational support prevented the registration of alternative candidates, although several other individuals did, albeit unsuccessfully, try to accomplish that task.[67] As a result, in the "founding" elections in Tatarstan in June 1991 there was only one candidate on the ballot.

The elections resulted in overwhelming support for Shaimiev, who received close to 71 percent of the vote. These elections represented more of an affirmation of the republic's statehood than a reflection of its democratic nature.[68] The introduction of the post of the president was seen as a sign of the realization of the republican sovereignty that was declared in August 1990. Mintimer Shaimiev, chairman of the Supreme Soviet of Tatarstan, was supported by the public as the person representing the republic vis-à-vis the center (the Soviet Union as well as the Russian Federation). Hence the republican presidency itself embodied Tatarstan's sovereignty and statehood. The election of the first president, therefore, played an integrative role in the political process, asserting Shaimiev personally as well as the position of the political establishment.

The extent of the regime's consolidation became apparent in the second election, held in March 1996, in which Shaimiev received 97 percent of the vote. This second presidential election was also held without alternative candidates, thus reflecting the monocentric nature of the political system. Of four individuals who wanted to register, only Shaimiev's candidacy was actually registered. Although the candidate from the Communist Party[69] was able to collect the required fifty thousand signatures, he decided to withdraw from the race. Two other contenders were unable to collect enough signatures.[70]

The three potential alternative candidates were in no position to compete with Shaimiev, whose reputation had grown dramatically since 1991. The 1994 bilateral treaty with Moscow enabled Shaimiev to create favorable conditions for the development of the republican economy. The treaty essentially amounted to the creation of a special regime regulating the relations between the center and Tatarstan, according to which the republic benefited from a favorable tax-sharing arrangement with the center.[71] Without strong and charismatic opposition leaders, the election outcomes were predictable. They were organized to serve as a demonstration of popular support for the regime and a confirmation of Shaimiev's position as the undisputed leader.

In the last presidential elections, in March 2001, for the first time the ballots included the names of alternative candidates. After Putin's federal reforms, the republican leaders could no longer hold elections without alternative candidates.[72] Also, in accordance with federal laws, governors were limited to two terms. Shaimiev already had been elected twice and could not legally run for a third term. Therefore, one of the main intrigues of this election was whether Shaimiev would receive legal permission to run for a third term. This task was accomplished when the State Duma adopted, in January 2001, an amendment to the federal law that allowed most of Russia's governors to run for a third term.

Shaimiev's campaign employed mostly traditional methods: numerous meetings with voters, some populist measures (such as adding 100 rubles to pensioners' allowance as "a present from the president"), and public praise in the local mass media (controlled by the government) for the achievements of the social and economic policies undertaken by the republican government. These achievements were packaged in the form of the internationally marketed "Tatarstan model" of economic and social transformation and included references to "compromising" but firm principles adhered to by the republican authorities in regulating the republic's relations with the federal authorities.[73]

TABLE 4.5. Presidential Elections in the Republic of Tatarstan

June 12, 1991	March 24, 1996	March 26, 2001	
Shaimiev 70.9%	Shaimiev 97.14%	Shaimiev	79.52%
		Shashurin	5.78%
		Grachev	5.47%
		Sadykov	4.43%
		Fedorov	0.49%
		Against all	2.81%

TABLE 4.6. Participation and Protest Vote in the Republic of Tatarstan

Presidential Elections	Turnout (%)		Against All (%)	
	Tatarstan	Kazan	Tatarstan	Kazan
1991	63	53	NA	NA
1996	78	73	2.8	3.1
2001	79	69	2.8	4.6

Four other candidates, including State Duma deputies Grachev and Shashurin; the leader of the republican branch of the CPRF, Sadykov; and one additional candidate from the party in power,[74] Aleksandr Fedorov, chief of Zelenodol'sk District, did not have a chance. They all stood independently, without attempting to join forces against Shaimiev. Their campaigns did not attract much attention from the press, which was largely controlled by the republican authorities. No major scandals erupted that could have provoked the public to vote unpredictably. As a result, Shaimiev received over 79 percent of the votes, while Grachev, who finished second, got only 5.5 percent. Table 4.5 provides detailed results. As opposed to the plunging participation rates and the growing vote against all candidates in Nizhnii Novgorod, turnout in Tatarstan grew, and the vote "against all" remained very low (table 4.6). But can we trust these figures?

Under the monocentric regime in Tatarstan—based on controlled media, economic resources, and, most important, centralized administrative resources—it is difficult to determine the extent to which electoral results reflect genuine support for the government. Local political experts have long warned about the "manufactured" character of results, about the use of administrative resources and other methods of achieving "correct" results in elections.[75] Indeed, the evidence of vote falsification and indiscriminate use of administrative resources in Tatarstan appears convincing and substantial.[76] Yet even with such evidence, it is possible to gauge the existence of real support for the republican leadership. Thus it has been noted that the pressure from and the involvement of the local administration in vote manufacturing and, specifically, in ensuring high turnout is more potent in the rural areas. The residents of big cities are more likely to escape the reach of the state and therefore have greater leeway in expressing their opinions. The urban population is also more sophisticated in its choice of media and has greater access to national newspapers, cable TV, and other, less biased sources of information. Therefore, one way to measure the impact of the administrative resource is to disaggregate the data on voter turnout and vote "against all" and compare republic-wide figures with those in the capital city of Kazan.[77] Given that Kazan authorities and specifically its former mayor, Iskhakov, were frequently seen as more autonomous from the republican government, there are reasons to suspect that voting figures in Kazan are more reliable in terms of reflecting public attitudes toward the political regime and political institutions in the republic. Even with such an adjustment, however, these figures (see table 4.6) reflect much greater turnout and a much lesser degree of protest attitudes in Tatarstan relative to Nizhnii Novgorod.

It has to be acknowledged that even when adjusting for the difference in the "electoral management" in rural areas and such a large capital city as Kazan, voting figures in Tatarstan are less reliable than those in Nizhnii Novgorod. Therefore, public opinion polls, especially those conducted by independent agencies, represent an alternative source of information about mass attitudes toward the regime. Public opinion polls also indicated a solid level of support and positive evaluation of the regional elites. In 1997–99 positive assessments of the president predominated both on the republican level and in Kazan (table 4.7). These attitudes have not changed radically in the following years. The survey held in Kazan ten days before the 2001 presidential election by *Vecherniaia Kazan,* one of the few opposition newspapers in Tatarstan, indicated that a considerable 65.2 percent of respondents would have voted for the incumbent president, Shaimiev.[78] Furthermore, public opinion polls conducted in the republic have revealed a consistent, more favorable view of society and politics in the Republic of Tatarstan than in Russia nationwide. The majority of respondents described the sociopolitical situation in the republic as calm and favorable while viewing Russia's condition as tense and crisis-prone (table 4.8). It is possible to interpret the results of this poll as an effect of political hegemony established in the republic and clever selling of the Tatarstan model by the authorities to the people rather than a sign of genuine appreciation of the regime's achievements. Although distinguishing between these two intrepretations seems impossible given the limitations of the data, for the purposes of my argument this difference matters less than the difference between the two political situations where such support is present or absent.

Could the respondents give more positive answers in Tatarstan because of the authoritarian situation in the republic? This expectation commonly arises regarding public opinion polls conducted in authoritarian settings. Indeed, analysts have observed that people in repressive regimes are less likely to be candid in their responses. This does not apply to Tatarstan, however, which is hardly a repressive regime controlled by police and eliciting fear of retribution. The authoritarian situation in Tatarstan is more constraining for intraelite relations in the republic rather than relations between the elites and the public. In postcommunist settings age (a proxy for the years spent under communism) has been shown to matter significantly for the honesty of respondents.[79] There might also be other factors associated with distrust and dishonesty in public opinion surveys. For example, the difference between the rural (more dependent on the authorities) and urban population might be substantial (as in the case with electoral voting). Based on these considerations and the different origin of the sources considered above—all of which point in the same direction—it appears possible to treat the data used in this study on the Republic of Tatarstan as no less valid than the data on Nizhnii Novgorod.

TABLE 4.7. Public Assessment of Regional Authorities in the Republic of Tatarstan

	Positive (%)[a]						Negative (%)[b]					
	1997		1998		1999[c]		1997		1998		1999[d]	
	RT*	Kazan	RT	Kazan	RT	Kazan	RT	Kazan	RT	Kazan	RT	Kazan
President	87	82	82	77	79.7	77	13	17	18	23	12.3	17.7
Adm./Govt.	66	54	61	50	NA	NA	34	46	39	50	NA	NA
Gossovet	59	51	57	44	NA	NA	41	49	43	56	NA	NA

Sources: Respublika Tatarstan v zerkale obshchestvennogo mneniia, 169; "Deiatel'nost' prezidenta RT, pravitel'stva i parlamenta v otsenkakh izbiratelei"; Mukhametshin 2000, 116.

Notes:

* RT = Republic of Tatarstan.

[a] This column includes those who answered "positively" and "satisfactorily" to the question, "How would you assess the work of the president/prime minister/parliament in the past year?" (with an exception for 1999; see note 116).

[b] This column includes those who answered "unsatisfactorily" and "not sure" to the same question.

[c] The figures for 1999 are from a different survey, indicating people who express "trust" or "trust rather than distrust" for President Shaimiev.

[d] These figures indicate those who "distrust" and "distrust rather than trust" President Shaimiev.

TABLE 4.8. Public Assessment of the Sociopolitical Situation in the Republic of Tatarstan and the Russian Federation

	Calm, Favorable									Tense, Crisis-Prone								
	1997	1998	1999	2000	2001	2002	2003	2004	2005	1997	1998	1999	2000	2001	2002	2003	2004	2005
Tatarstan	65	16	55	63	69	67	65	72	65	28	80	37	28	25	27	28	25	27
Russia	16	2	7	21	41	31	32	32	39	76	95	88	69	51	60	69	51	60

Source: Isaev 2005.

In brief, the data considered above reflect a considerable degree of public recognition and even support for the authorities in the Republic of Tatarstan. It appears reasonable to suggest, therefore, that the political system constructed in Tatarstan in the 1990s enjoyed a higher degree of legitimacy than the one that emerged in Nizhnii Novgorod. This legitimacy was based on the ideological "production" of the Tatarstan model as a stable and peaceful republic that avoided the impoverishment and political instability experienced by many other regions in Russia. The noncompetitive nature of the regime allowed the government to promote this Tatarstan model and influence positively the public assessment of economic, social, and political realities in the republic. Any potential opposition forces were dealt with before they presented a real danger to the regime, and Tatarstani voters have never experienced the methods of electoral struggle that led to the acute revulsion against regional politics in Nizhnii Novgorod in 2001–2. The political-economic system built in the republic during the 1990s appeared much more stable and accepted by the public than the one in Nizhnii Novgorod.[80]

Many local experts wondered about the reasons for the use of administrative resources in the republic where residents supposedly would have voted for Shaimiev anyway. The explanations advanced for such seemingly irrational actions are related to two important features of the political regime in Tatarstan. On the one hand, a high degree of popular support, as seen in the electoral results, provided the Tatarstani political elite with greater bargaining chips with Moscow. On the other hand, the meso-elites on the regional level in Tatarstan were motivated to deliver record voting results favorable to the authorities to show their loyalty and score points with the president. As noted by local observers, there was a tradition of informal competition between meso-elites for "best" voting results, indicating the presence of a systematic pressure to deliver votes.[81] Ironically, the heavy-handed interference of administrative resources (felt in some regions in the republic more than in others) had likely had a damaging effect on genuine public support for the government even when officially delivering higher support figures. A reliance on the Tatarstan model to ensure public support would probably have been sufficient.

A similar legitimation model (even if with different ideological content) did exist in Nizhnii Novgorod under Nemtsov's governorship, when the region was promoted as a pioneer of democratic and market reforms.[82] Until 1997 this model was not seriously challenged by political competitors, and the public maintained a positive evaluation of the regional government. After Nemtsov's departure, however, the model was discredited by his political opponents, who focused on the deteriorating economy and grim social realities. Afterward, no political actor was able to develop any legitimacy claims or the legitimation model such as the one that existed under Nemtsov. The logic of political struggle and mutual public accusations devoured all the actors.

Theoretical Observations

If democracy is viewed as "a system of organized uncertainty," in which actors know the rules but do not know the outcomes, and if the electoral process is the principal rule governing transfer of power, then Nizhnii Novgorod was a democracy because there the electoral process functioned properly in a sense of creating uncertainty as to who would come to power next.[83] What observations can be made with regard to functioning of competitive elections and their impact in Nizhnii Novgorod? First, an electoral system with genuine contestation does not deter informal arrangements among political and economic elites. Informal elite networks can coexist with electoral institutions that are functioning under conditions of political contestation. This observation supports earlier studies about weak political parties in Russia and highlights the role of informal elite networks as party substitutes.[84] Second, the causal links asserted earlier that electoral democracy undermines crony capitalism and that political competition leads to better governance and less corruption[85] needs, as regards systems like Russia's, to be reversed. When political competition is combined with crony capitalism, the electoral system itself is undermined by crony capitalist arrangements along with the main political actors. How does this happen?

The delegitimization of the electoral process and the ruling elites occurs as an unintended consequence of interelite clashes that become publicized during electoral campaigns. As the EPNs compete for state resources and elected posts, they have strong incentives to use their media outlets to expose compromising material aimed at delegitimizing their opponents. The political struggle turns into information warfare among the key competitors, with the issue of corruption turned into a political tool and an array of other manipulative tools used to obtain the desired results. In the course of such wars, all the parties are discredited. As the official authorities get involved and try to "fix" the vote or interfere with election results using administrative resources,[86] they expose their crony, self-serving nature as well. What is even more important, the institutional framework used in the political struggle—the electoral mechanism—also undergoes a process of delegitimization. Faced with consecutive rounds of dirty, competitive elections, which turn issues of vital importance, such as water provision, into political hot-button ones, the public perceives the electoral process as the instrument for pursuing elite interests rather than a means to project the public will.

The increased political competition in Nizhnii Novgorod did not make regional politics more democratic in public eyes or the government more accountable. Its actual impact was felt mostly in the changing methods of electoral struggle and the explosion of creativity in the field of political technologies and negative campaigning. This impact was rejected by a public disgusted by the regional elites and the games they play—including the game of elections that, despite their competitive nature, could not ensure accountability and good governance in the region. The only result of competition under such circumstances was the public's heightened sense that private interests dominate the state, with an ensuing retreat into political apathy and protest voting.

Political regimes lacking meaningful political competition avoid such negative tendencies. In relatively secure monocentric regimes elections do not introduce uncertainty because the dominant network has greater influence over the election results through controlling public opinion and administrative and economic resources. Such control over the electoral process and public opinion is enabled by official control of the mass media, lower-level government officials, and key economic elites in the region. The authorities do not have to resort to force or blatant manipulation to change voting outcomes. They influence the public on the level of perceptions and attitudes and deal with potential rivals before they even emerge. The public does not face an outpouring of corruption charges;

instead, enabled by official control over the mass media, the government projects its claims for legitimacy by developing a set of ideas that play into the public's hopes and fears and present the situation in the republic as more successful than in other regions. Hence not only are public perceptions of corruption and cronyism controlled in such systems, but the absence of strong opposition voices allows the ruling elite to develop a positive image of the situation in the republic.

Politicizing the provision of public goods could not have happened in a politically integrated regime such as Tatarstan's. Since elections there are used as a legitimizing tool for the regime rather than an instrument of power struggle, if anything, the provision of public goods could only improve before elections. The integrated political and economic elite in such a system has a common interest in ensuring the legitimacy of the regime rather than in undermining it. The centralization of state resources is helpful in this regard: instead of being used for discrediting political competitors, resources are used to enhance support for the dominant power structures.

The Sorry Fate of Regional Elections in Russia

Albeit an extreme case, Nizhnii Novgorod is representative of the situation that existed in many regions of Russia from the mid-1990s up to 2004, when President Putin decided to abolish gubernatorial elections. Political rivalries between informal elite groups in the regions were manifested in messy and bitter electoral campaigns that turned the regional political scene into a trial field of manipulative technologies, provocation schemes, and corruption scandals. Dirty tricks *(chernye tekhnologii)* became an accepted part of elections. Their wide usage contributed to and reflected the emergence of numerous political consultancy firms, PR agencies, and political spin doctors who used various, sometimes openly illegal methods of promoting their candidates. Commentators in the Russian media and, subsequently, other students of Russian regional politics started to refer to various methods of electoral manipulation by the name of the region where a specific method or tactic was used first. Joel Moses, for example, mentioned the "Belgorod alternative," the "Briansk alternative," the "Kursk alternative," and the "Orel alternative" of electoral tactics used in the regions during 1999–2000.[87] The "Belgorod alternative" involved changing the scheduled election date and reducing the margin necessary to win. The election date was moved forward by eight months, so that opponents would have less time to prepare, and election laws were changed to allow for a victory with a simple plurality. Andrew Konitzer-Smirnov observed that the Belgorod alternative was used fully or partially in the Kirov, Altay, Murmansk, Pskov, Briansk, and Volgograd regions.[88]

The "Briansk alternative" involved clone candidates of the type discussed above in the case of the Nizhnii Novgorod region. This method became especially popular across Russia and even beyond it and was applied not only to candidates but also to parties.[89] The "Kursk alternative" was the most famous case of federal intervention in the electoral process in the regions. In Kursk the region's popular incumbent, Aleksandr Rutskoi, was removed from the ballot just a day before the election in October 2000. The last-minute decision by the regional court to change the ballot (accusing Rutskoi of violating campaign rules by not disclosing information about his property and income) evidently originated from the Kremlin, which was eager to replace the outspoken incumbent. The trend of the Kremlin's meddling in regional elections grew under Putin as his administration tried to oust those governors deemed "inconvenient" and secure the election of more suitable candidates, that is, candidates loyal to the Kremlin.[90] The "Orel alternative" appeared even earlier, in 1997, when all the most serious challengers were excluded from the electoral race and a heavyweight incumbent governor, Yegor Stroev, ran against an unknown candidate, winning with over 95 percent of the vote. This scenario was also successfully implemented in other regions.[91]

Candidates seeking to challenge the incumbents deployed similar methods of black or gray PR. They also hired political technologists and relied on dishonest tactics to undermine opponents. Some analysts have even suggested that black PR practices in Russia can be viewed as a "weapon of the weak" used in the competition with an incumbent and other candidates who have access to the administrative resource.[92] One of the most common strategies involved manipulating the media and deploying the weapon of *kompromat* (compromising materials) for discrediting opponents.[93] Kompromat had multiple uses: it could be used in bargaining as an instrument for "informal persuasion." Those in possession of kompromat could blackmail their opponents and achieve their goals using the threat of exposure. In the electoral struggle, though, when the main goal is to publicly discredit an opponent, kompromat is used in the context of framing an information attack on the opposing candidate. Thus a well-known governor of Sverdlovsk, Eduard Rossel', underwent an intense media attack that involved accusations that he had tight links to the Uralmash criminal group and portraying him as the "godfather of Sverdlovsk mafia."[94] Another heavyweight in the Russian regional politics, Mayor Luzhkov of Moscow, also suffered several excruciating media attacks, with the most devastating one conducted on the ORT TV channel by Sergei Dorenko in fall 1999.

Given the destructive capacity of kompromat, it became a commodity in high demand during the 1990s and 2000s. Both state-based security agencies and private firms engaged in collecting information that was a potential blackmail tool. When the facts were not available, kompromat could be fabricated and used equally effectively because no one really checked whether it was authentic, and no one was prosecuted for the dissemination of inaccurate information. Since the media sources in the 1990s were controlled by those who were directly engaged in political fights, the press was exploited for political purposes and, as a result, kompromat "dominated the Russian press, television and Internet."[95] Given the legacy of the dry official press of the Soviet period, such information wars shocked the public. Initially, the public became interested and even excited about this side of "glasnost" in Russia. The extent of these public "revelations," however, eventually led to growing distrust of the media and especially the press.[96] In 2000, for example, over 60 percent of Russian citizens did not trust the media.[97]

Regional electoral campaigns marred by a variety of tricks and schemes could not avoid having an impact on how the elections themselves were perceived by the public. By the early 2000s most of Russia's citizens shared the perception that democratic institutions on the regional level had failed. The manifestation of this popular outlook took different forms, both behavioral and attitudinal. Some signs of disenchantment with how political institutions performed appeared in voting behavior and the growing protest vote, especially on the regional level. Until 2005 Russia's elections preserved a peculiar feature of Soviet voting procedures: citizens could vote against the party-nominated candidate by crossing out his name on the ballot.[98] In the Russian electoral system, since December 1993, this feature became the option to vote against all candidates and was intended to increase the legitimacy of the elections and widen the choice available to the electorate. In practical terms, this voting option was expected to increase voter turnout. Its effect, however, went beyond the one originally planned by the policy makers.[99] How did the Russian citizens use this option over the period 1993–2005, when this ballot choice was available?

Apparently, with the passage of time, the Russian electorate increasingly preferred a vote against all candidates at all administrative levels. In 1995 the "against all" vote in State Duma elections was among the top four electoral options in almost two-thirds and, in 1999, in four-fifths of constituencies.[100] In 2002–3 the "against all" option was one of the top competitors for gubernatorial or mayoral seats in Nizhnii Novgorod, Norilsk, the Komi republic, and the territory of Krasnodar. More and more people chose to reject all real candidates in the elections across Russia and opt for "against all." Reacting to this dangerous trend leading to absurd electoral outcomes, Russia's Central Electoral Commission imposed restrictions on campaigning for the "against all" choice made available to Russian citizens on the ballot,[101] and later, in summer 2005, it took a more radical step: the option of voting against all candidates was abolished. Apparently, the government and the legislators decided, "no candidate, no problem."

Dealing with the symptoms of the problem, however, did not mean resolving the problem itself. Some scholars who have explored the "against all" vote in Russia attributed it to political protest and disenchantment with the political system.[102] It was suggested that this peculiar option available to Russian voters served as a democratic "safety valve" that allowed for "institutionalized protest voting."[103] Revealingly, a significant correlation was found between the regional-level vote "against all" during the 1990s and the proportion of ethnic Russians living in a region.[104] The voters from the ethnic republics were less likely to opt for this protest vote. Taking into account that ethnic republics during the 1990s tended to be significantly less competitive than Russian-dominated regions,[105] political competition is the likely intervening causal factor that explains the higher degree of protest and disappointment in the regions with a higher proportion of Russians.

Perhaps the best attitudinal manifestation of public disappointment with regional elections is the reaction of the Russian people to Putin's decision to abolish gubernatorial elections entirely. Announced after a school tragedy in Beslan in September 2004, this decision appeared to be an illogical reaction to the problem of terrorism in Russia. After all, what is the link between terrorism and elections? However, as noted in the introduction, Russian citizens did not oppose this action, which, in effect, stripped them of their democratic rights. In fact, the balance between those who disapproved of this decision and those who supported it quickly shifted in favor of Putin.[106] Clearly, most voters in Russia did not believe that they lost something of value with the elimination of gubernatorial elections. Rather, they bought into the promise of more order and stability and less waste and chaos in the new, appointment-based system of regional power. One of the popular justifications used for this reform pointed to an annual savings of $1 billion, previously spent on the "gray" electoral market by competing candidates.[107] This public reaction is ironic and lamentable in light of studies that have revealed the positive role of regional elections in Russia in holding governors accountable for regional economic performance.[108] Frustration with the electoral process and the methods of political struggle did not allow for a more rational assessment of the pros and cons of the electoral process. Such an unfortunate outcome— of undervalued elections that might have served a real accountability function—reinforces the significance of the argument advanced in this chapter. The effects of political competition in the context of crony capitalist systems deserve special consideration. The manifestations of political competition in electoral campaigns play a key role in shaping public perceptions of elites and political institutions. The database of expert analysis of gubernatorial elections (summarized in table 4.9) produced by the Carnegie Moscow Center reveals similar patterns in other regions of the Russian Federation.[109] Heightening political fragmentation manifested in intense information warfare and nasty electoral campaigns alienated the public from the elites and discredited the electoral system.

TABLE 4.9. Experts' Assessment of Selected Gubernatorial Elections, 1998–2002

Region	Date of Election	Competitive/Noncompetitive; Use of Black PR	Electoral Impact on Civil Society and Black PR Effect*
Mordovia	02/1998	Not competitive, no black PR	Neutral assessment of the election and its impact
Vladimir	12/2000	Not competitive, no black PR	Neutral assessment of the election and its impact
Ivanovo	12/2000	Competitive; no black PR	Election had no impact; neutral assessment
Ryazan'	12/2000	Very competitive; black PR	Negative impact of black PR on public attitudes toward both politicians and elections
Murmansk	03/2000	Competitive, black PR	Mixed effect of the election: it stimulated political apathy, distrust of authorities and electoral mechanism itself but also represents a feedback mechanism between the authorities and population
Tambov	12/1999	Very competitive, black PR	Elections not considered important by the public but tolerated
Lipetsk	04/2002	Competitive, no black PR	Potential positive impact of election
Voronezh	12/2000	Competitive, black PR	Negative impact of information war on civil society
Kursk	10/2000(i) 11/2000(ii)**	Competitive, black PR	Mixed impact of elections on civil society: both positive and negative effects
Bryansk	12/2000	Very competitive, widespread black PR	Election had negative impact on civil society; use of black PR leads to distrust of authorities and the electoral mechanism
Marii-El	12/2000	Very competitive, widespread black PR	A negative impact of black PR is acknowledged, as well as a positive impact of power transfer in the region
Penza	04/1998	Competitive, no black PR	Positive impact of competition; free press often used as a tool to manipulate public opinion
Chuvashia	12/2001	Very competitive, black PR	Elections do not stimulate civil society; main regional political cleavage leads to fragmentation and polarization of the polity
Bashkortostan	06/1998	Not competitive but scandalous	Negative impact of the election; relatively high protest vote (17% voted "against all")
Samara	07/2000	Not competitive	Mixed assessment: elections are controlled and thus do not function properly; but any election has an inevitably positive impact on civil society
Saratov	03/2000	Not competitive, black PR	Elections discredited as a result of gross manipulation of electoral rules by the authorities
Ulyanovsk	12/2000	Competitive, black PR	Positive impact of power transfer on civil society
Komi	12/2001	Very competitive, black PR	Negative impact of black PR on voters
Nizhnii Novgorod	07/2001	Very competitive, black PR	Negative impact of scandalous elections on public perceptions

* In the absence of a clear positive, negative, or mixed assessment of the election's impact on the public, I use the term *neutral assessment*.
** Runoffs.

Political Competition and Public Perceptions of Corruption in Russia's Regions

As I argued above by contrasting the cases of Nizhnii Novgorod and Tatarstan, in the context of crony capitalism political competition undermines public trust in competitive elections and regional elites by increasing public perceptions of corruption.[110] This argument is based, however, on the analysis of cases that represent extreme opposites in terms of political competition levels. To test this observation more systematically I used a cross-regional data set on corruption perceptions produced in 2002 by Transparency International (TI) in collaboration with the Information Democracy Foundation (INDEM). While this data set has been used to examine the causes of corruption across Russia's regions,[111] I used it to examine whether people in politically competitive regions are more likely to have greater *perceptions* of corruption.

The data set covers forty of the eighty-three regions of the Russian Federation and combines perception-based and experience-based data. To evaluate public perceptions of corruption in the regions, the survey conducted by TI and INDEM included assessment questions (e.g., "How would you estimate the level of corruption in the following institutions?") and questions about people's personal experience with corruption (e.g., "When did you have to informally influence an official using a bribe, gift, service or other means in order to solve a problem?"). The data also include indicators of public perceptions of corruption on the local, regional, and federal levels, as well as across the various branches of power (executive, legislative, and judicial), and indicators of public trust in local, regional, and federal authorities, thus allowing a test of the link between perceptions of corruption and public trust in authorities.[112]

To analyze how public perceptions of corruption might depend on regional political competitiveness, I had to assess the level of competitiveness in Russia's regions. I used two measures of political competitiveness adopted from a wide-scale "Democratic Audit of Regions" conducted by Obshchestvennaia Expertiza (Public Expertise).[113] A proxy for political competition (or lack of it) in the regions that is specific to Russia under President Putin is the degree to which the new party of power, United Russia, has monopolized the regional parliaments.[114] The success of United

Russia in the regional legislature has reflected the degree to which the regional authorities—for the most part allied with the party of power—control the political space and the administrative resources.[115] Even the most recalcitrant and autonomy-minded governors under Putin preferred a bandwagoning strategy: join and support United Russia. Anecdotal evidence from the most centralized and tightly controlled regional regimes in Russia (i.e., Tatarstan and Bashkortostan) confirms that the domination of the United Russia party reflects the political monopolization in the region. These two republics are, for example, among the top five regions with the highest percentage of United Russia members in their regional parliaments. It is clear that these percentages do not reflect any special ideological appeal of United Russia in these regions but rather effective control of administrative resources by the regional governments and absence of any organized opposition. Hence the higher the proportion of United Russia deputies in the regional legislature, the lower the degree of political competition in the region. This indicator of political competition was therefore constructed by subtracting the proportion of seats controlled by United Russia from 100. The second indicator is based on the results of a broader assessment of regional democracy that includes eight different indicators of democracy.[116] Based on these indicators, the analysts working on the Democratic Audit of Regions divided all regions into five categories (from 1, least democratic, to 5, most democratic).[117]

To test the impact of political competitiveness on corruption perceptions in Russia's regions, I estimated two multivariate linear regression models by the ordinary least squares (OLS). I used several control variables that could influence corruption perceptions in the regions.[118] Specifically, my model included indicators for press freedom,[119] regional economic development (using gross regional product data),[120] number of pensioners (retired people) in the region, and the regional level of unemployment.[121] The first model explaining perceptions of corruption in Russian regions included, as predictors, indicators of corruption experience, gross regional product,[122] freedom of the press, political competition, unemployment rate, and proportion of pensioners. The results of this test are reported in table 4.10.

The main finding from testing this model is that perceptions of corruption are higher in regions with higher political competition levels. The

TABLE 4.10. Model 1

	Regional Corruption	Federal Corruption
Experience	−.09 (.07)	−.06 (.05)
Free press	.15 (.07)*	.09 (.05)
Political competition	.09 (.04)*	.04 (.03)
LogGRP	−.09 (.03)**	−.04 (.02)
Unemployment rate	−.17 (.55)	−.3 (.4)
Pensioners	−.10 (.28)	−.09 (.2)
Constant	1.73 (.46)	1.18 (.33)
N***	39	39
R-squared	.38	.21
F-statistics	3.3	1.41
Prob>F	.01	.2

* Significant at less than 5 percent.
** Significant at less than 1 percent.
*** N = 39 because the value on political competition for one region was missing.

relationship between the variable of political competition and perceptions of corruption is significant at 95 percent confidence interval and is substantial, with a coefficient of .09. This empirical finding provides strong support for theoretical observations based on the two case studies discussed in this book. In addition, some of the control variables used in this model are statistically related to corruption perceptions. Specifically, the model reveals that perceptions of corruption are higher in regions with freer press and lower levels of economic development. It appears that the mass media plays a more immediate and significant role in shaping public opinion and, specifically, public perceptions about corruption.

The earlier study of regional corruption in Russia revealed a strong link between regional economic development (measured using gross regional product data) and corruption perceptions, interpreted as a link between economic development and corruption.[123] This model confirms the earlier finding. However, the "objectivist" interpretation of this finding provided in the previous study can be challenged. The factors related to economic development might not necessarily work to reduce state officials' incentives for corruption and lower acts of corruption; instead, people in poorer regions might simply tend to think that corruption is higher than those living in the richer regions. Looking at this correlation from the perspective of perceptions of corruption rather than real corruption adds this other potential interpretation of the nature of this link, as considered in the next section.

The same predictors were also tested with the dependent variable of public perceptions of federal-level corruption (see table 4.10). This model demonstrated that the regional-level predictors (regional economic development, press freedom, political competition, and proportion of retired people living in the region) do not have much to do with public perceptions of corruption on the federal level. Apparently, people do not perceive all governmental levels as equally corrupt; different factors seem to determine public perceptions of corruption on different levels of government.

When the insignificant variables are removed from the equation, the model yields results that highlight once again that political competition levels influence corruption perceptions. Among the control variables, only regional economic development (measured through gross regional product) appears to still be related to corruption perceptions. The variable of free press is significant only at 10 percent confidence interval; furthermore, the impact of political competition appears more robust than the press freedom variable (table 4.11). This finding points to the complex role of the press in Russia and to the entangled nature of the media-political relationship in that context.[124] The arguments involving the concept of press freedom in the Russian context must be careful not to assume a liberal model of relationships between press and politics. Although many observers consider the Russian press free in the 1990s—and it surely was much freer, relative to current Russia—it was not autonomous from private influence. To the contrary, financially dependent on their owners, media outlets could not fulfill the expected public function of providing unbiased information and, as discussed earlier, more often served as a conduit for political competition among rival elite groups.

The second model used an indicator of democracy instead of political competition in the regions.[125] Having a limited number of observations, I excluded control variables for the unemployment rate and the number of pensioners (which did not reveal a statistically significant re-

TABLE 4.11. Model 1 (Reduced Specification)

	Regional Corruption	*Federal Corruption*
LogGRP	−.07 (.0206)**	−.03 (.0151)
Political competition	.10 (.0415)*	.04 (.0304)
Free press	.11 (.05)	.07 (.04)
Constant	1.40 (.2155)	.89 (.1578)
N	39	39
R-squared	.36	.16
F-statistics	6.44	2.25
Prob > F	.001	.1

* Significant at less than 5 percent.
** Significant at less than 1 percent.

lationship to corruption perceptions in the first model) in order to maintain parsimony in the model. Therefore, this model included four dummy variables of democracy and controlled for gross regional product and press freedom (table 4.12).

This model also produced robust results. Together, the predictors account for 54 percent of the variation in the public perceptions of corruption across the regions and the results appear very similar to the first model. The estimated coefficients show that perceptions of corruption in the regions increase with the level of democracy and decrease with the level of economic development. At the same time, the coefficients are significant only at the lowest level of democracy. With the move away from the most authoritarian, least competitive system toward a more open system, the relationship between the level of democracy and corruption perceptions continuously decreases. This finding seems to highlight that public perceptions of corruption in a strictly controlled authoritarian system are based solely on the control over information available to the public and effectiveness of propaganda advanced by the political regime. Public perceptions and public opinion can be successfully controlled only in the absence of *any* democratic features in the regime, at the lowest possible degree of democracy. Any degree of regime liberalization away from a tightly controlled, nondemocratic regime results in government losing the capacity to control public opinion and corruption perceptions.

TABLE 4.12. Model 2

	Regional Corruption	Federal Corruption
Dem1	−.0998 (.0266)**	−.0421(.0208)*
Dem2	.0052 (.024)	−.0029 (.0188)
Dem3	.0323 (0204)	.0269 (.0159)
Dem5	.0207 (.0187)	.0083 (.0146)
LogGRP	−.0692 (.02)**	−.0342 (.0156)*
Press freedom	.08 (.06)	.07 (.04)
Constant	1.4036 (.2105)	.9694 (.1643)
N	40	40
R-squared	.54	.30
F-statistics	6.35	2.40
Prob > F	.0002	.05

* Significant at less than 5 percent.
** Significant at less than 1 percent.

This finding resonates with the studies of color revolutions in the post-Soviet region that pointed to the vulnerabilities and instability of competitive authoritarian regimes even with limited political pluralism.[126] According to a number of scholars, color revolutions can be avoided only in very centralized political systems that do not leave any space for open political expression and competition.[127] It is apparent from this analysis that such authoritarian control also allows for managing public perceptions of corruption.

The variable of press freedom was not statistically significant in this model. It seems that the various indicators used to form an indicator of democracy override the press freedom indicator. Also, the same model run against the indicator of federal corruption perceptions yielded the results that differed from the first model. This model shows statistically significant correlation between regional-level indicators of democracy and economic development and public perceptions of corruption on the federal level. In less democratic and more developed regions, people tend to think better not only of the regional level but also of the federal level government. This finding illustrates yet again why perceptions of corruption should not be used as a proxy for corruption itself. The regional-level indicators of democracy and economic development are hardly linked to the presence of real corruption in the federal center. But it does seem plausible to expect that if people are relatively more satisfied with their lives on the regional level, then their vision of the government on various levels is more favorable than in those regions where people are frustrated—whether with their living conditions, the perceived political games played by elites in the electoral campaigns, or some combination of these factors. In either case, the issue of real corruption does not seem to be directly linked to these perceptions.

In short, the impact of regional political competition on public perceptions of corruption appears to be the most noteworthy finding of this statistical analysis. It confirms the analysis advanced earlier in this chapter as well as observations of other analysts of regional politics in Russia who have long noticed the "dark side" of political competition.[128] The more uncertainty and competition political actors faced, the more they were prone to employing political consultants and relying on a wide range of dirty tricks and manipulation. The unintended result of these electoral ploys was to bury the public in piles of compromising materials, thus raising public perceptions of corruption and undermining trust in all elites involved in these political battles.

This finding is somewhat controversial when considered along the arguments suggesting that increased political competition reduces corruption.[129] It does not entirely challenge the results of these recent studies that link political competition to lowering corruption because that effect might be a longer-term outcome of political competition, or, even more likely, such an effect might result from a combination of factors that could include political competition as one of several ingredients necessary for reducing corruption. Political competition might be a necessary but not sufficient variable. This finding does, however, call for more careful use of subjective measures of corruptions in corruption studies because it shows that political competition promotes popular beliefs about corruption in the short term. Even when political competition might work to decrease real corruption, on the level of perceptions the situation might be worsening. This finding is also controversial empirically because according to these data Bashkortostan, one of the most authoritarian regimes in Russia, frequently noted to be a corrupt crony system, ranks as the cleanest region in terms of corruption perceptions. Using corruption perceptions data for measuring corruption in Bashkortostan is therefore meaningless. In view of my argument that political competition promotes popular beliefs about corruption, such an outcome appears completely logical, however. So even if the earlier studies are accurate in their predictions that political competition works to decrease real corruption, on the level of perceptions the impact might differ. In this case the same factor might be "pushing" in different directions and work at cross-purposes, with the indeterminate final result. It is noteworthy because the impact of corruption perceptions is associated with high political costs, as demonstrated in this book.

The link between increased public perceptions of corruption and press freedom, uncovered by the first model, also deserves special attention. On the surface it appears that the free press functions in Russia as expected by classic democratic theory: it provides greater information about governmental misconduct, thus educating the public about how corrupt the government is. Logically, the people must react by "throwing the rascals out" in the next elections, and the new politicians must presumably be less corrupt. That is why generally, in older democracies, freer press is associated with less corruption, and that is why free press is frequently prescribed as a tool for fighting corruption. This logic fails in the Russian context, however, where free press does not mean independent press and where media outlets have been *instrumentalized* for advancing political and economic interests of their owners and sponsors. As illustrated in earlier chapters, during the 1990s media resources became an important asset coveted by national and regional-level business magnates. This asset was employed in political and economic struggles between the oligarchs and vis-à-vis the state.[130] Therefore, the propensity of the press to publicize and focus on corruption issues differed in the regions, depending on the degree of political and economic competition. Freedom of the press, as expressed in the presence of various owners and a lack of governmental monopoly, did not ensure the functioning of the press as the "fourth estate," that is, as guardian of the public interest and watchdog on governmental activities. Therefore, the analytical lens other than a liberal model of press and media is necessary to fully capture the role of the media in the Russian context. Anthropologists, more sensitive to differences in context, have been quicker to react and have advanced the concept of media-political clientelism to characterize such apparently non-Western workings of the media.[131] Political scientists should integrate this understanding to modify and improve their theories as well.

Conclusion

The causal mechanism linking crony capitalism to instability through the intervening factor of political competition hinges on public perceptions of cronyism and corruption of elites and the main institutions structuring the political field. These perceptions of cronyism and the prevalence of private interests of wealth and power undermine public trust and support for the political regime and breed apathy, cynicism, and protest against the system. This chain of causation then turns into a vicious circle as elites try to use corruption issues for mobilizing public support in their political rivalries, thereby contributing further to the growing perceptions of corruption and public skepticism.

This chapter illustrates this logic by exploring the delegitimization of the regional elites and the electoral process in Nizhnii Novgorod and by a statistical analysis of the effect of political competition levels on public perceptions of corruption in forty other regions of Russia. It appears that, at least in the short run, a crony capitalist institutional order brings political competition and the electoral process into contradiction. To the extent that elections are competitive and function as a mechanism of power transfer creating political uncertainty, competing elites have to engage the public. Driven by the high stakes involved in the outcome of elections, the candidates engage in all-out information wars and invent dirty political technologies that inadvertently undermine the elites as well as the electoral process itself. Drawn into the open rivalry between EPNs, members of the public sense that they are constantly being manipulated and come to view the electoral process as a mechanism of power struggle rather than a process through which the common will is expressed. These tendencies played out in most other regions of the Russian Federation and were avoided only in fully centralized, noncompetitive regimes with controlled information flows and managed public opinion, such as the system built in Tatarstan.

CHAPTER 5

Corruption and Democracy under Yeltsin and Putin

Democracy in Russia is serious and long term. Social life in Russia will become more complicated as the democratic institutions develop further. Therefore, in our political work we will have to pay more attention to convincing and explaining.
—Vladislav Surkov, presidential aide, in a speech to students
at the United Russia party school, February 7, 2006

This chapter examines the evolution of political competition in postcommunist Russia to explore on the national level the argument developed earlier based on two subnational cases. The two periods in Russian politics that can be distinguished in terms of political competition are Yeltsin's and Putin's presidencies, while Medvedev's presidency could be seen as a continuation of Putin's era. While distinct politically, these two eras can both be characterized as crony capitalist, though the type of corruption and the form of political-economic fusion underpinning the system are different. The competitive regime constructed under Yeltsin faced a crisis of legitimacy by the late 1990s. Public attitudes toward Yeltsin himself, his government, and the institutions of democracy deteriorated, while public apathy and cynicism, abstention from voting, and protest voting increased. The policies undertaken by Putin and his team reversed these tendencies and rebuilt state legitimacy on a new, noncompetitive basis. I argue therefore that the authoritarian turn under Putin is best comprehended as a logical response by the Russian political elite to the challenges that emerged under Yeltsin's competitive crony system. Putin broke away from vicious, destabilizing cycles of rival elites openly clashing over property and state power and undermining the legitimacy of state authorities and political institutions in the process of these clashes. Instead, he constructed a political regime based on the centralization of state authority, consolidation of economic resources, and strict control over the media, which was mobilized to promote the state's policies. The crony character of the institutional order underpinning this new, noncompetitive political system did not change. Collusion between political and economic elites and unstable property rights remained at the core of the system, while the amount of corruption, if anything, only increased.[1] Interelite clashes over power and wealth moved to the corridors of power, hidden from public sight. Elections under Putin have progressively lost the uncertainty of outcomes that existed under Yeltsin. The competitive cronyism of Yeltsin's era was thus displaced by noncompetitive cronyism under Putin.

Yeltsin's Russia, riveted by political conflict and competition between informal elite factions, closely resembles the political system in Nizhnii Novgorod. By the second half of 1999 Russia's political regime was at a high point of contestation; some of the most influential regional elites combined forces with the former prime minister and the mayor of Moscow in an attempt to take control of national politics. The amount of negative campaigning also reached its peak, with an attempt by the Kremlin to discredit the rival elites. The political crisis was looming when the terrorist acts attributed to the Chechens shattered the remaining fragile order and certainty in the society. When Putin came to power in the midst of the crisis, he initiated a strategy of gradual political and economic centralization and consolidation of control over media sources. An analysis of Putin's policies reveals that his overall strategy has a striking resemblance to the policies of the Tatarstani government in building a consolidated political system. The consequences of his policies are also similar to the political outcomes in Tatarstan: Putin's leadership became associated with bringing back stability and order and earned Putin high popularity

ratings and mass support, although the deep-rooted problems of cronyism remained in place.

In this chapter I first address the issue of Russia's crony capitalism
and its transformation under Putin and then explore the Russian political landscape as divided into two distinct periods: (1) a competitive regime under Yeltsin and (2) gradual consolidation of a noncompetitive
regime under Putin continuing under President Dmitry Medvedev. Following the analysis of similarities and differences of two regimes, I draw
attention to public attitudes and their evolution in Russia over the length
of postcommunist transformation, especially with regard to attitudes toward presidents, political institutions, elections, democracy, and corruption. This overview provides additional support to the argument advanced
in this study about the perils of political competition under crony capitalism. After chaotic years of competitive politics under Yeltsin, Putin's cen-
tralizing policies worked to reestablish the connection between the Russian state and its people. Although cronyism remained an inherent part of
the political-economic system constructed under Putin, a different type of
politics, one that emphasized stability, unity, and integration, mitigated
its negative effect on public opinion.

Russia's Crony Capitalism: "State Capture"
versus Systematic Corruption

The oligarchic capitalism that emerged in Russia under Yeltsin has been
the subject of much research.[2] Many analysts have conceptualized the phenomenon of oligarchs dominating the state and the economy as a case
of "state capture."[3] The informal networks and linkages that permeated
the top echelons of the state under Yeltsin are identifiable, especially
starting with the infamous loans-for-shares deal in which the bankrupt
federal government traded ownership of some of the most profitable sectors of industry in exchange for loans.[4] The few bankers that were among
the winners of the loans-for-shares auctions then contributed generously
to Yeltsin's presidential campaign.[5] This scheme demonstrated clearly the
principal incentives behind the emergence of informal EPNs: the politicians' need for financial resources to ensure electoral victory and the busi-

ness elites' need to secure and enhance their property rights. In 1996 Yeltsin needed financial resources to wage a successful reelection campaign, while the bankers sought an expansion into the industrial sector and, in some cases, acquired state positions, enabling influence over state policy making.

Later in the 1990s, in the last few years of Yeltsin's presidency, the state was dominated by the Family, another identifiable informal network that included members of Yeltsin's family as well as infamous oligarchs (most notoriously, Boris Berezovsky). The two-sided exchange in this network—of political support on the one hand and favors of an economic nature on the other—has been accepted by now as common knowledge about Yeltsin's regime. At the same time, similar informal networks permeated the state on all levels, not only at the top of the power pyramid.

The logic of crony capitalism played out strikingly when a new president took office. Despite being the chosen successor, Putin intended to reshuffle the relationship between the state and big business. In these circumstances, the need on the part of the asset holders to secure their assets by getting political support became painfully obvious. The "degree of pain" that could be inflicted on the previously powerful oligarchs ranged from sending them into exile and expropriating some of their possessions to sending them to jail and seizing most of their assets.[6] Putin has changed most aspects of business-state relationships that prevailed under Yeltsin. Therefore, here I focus more on his presidency and examine the nature of the political-economic system that emerged in Russia under his leadership. While different in nature from Yeltsin's system of cronyism, Putin's Russia can still be characterized as a variant of crony capitalism. It is cronyism in the sense that the rule of law is absent and property rights are not guaranteed but depend on selective rewards and punishments from the state. At the same time it differs from the state capture model that prevailed under Yeltsin and is better characterized using the model of "systematic corruption" proposed by John Wallis in his analysis of the evolution of relationships between markets and politics in the United States.[7] What is systematic corruption, and how is it different from the form of crony capitalism that emerged under Yeltsin?

Crony capitalism is a political-economic phenomenon in that it involves both state and business actors and has both economic and political implications. The terms of the relationships between state and business actors can also vary in that at any given time one side can be more powerful than the other. In the state capture model, certain businessmen (in Russia, the so-called oligarchs) appear as a stronger party in this equation. The alternative model involves the state dominating in this relationship. When certain businessmen dominate the state, private economic interests are pursued through the political process, representing a case of "venal corruption," or economics corrupting politics.[8] When the state is the dominant actor and uses economic favors to advance political domination, it is a case of systematic corruption, or politics corrupting economics.[9] More specifically, systematic corruption involves deliberate creation of rents "by limiting entry into valuable economic activities" for political ends.[10] The rents created by the government bind the interests of rent recipients to the government and enable the creation of a coalition that can dominate the government.[11]

According to this distinction, Putin's Russia is better understood as the latter case of systematic corruption because the government has initiated a consistent strategy of reclaiming and constructing new levers of control over the economy. From the beginning of his term as president, Putin announced the policy of "equidistancing" of oligarchs and, in his regular meetings with key business elites, conveyed new rules of engagement between the state and big property holders. While the policy of equidistancing in reality resulted in the emergence of new oligarchs close to the Kremlin, the new rules of state-business relations established expectations of political loyalty to Putin and his regime, nonparticipation in politics and acceptance of a new role of big business as a promoter of state interests. To make these rules credible and set the boundaries for independent elite behavior, Putin used selective punishment, as in the 2003 Yukos affair, which ended in the long-term imprisonment of Mikhail Khodorkovsky, owner of the Yukos oil company and the richest oligarch in Russia at that time.[12] Putin's strategy also involved direct nationalization of Yuganskneftegaz, the core company remaining from Yukos. Furthermore, the cases of Roman Abramovich unexpectedly selling his Sibneft' oil company to Gazprom[13] and Mikhail Gutseriev being pressured to sell his Russneft' oil company to Oleg Deripaska[14] reveal very clearly both the Kremlin's attempt to establish control over the energy sector and the dangers of not being part of Putin's "clan."

The energy sector was not the only sector over which the Russian government sought control. State expansion extended into other areas deemed strategic. In 2006 the Kremlin approved a merger of eight aircraft plants into a giant state-controlled holding called United Aircraft Corporation (OAK).[15] Earlier, in 2005, Rosoboronexport, the state-controlled arms exporting company, acquired control of AvtoVAZ, the largest automaker in Russia. Transformed into Rostekhnologii (RTC) it later obtained stakes in many other companies around Russia, including a big stake in KamAZ.[16] The establishment of the state-controlled United Shipbuilding Corporation (OSC) in 2007 based on the merger of several smaller shipbuilding companies added to the trend of enlarging and strengthening state holdings in the strategic sectors of the economy. All these moves seem to be indicative of the Kremlin's developmental ambitions pursued through the strategy of creating state-controlled industrial champions. These state actions are sometimes criticized by observers as aimed at providing plump jobs for state bureaucrats rather than economic development. The economic logic behind this strategy is seriously doubted by many analysts, especially in the face of Russia's falling competitiveness in the world economy.[17] On the other hand, some analysts hold a more sanguine view about the developmental intentions of the Kremlin. Thus Stanislav Markus (2007) has argued that Putin's presidency is characterized by a greater institutionalization of business-state relationships expressed through the increasing role of business associations such as the Russian Union of Industrialists and Entrepreneurs (RSPP), the Union of Business Associations of Russia (OPORA), and the Chamber of Commerce and Industry (TPP). According to Markus, these associations were encouraged by the Kremlin to articulate their interests and participate in policy making in order to compensate for the inefficient and incoherent state.[18]

Overall, the general strategy of Putin's administration vis-à-vis economic entities in Russia seems to clearly distinguish the special role played by the strategically important big businesses in the national economy. Even when not state controlled, large property holdings in Russia are viewed by the Kremlin as essential for promotion of state interests and state building. As a result, large-scale private property in Russia could be considered, more realistically, *conditional*.[19] Private property in the Western sense is historically associated with the bundle of rights that allow owners of property not only to control its use and the profits it generates but also the freedom to sell and dispense with the property in the manner they see fit. Some of these rights are heavily constrained in Putin's Russia. The owners of most important industrial resources are likely to face restrictions if they want to sell their assets to foreign investors. Foreign participation in Russia's energy projects was also considerably curtailed under Putin. Even large-scale domestic mergers had to get approval from the Kremlin.[20] Perhaps most notoriously, large property owners have to be always ready to give up their assets in the event the Kremlin wants to nationalize them. The unexpected 2006 sale of Sibneft' to Gazpromneft' (owned by Gazprom) and the economic effect of Putin's attack on Mechel in 2008 were revealing in this regard.[21] There are other restrictions related to the conditions under which even such already limited property rights could be retained. Large asset holders in Russia cannot participate independently in politics. This opportunity was deterred early on in Putin's presidency using the very effective strategy of selective punishment.

In addition to these broad limitations on property holders, there are informal obligations, such as "voluntary" donations to various Kremlin-initiated projects. The reconstruction of the Konstantinov palace in St. Petersburg, for example, was funded by private donations from big businesses. Such a practice was especially widespread in the regions of Russia during the 1990s. Putin transferred it to the national level while at the same time criticizing and trying to uproot this vassalage model in governor-business relationships in the regions.[22] These practices continued under President Medvedev and were propelled by now–Prime Minister Putin.[23]

To summarize, Putin's policies did not bring the proclaimed separation between government and big business. If anything, the fusion of state and big business was strengthened. The crony capitalist nature of the political-economic system persisted: the system lacked clearly defined rules of the game and secure rights to property applied equally to all economic actors. Selective rewards and punishments were as characteristic of Putin's era as Yeltsin's. However, the new system featured a new pattern of domination and resembled a case of systematic corruption, characterized by the use of economic means for political ends.[24] As succinctly stated by Easter, "In contemporary Russia, state concessions are not managed directly by state ministries and agencies, as was the case in the command economy. They are farmed out to politically favored corporate executives, who are charged with turning a profit while navigating the pitfalls of global capitalism and fulfilling state-determined social [and, I would add, political] obligations."[25]

Political Contestation under Yeltsin

Yeltsin's Russia allowed for a fair degree of political pluralism (albeit often perceived as disorderly), despite the occasional completely nondemocratic actions of the president, such as the shelling of the parliament in 1993.[26] This pluralism was manifested in wider representation of political parties in the State Duma, in the proliferation of independent media, in the vibrant electoral campaigns in the regions of Russia as well as nationwide, and even in the number of candidates in the presidential races. Below I focus on three periods of especially intense political confrontations that illustrate the presence of political alternatives to Yeltsin and his agenda.

The first confrontation involved the executive and parliamentary branches of power in 1992–93, when the Congress of People's Deputies became the focal point of conservative forces opposed to Yeltsin's economic reforms. Reacting to Yeltsin's assumption of extraordinary executive powers in March 1993, the parliamentarians voted to impeach him, but the vote failed by a narrow margin. This conflict culminated in September, when Yeltsin decreed the dissolution of the unruly Congress of Deputies and used tank artillery to bombard the White House, where the parliamentarians were barricaded. The ultimate victory in this conflict enabled Yeltsin to push through the adoption of a super-presidential constitution in December 1993.[27] Even with this constitution, the legislative branch (State Duma) did not lose its relevance. In contrast, the 1993 and 1995 parliamentary elections resulted in the parliament being dominated by parties opposed to Yeltsin: Vladimir Zhirinovsky's Liberal Democratic Party of Russia [LDPR] and the Communists. In the 1995 election Our Home Is Russia, the party favored by the Kremlin and considered the party of power gained only about 12 percent of the seats. The State Duma was thus able to defy Yeltsin on some issues; it rejected his legislative initiatives, voted no confidence in the government,[28] and forced the withdrawal of his prime minister nominations.[29]

The second political moment that highlighted the existence of the political alternative to Yeltsin was the 1995–96 electoral season. The 1995 parliamentary elections showed that the Russian public did not support the government. The Communist Party won the biggest share of the vote (22 percent), while Zhirinovsky's LDPR captured second place with 11 percent. The party of power led by Prime Minister Viktor Chernomyrdin won only 10 percent of the vote. Popular support for Yeltsin had also dwindled. His ratings fell to single digits by January 1996, while popular support for Gennady Zyuganov, leader of the Communist Party of the Russian Federation, grew. Few people believed that Yeltsin could win reelection; in fact, many analysts predicted that the election would be postponed. Some of Yeltsin's core advisers counseled him to postpone the election and even announced this idea publicly.[30] The events of 1996, however, unfolded in a different direction. Instead of postponing the election, Yeltsin changed his campaign team from the one led by Oleg Soskovets and Aleksandr Korzhakov to the team led by Anatoly Chubais and backed by major Russian businessmen such as Berezovsky and Gusinsky. In the end, the new strategy polarized the election into pro-reform and anti-reform camps; the enormous financial resources mobilized with the help of the state and the Russian bankers and a massive media campaign aimed at improving Yeltsin's image and tarnishing Zyuganov's shifted popular opinion in favor of Yeltsin and allowed him to win reelection.[31]

The early years of Yeltsin's second presidential term were characterized by intense competition among rival economic-political clans competing over lucrative privatization deals.[32] Engaged in all-out information warfare, competing oligarchs made personal accusations and allegations of corruption in rival media sources. The fighting became especially intense in 1997–98. At one point Yeltsin had to interfere in an attempt to persuade the rival parties to limit their conflicts,[33] but that interference did not change either the crony nature of Russian capitalism or the competitive nature of Yeltsin's regime.

Finally, a serious political challenge to Yeltsin emerged in 1999, with the political mobilization of regional leaders behind the figures of Prime Minister Primakov and Moscow's Mayor Luzhkov. The result was the formation of two political parties, Luzhkov's Fatherland (Otechestvo) and selected regional leaders' All Russia (Vsia Rossiia). The electoral bloc combining these two parties and known as Fatherland–All Russia was expected to dominate in the 1999 State Duma elections but, outmaneuvered by the Kremlin, did not meet widespread expectations. Realizing the ultimate stakes—controlling the presidency—the Kremlin initiated a vicious information attack on its political opponents, in particular the Fatherland–All Russia bloc. Using an influential anchorman as its mudslinger, the Kremlin targeted Primakov and Luzhkov. In a single broadcast Primakov was indirectly accused of plotting the assassination of a foreign head of state, traveling to Germany for medical treatment that he could have received in Moscow, and even trying to undermine the Russian position during the war in Kosovo. His age and his health were also consistently questioned to undermine his fitness for the presidency. Luzhkov, in turn, was accused of ordering the 1996 murder of an American businessman, Paul Tatum, and having links with the Japanese doomsday cult Aum Shinrikyo.[34]

The Kremlin succeeded in discrediting its competitors and attained its goal of preventing the OVR electoral bloc's domination in the State Duma, promoting instead the newly formed Unity party.[35] The results of the 1999 parliamentary elections resolved the political struggle strongly in favor of the Kremlin. The 2000 presidential elections did not, therefore, involve intense competition. Not surprisingly, the degree of negative campaigning was very low. Putin rarely attacked his main opponents, Gennady Zyuganov and Grigory Yavlinskii. They resorted to this tactic more often than Putin but nothing resembling the dirty tricks and mudslinging of the previous presidential campaign.[36]

All in all, the political regime under Yeltsin was neither consolidated nor backed by strong institutions. While Yeltsin's tsarlike personality led at times to high-handed decisions, bearing more resemblance to autocratic rule, the overall political system remained relatively open.

Political Consolidation under Putin

Putin was appointed prime minister in August 1999, at a time of very feeble presidential authority and growing political challenge from the Primakov-Luzhkov bloc. After the victory of the Kremlin-backed Unity party and Yeltsin's surprising decision to resign, the situation turned very favorable for Putin, Yeltsin's designated successor. After his decisive victory in the 2000 presidential elections, Putin initiated a set of policies aimed at "correcting the errors of the past" and, step by step, replacing the perceived chaos and anarchy of the Yeltsin era with a stable and predictable political system. This system was to be based on the proclaimed "dictatorship of law" and the restoration of the chain of command, or so-called power vertical. In real life, this meant constructing a system in which everyone knows *kto v dome khoziain* (who is master of the house). Accomplishing this ambitious political agenda involved reforming the central government's relations with the regional elites, oligarchs, and the public as well as creating a strong organizational basis for the political regime relying on the dominant party of power.[37]

Federal Reforms

Putin started with the reform of federal-regional relations. Given that the greatest challenge to the Kremlin emerged out of the political mobilization of regional elites prior to the 1999 parliamentary elections, the need to establish greater control over regional elites was obvious. In May 2000 Putin created seven federal districts, to which he sent hand-picked presidential envoys. In effect, this was a new administrative structure superimposed on the then-existing division of the Russian Federation into eighty-nine constituent units.[38] The envoys were charged with regaining control of federal functions lost to the regions in previous years, increasing the effectiveness of federal agencies, and, in general, ensuring that the president's policies were implemented in the regions.[39] The actual implementation of these tasks involved numerous subprojects and initiatives, including harmonizing regional legislation with federal laws, preparing socioeconomic development plans for the districts, setting up public chambers in the regions for direct contact with the population, and controlling personnel hires in federal offices.[40]

The federal reform also entailed reorganization of the Federation Council. Specifically, Putin prompted regional governors and speakers of regional legislatures to give up their seats in the upper chamber of the Russian parliament. The new rule postulated that the regional executive and legislative branches send one delegate each to the Federation Council. In effect, this change deprived governors of the legislative immunity they possessed due to their representation in the upper chamber and reduced their direct lobbying capacity in Moscow. The Federation Council's role as the lobbying venue for regional interests significantly decreased as a result. Another legislative innovation aimed at enhancing control over regional governors involved adopting a law that allowed federal authorities to fire governors and disband regional legislatures in cases when they violated federal laws. Although these measures were never put into practice, they provided for an additional check on the conduct of regional elites. In parallel with these measures, Putin initiated revision of the tax code, shifting the balance of taxes in favor of the federal center. The new division of taxes resulted in greater centralization of resources in Moscow and was another blow to the governors' power.

All these measures effected significant recentralization of the Russian Federation, taking away the regional autonomy allowed under Yeltsin and placing the regional leaders under tighter control of Moscow.[41] This process came to its logical conclusion with the abolition of gubernatorial elections proposed by Putin in the aftermath of the hostage-taking tragedy in Beslan in September 2004 and enacted in January 2005. With this measure, the top-down hierarchy of federal power was reconstituted, and the regional governors lost their independent legitimacy base conferred on them through regional elections.[42] The federal reform, however, was only one of the items in Putin's overall agenda of building a coherent, centralized political system. In addition to the regional governors, the central authority had other potential political challengers: the rich and powerful businessmen who influenced the state decisions under Yeltsin.

Putin and the Oligarchs

The changing nature of state-business relations in Putin's Russia was discussed above. Here I focus on certain previously powerful oligarchs and their fate under Putin. The neutralization of oligarchs required concerted action on the part of Putin's administration. On the one hand, Putin had to subdue the most powerful members of this group, in particular, Berezovsky, the most politically entrenched oligarch, who masterminded

Putin's ascent to power but, shortly after, became critical of Putin and his policies. The Kremlin reacted by forcing him to give up his control of the ORT channel and opening a criminal case regarding the misappropriation of Aeroflot, Russia's largest national airline company, funds. Faced with criminal charges, Berezovsky decided to flee Russia (he now resides in London).[43] A similar fate awaited another powerful oligarch, Gusinsky, who controlled the popular NTV channel. By 2001 NTV was the only TV channel in Russia that openly criticized Putin, especially for the war in Chechnya. Within a year NTV was taken over by the state-controlled Gazprom, while Gusinsky escaped to Spain after being charged with embezzlement and money laundering.

The third and most radical *razborka* ("setting things straight") involved Khodorkovsky, Russia's richest oligarch, who was accused of tax evasion, arrested, jailed, and sent to Siberia in 2003–4. Most observers viewed Khodorkovsky's arrest as politically motivated, noting that he funded several opposition parties and hinted at his presidential ambitions.[44] Despite less politically flavored plausible hypotheses concerning Putin's decision,[45] the selective nature of this arrest made it political and evoked international repercussions. Khodorkovsky's oil company, Yukos, was split up and its biggest asset, Yuganskneftegaz, bought in a 2004 auction by the state-controlled Rosneft'.[46] The company eventually faced bankruptcy in 2006 and its remaining assets were sold off in an auction in May 2007. In a populist fashion, Putin announced in his 2007 annual state of the nation address that the proceeds from auctioning off Yukos assets would be used to build houses, roads, and other infrastructure.[47]

The selective purging of powerful Yeltsin-era oligarchs did not bring an end to cronyism. Many analysts have noted the emergence in Putin's Russia of new state and business elites originating from or having strong links to security services and law enforcement bodies.[48] The term *siloviki* is colloquially used to describe part of the elite in Putin's Russia. Indeed, Putin's presidency had empowered this new group of individuals, many of whom have close connections to Putin. The key members of this group now hold top positions in the Kremlin and government ministries and control state-owned enterprises and private companies.[49] This group, also referred to as *"silovarchs,"* can be seen as the single most important beneficiary of Putin's term in power.[50]

Putin and the Mass Media

Along with reining in business moguls and the regional elites, the Kremlin consolidated its control of key media. This was the central part of Putin's strategy aimed at controlling public opinion in Russia and changing the relationship between the state and the public. If there is one thing Putin had learned well in the Soviet security service, it must be the importance of information for controlling the hearts and minds of the masses.[51] The Soviet government's intense use of propaganda and counterpropaganda is well known. This tradition, sidelined under Gorbachev and Yeltsin, seems to be on a path to revival in Russia in the past few years.[52] Putin's interest in controlling the flow of information was already obvious in 1999, when he was prime minister. The second war in Chechnya, responsible for the quick rise of Putin's political persona, was the first subject the news coverage of which was carefully regulated by state authorities. Putin established the Russian Information Center to manage reporting on the war, which was referred to in official statements as an "anti-terrorist operation." Access to news on this topic was restricted to official press pools; "unreliable" journalists were denied accreditation.[53]

Putin's understanding of the destabilizing potential of critical news reporting became even more evident early in his presidency, in September 2000, when he signed the Doctrine of Information Security. This doctrine juxtaposed the individual's right of access to information to the interests of society and the state, emphasizing the latter and specifically the need to "maintain accord in society" and ensure "political, economic, and social stability."[54] This doctrine signaled the government's intent to strengthen state control over the mass media. The realization of this intent was already under way. As discussed above, soon after becoming president, Putin waged campaigns against selected oligarchs who controlled massive media empires. An array of criminal investigations and police raids was initiated against the Media-Most empire, controlled by Vladimir Gusinsky. Gusinsky himself was arrested in June 2000 and released after agreeing to sell a controlling stake of Media-Most to Gazprom.[55] As a result of this deal, part of Gusinsky's Media-Most, NTV, the third-largest TV network in Russia and second in popularity ratings, fell under state control, though indirectly, through management by Gazprom. Not only NTV but also such popular publications as the weekly magazine *Itogi* and the daily newspaper *Segodnya* owned by Media-Most fell under Gazprom's influence.[56] A similar fate awaited Boris Berezovsky's media empire. After months of criminal investigations and the arrests of Berezovsky's business partners, in December 2000 he agreed to sell his ORT (the largest TV network in Russia) shares. In 2001 Berezovsky also lost the remaining TV-6 network, which was ordered to be liquidated after several court rulings.[57]

This trend did not end with expelling the powerful Berezovsky and Gusinsky. In 2005 the Kremlin mounted pressure on REN-TV, then considered the only remaining liberal TV network in Russia.[58] REN-TV was co-owned by Irena Lisnevskaya and Unified Energy Systems (EES), headed by Anatoly Chubais. Both Chubais and Lisnevskaya sold their shares in 2005, with EES's stake purchased by Alexei Mordashov, the pro-Kremlin magnate controlling the metallurgy company Severstal.[59]

The Kremlin reestablished the Soviet tradition of regular meetings with the editors in chief of major state-controlled newspapers and magazines to convey the correct line in reporting on the most controversial issues, especially with regard to Chechnya.[60] The pool of Russian journalists had been differentiated by the Kremlin into "good" and "bad" ones, in accordance with the degree of loyalty they had shown toward the political regime. Those considered "good" received invitations to meetings at the Kremlin and received favorable treatment by the presidential administration; the "bad" (read: more critical) ones were mostly ignored.[61] Still, the overwhelming state control of major TV networks and channels is probably the most effective of the Kremlin's propaganda instruments. Because of the cost, newspaper and magazine circulation had dropped sharply in Russia in the past two decades.[62] Meanwhile, television has enjoyed the status of the most popular source of entertainment. The main TV channels, such as Channel One and RTR have a potential audience of 95 to 98 percent of the country's population.[63] They therefore have huge influence on public opinion.

Building the Party of Power

Last but not least, the centralization of political power under Putin involved another important project, building the dominant party, which was led by the main Kremlin ideologist, Vladislav Surkov.[64] Recent scholarship has paid much attention to the central role of strong parties in the maintenance of authoritarian regimes around the world.[65] Strong party organizations help manage elite conflict, enhance the rulers' capacity to win in elections, enable rulers' control over the legislature, and facilitate executive succession.[66] It appears that Putin learned these lessons well, because the construction of the party of power was strongly promoted in the years of his presidency. Curiously, the Unity electoral bloc that dominated in the 1999 parliamentary elections actually started as a "presidential election tactic" designed to divert votes from the Fatherland–All Russia bloc.[67] The alliance of Primakov and Luzhkov in Fatherland–All Russia, supported by such powerful regional bosses as Mintimer Shaimiev, president of Tatarstan, and Vladimir Yakovlev, governor of St. Petersburg, represented formidable opposition to the Kremlin and a robust alternative in the upcoming presidential elections.[68] In this uncertain political context, Unity was primarily conceived as a "weapon in the struggle for the presidency."[69] Its decisive electoral success led to the reassessment of its potential as a permanent party of power that might ensure political stability in the long run.

The building of the dominant party started after the 2000 presidential election. In a classic bandwagon effect, the two main losing parties composing Fatherland–All Russia merged in 2001 with Unity. The new party, United Russia, became a massive party of power, but, unlike earlier versions such as Russia's Choice and Our Home Is Russia, this was to be a much more effective organization. It occupied a centrist position and was therefore able to avoid the legislative gridlock and overcome the presidential-parliamentary deadlock characterizing the relations between the State Duma and the Kremlin under Yeltsin.[70] Since 2003 the Kremlin invested even more effort in promoting United Russia in the regions as Putin's team realized that it needed the governors' administrative resources to ensure victory.[71] Membership in United Russia grew very rapidly, supported by its numerous regional branches. By 2008 the self-reported party membership had reached around two million. The state bureaucracy was, of course, the driving force behind its expansion. It has been even nicknamed "a labor union of bureaucrats."[72] The major achievement of the party was a landslide victory in the 2003 and 2007 parliamentary elections, which produced a pro-presidential one-party majority in the State Duma. By 2008 the party also controlled a majority of seats in regional legislatures.[73] Currently, the party involves not only civil servants and regional elites but also many ordinary folks who view membership in the United Russia as a resource for career advancement.[74] In that, the party resembles the role played by the Communist Party of the Soviet Union.

In brief, Putin's presidency took Russia from a competitive, oligarchy-based system in the direction first of a "managed democracy"[75] and later of a "bureaucratic authoritarian" political system.[76] Whatever the label is, the essential elements of the political system that evolved under Putin included establishing control over regional leaders, the oligarchs, and the mass media (television specifically); drastically limiting political opposition; and securing single-party domination in the parliament. This "creeping authoritarianism" ultimately led to Freedom House categorizing Russia in 2004 as "not free." This assessment was supported by other Western institutions, such as the rating agency Standard & Poor's, which warned in its annual country report that businesses in Russia are subject to a "centralized and personality-driven political regime."[77]

Such negative assessments originated mostly in the West. Russian insiders perceived things differently. In a striking contrast to such gloomy warnings, Bill Browder, CEO of Moscow-based Hermitage Capital,[78] noted that "a nice, well-run authoritarian regime is better than an oligarchic mafia regime—and those are the choices on offer."[79] Browder's preference for a well-run authoritarian regime as opposed to an oligarchic regime seems to be seconded by the majority of Russian people.

The Evolution of Popular Attitudes and the Puzzle of Putin's Popularity

Popular attitudes toward the government in Russia experienced a roller-coaster ride, reaching the heights of euphoria and hope in the new president in the early 1990s and then rapidly descending into distrust, cynicism, and apathy to the government by 1995 and, even more pronouncedly by 1999, and, finally, finding new hope and rising to new heights starting in 2000, with the election of yet another new president. Below, I first focus on the evolution of popular attitudes toward Russia's political system, reviewing how Russian citizens viewed their two presidents, country's political regime, political parties, elections, and democracy in general.

After assessing the political aspect of popular attitudes, I turn to the issue of corruption and evaluate the dynamics of public perceptions of corruption in Russia. Finally, I suggest an interpretation of the data presented in the context of changing political competition levels in Russia and advance an explanation for Putin's unwavering popularity with the masses.

How Do Russians View Their Presidents?

A charismatic politician, Yeltsin was elected Russia's president on June 12, 1991, at the height of his popularity, as a leader advocating more radical political and economic reforms and representing a real alternative to a more hesitant and cautious Gorbachev. The euphoric period did not last long, however; starting in 1992 Yeltsin's popularity started to decline (fig. 5.1).[80] It plunged to single digits by January 1996, when the second presidential elections were held. Only through the efforts of the entire state apparatus and the richest oligarchs, who mobilized their massive financial and media resources behind the incumbent, was Yeltsin able to win in that 1996 race. His second term did not bring him much public support. Seriously ill, he had to withdraw from day-to-day administration and governance, only making abrupt appearances to change personnel and reshuffle the cabinet. Yeltsin's popularity hit rock bottom in 1998 following the devaluation of the ruble and remained there until the end of his presidency.[81] By 1999 his political weakness was so pronounced that the nation was saturated with frequent rumors about his resignation. The negative attitudes were reflected even in the polls after Yeltsin's dramatic resignation on December 31, 2000. Evaluating the historical impact of Yeltsin's era on Russia, 67 percent of respondents in January 2001 (right after Yeltsin's decision to resign) thought that it was more negative than positive, and only 15 percent assessed his era as positive.[82]

The dynamics of popular approval for Russia's second president caused much controversy. Putin, practically unknown to the public until his appointment as prime minister in August 1999, rapidly garnered popular support as a result of his tough stance on the Chechnya issue and maintained remarkably high approval ratings since his election as president in March 2000. Putin was unscathed by events potentially very damaging to his popularity, with his approval ratings remaining at 70 to 80 percent, creating what became known as "the Putin phenomenon" (see fig. 5.1).

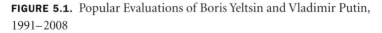

FIGURE 5.1. Popular Evaluations of Boris Yeltsin and Vladimir Putin, 1991–2008

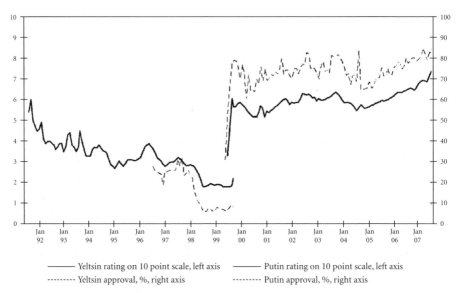

———— Yeltsin rating on 10 point scale, left axis   ———— Putin rating on 10 point scale, left axis

-------- Yeltsin approval, %, right axis   -------- Putin approval, %, right axis

Source: Treisman 2008.

Note: "Yeltsin approval" is percentage of respondents saying on the whole they approve of Yeltsin's peformance; likewise for "Putin approval." Ratings on 10-point scale are average answer to question: "What evaluation from 1 (lowest) to 10 (highest) would you give the President of Russia (name of president)?"

The level of support for Putin was not affected by the loss of the submarine *Kursk,* airplane crashes, or the tragedies of Nord-Ost and Beslan. On the contrary. Some pollsters observed that after such cataclysms Putin's ratings went up, leading some observers to comment on Russia as a country of masochists.[83] Indeed, Putin was able to maintain such remarkable high ratings until the end of his term in 2008 and even after that, as Russia's prime minister, economic crisis notwithstanding.[84]

Public Attitudes toward the Regime, Political Parties, and Elections

The discussion of the dynamics of regime approval in Russia is informed in this section by the work done by the Center for Study of Public Policy at the University of Strathclyde. The New Russia Barometer (NRB) survey, conducted in Russia by the respected Levada Center, has traced popular attitudes toward the Russian regime since 1992. The dynamics of regime approval reveal the relatively low rating for the Yeltsin regime in 1992–99 (ranging from a low of 14 in 1992 to a high of 38 in 1996, when measured on the scale from negative 100 to positive 100) and the steadily rising approval rating under Putin, starting in 2000 (from 37 in 2000 to 65 in 2004).[85] Those with negative perceptions of the regime had always outnumbered positive evaluations throughout Yeltsin's era. Under Putin, this situation changed as a majority of Russians seemed to endorse the regime.[86]

While the public evaluation of the regime has shifted in Russia, distrust of political parties has not changed. Political parties have consistently been among the most distrusted institutions in Russia throughout Yeltsin's and Putin's eras. Only 9 percent of respondents expressed trust in political parties after the parliamentary elections in 1999, while 75 percent actively distrusted them.[87] By 2001 the number of people trusting parties was about 6 percent.[88] Apparently, Putin's presidency has not brought any change in this realm. Despite the resources channeled to United Russia, public distrust for political parties did not lessen and United Russia's membership grew more because of the administrative resources mobilized by political elites than because of ideological party believers.[89] The high degree of public distrust of parties in Russia is reasonable. Over the 1990s political parties became the favorite item in the political technologists' toolbox and were actively used for manipulating electoral outcomes. The spurts of political creativity around election times led to the emergence of "scarecrow" parties frightening the electorate (as the Communists were presented in the 1996 presidential elections), "neophytes" exploiting public disillusionment with politics and using an outsider status, "false aerodrome" parties created to fail and divert criticism, spoiler parties to steal votes from the real competitors.[90] Clearly, political parties in Russia have not become an institution aggregating and representing various societal interests in accordance with democratic theory. They are rather instruments for "managing" electoral outcomes and promoting specific politicians. Putin has not been able to change the skeptical view of political parties in Russia; in fact, he has probably reinforced it by refusing

FIGURE 5.2. Changing Russian Views on Elections (% of respondents who favor canceling elections)

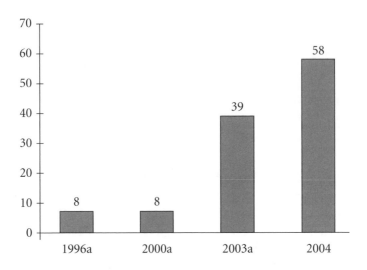

Source: Rose, Munro, and Mishler 2004, 11.

to join any party. Even his decision to lead United Russia when he became prime minister under President Dmitry Medvedev did not cause him to become a member.

While distrust for political parties has been pervasive and consistent over the 1990s, public attitudes have revealed a negative trend in regard to another democratic institution in Russia, namely, elections. In the early 1990s numerous surveys indicated high levels of support for competitive elections.[91] However, already by 1996–97 researchers had noted that this support was declining.[92] The Russian public's faith in the electoral process continued to erode subsequently, as is clearly reflected in the change of perceptions about the need for elections. By 2003–4 the number of people favoring the cancellation of elections had sharply increased (fig. 5.2). This trend was also manifested in the indifference among the public when Putin abolished gubernatorial elections. Not only that people did not protest that their rights were abrogated, but surveys demonstrated a growing number of people approving this decision.[93] More respondents approved of Putin than disapproved in regard to the abolition of gubernatorial elections. Russian pollsters have pointed out that the tendency for elections to become devalued among the public continued after 2003.[94]

How Do Russians View Democracy?

The opinion polls studying public attitudes toward democracy in Russia have produced contradictory evidence. This is to be expected: given the wide divergence of views in academic circles as to what constitutes a democracy, the complexity of popular perceptions of this term could be anticipated. Most opinion polls reveal that Russians have valued and still favor democratic ideals and principles.[95] However, more recent polls show a certain shift in the regime type preferred for Russia. When asked in 1998 a general question about an ideal regime for Russia,[96] most respondents preferred their country be a democracy, not a dictatorship.[97] In recent years the survey results have been more conflicting. Some of Russia's polling agencies increasingly talk about popular disaffection with democracy and a shift in preferences toward more authoritarian forms of government. Thus in 2005, 51 percent of respondents thought that Russia needs a president-dictator.[98] Echoing this popular mood, some analysts suggested that the 2008 elections would bring to power a president similar to Lukashenka, president of Belarus, and Nazarbayev, president of Kazakhstan, both well-known authoritarian leaders in post-Soviet Russia.[99] Other pollsters have found that a majority of Russians still reject all authoritarian alternatives and prefer a democratic regime.[100]

An understanding of such contradictions is not possible if we do not inquire into the popular meaning of democracy in Russia. Specifically, what do Russians view as necessary for the government to be democratic? The NRB survey shows that people widely agree that democracy must involve the rule of law ("equality of all citizens before the law"), multiparty elections, and economic welfare.[101] Given the absence of the rule of law and widespread economic welfare, it is not surprising that most Russians do not view Russia as fully democratic; most place it somewhere at the midpoint between democracy and dictatorship.[102] At the same time, it could also have been expected that if the system of the 1990s was in fact associated with democracy, then such an association could have given democracy a bad name for the majority of Russians. Therefore, these contradictory findings of the opinion polls—some suggesting that Russians still support democracy and others pointing to shifting preferences—might all be reflecting the same thing: people support a more ideally understood concept of democracy (when it is coupled with a functioning state and the rule of law) but reject its deformed implementation in the 1990s.

The Dynamics of Corruption Perceptions

Earlier in this chapter I discussed the changing nature of corruption in Russia. Was this difference reflected in the subjective evaluations of corruption in Russia? Even more important, was the declining political competitiveness under Putin paralleled by lessening public perceptions of corruption, as could be expected from the argument advanced in this book?

The most systematic assessment of corruption perceptions in Russia (as in many other countries) is done by Transparency International, a leading international organization that conducts regular surveys to assess the level of corruption in countries around the world. TI data allow for tracing corruption perceptions in Russia in the period from 1996 to 2008 (fig. 5.3). The pattern that stands out is largely supportive of the argument about the impact of political competition under crony capitalism, especially for the period 1996–2004. The TI data demonstrate that in the period 1996–2000, under the more competitive regime of Boris Yeltsin, there was an identifiable negative trend of increasing perceptions of corruption (from 2.6 to 2.1).[103] This trend then reversed in the first term of Putin's presidency. During 2001–4 public perceptions of corruption declined from 2.1 to 2.8. Hence Russia nationwide reveals a trend similar to that found in its regions: greater competitiveness seems to be associated with higher perceptions of corruption, while a more controlled public space and restricted opposition under Putin produced, at least in the first four years of Putin's presidency, decreasing subjective evaluations of corruption by the people. Even further, the TI data arguably allow for establishing a direct link between the most intense electoral campaigns and the resultant public views on corruption in Russia. Indeed, if information wars and negative campaigns have a direct impact on corruption perceptions,

FIGURE 5.3. Transparency International Corruption Perception Index

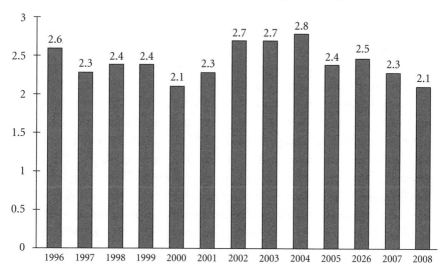

Source: Transparency International (www.transparency.org).

then it could be expected that there would be a sharp rise in corruption perceptions following the most intense 1999 electoral season in Russia. The TI data confirm this by a more substantive, three-decimal-point drop (from 2.4 to 2.1) in the index of corruption perceptions in 2000, whereas the previous three years were characterized by a relative stability (2.3–2.4) in subjective evaluations of corruption.

However, contrary to my expectations, this trend seems to have reversed in 2005, which stands out as a year in which the TI assessment of corruption perceptions in Russia fell sharply, from 2.8 to 2.4 (bringing Russia from 90th place in 2004 to the lowest-ever 126th place, which it shared with Niger, Albania, and Sierra Leone). Furthermore, after slightly rising in 2006, Russia's ranking in corruption perceptions continued to drop in 2007–8. It appears that the early Putin years of more positive evaluations of the corruption situation in Russia have given way to more skeptical views. How can this shift be explained?

One potential explanation might be found in the studies done by the INDEM foundation, a Russia-based nongovernmental think tank. In their report "The Diagnostics of Corruption in Russia: 2001–2005," INDEM scholars noted, among other things, that the economic growth and increasing prosperity in Russia were paralleled by an increase in bribes: the average bribe size in 2005 was thirteen times higher than in 2001.[104] Various other commentators have also noted that as the economy grew in the 2000s, the amount of resources flowing in the informal sector skyrocketed.[105] It appears plausible to suggest that Russia's sliding position in TI rankings on corruption perceptions since 2005 might reflect the fact that popular perceptions of corruption started to catch up with the reported dramatic increase in corruption and especially in the amount of bribes given out in real life in Russia. A quick look at the methodology used by TI further clarifies this puzzle. To produce the Corruption Perception Index (CPI) indices, TI relies on evaluations done by country experts and business leaders, who are likely to be much more aware of the real situation and trends in the extent of corruption plaguing a country. These assessments therefore might differ significantly from popular views on corruption levels in Russia. Indeed, Stephen White and Ian McAllister, who have conducted studies on how ordinary people in Russia perceive corruption levels, report that popular perceptions of corruption under Putin have in fact been decreasing despite the fact that real corruption levels have reportedly grown (fig. 5.4).[106]

Connecting the Dots: Cronyism, Competition, and the Puzzle of Putin's Popularity

To the question, "What do you think is the biggest obstacle to Russia becoming a normal society," a majority of Russians (66 percent) responded government corruption and nonenforcement of laws.[107] The Putin phenomenon and the unwavering public support enjoyed by Russia's second president should be understood in the context of how Russian citizens view the major problems plaguing their state and society. Russia's authoritarian turn under Putin is not an unexpected and annoying detour from the democratic path that Russia had been following before he came to power. It originates from the fissures that had developed in the crony capitalist institutional order during the 1990s. Specifically, it is a counterreaction to the destabilizing dynamics of the competitive, oligarchic sys-

FIGURE 5.4. Public Views of Government Corruption in Russia, 2001–2008

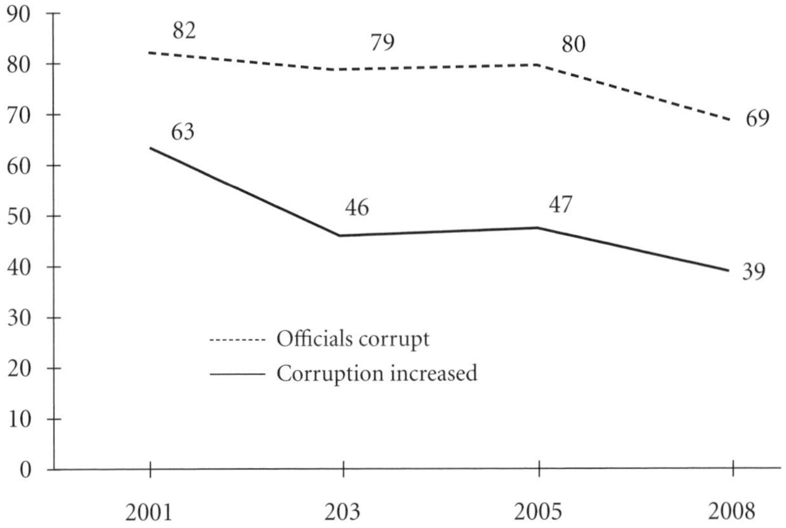

Source: White and McAllister, unpublished manuscript (data based on 2000 NRB and 2003, 2005, and 2008 Russian surveys).

tem that has emerged in Russia during the 1990s. The manipulative tools and technologies used by political and economic elites during the much-publicized struggles for power and property brought the issue of corruption to the surface, undermining public faith in the state, political institutions, and the ruling elites. By the late 1990s a new political momentum rose in Russia. It was characterized by the demand for a new "political formula" if the political authorities were to maintain control. Putin reacted "adequately" to this new political context. Unable (and unwilling) to root out crony capitalism, he restricted political competition and power struggles, thus removing the main "trigger" undermining public faith in state institutions and the political regime, and focused on recovering (first of all in public eyes) the public purpose of the state. This, I argue, is the primary reason for his lasting popularity and consistently high and robust approval ratings that have puzzled numerous analysts.[108]

Stability, order, and economic growth are claimed to be among the primary achievements of Putin, whose leadership is perceived to be based on a philosophy combining reform and order and the pursuit of centralization for the sake of modernization.[109] However, if one looks into what was really required for that stability to be attained, then the most conspicuous policies of the new president were related to the elimination of freedom of the press in the country.[110] The rowdy 1990s were replaced by the tightly controlled official media featuring self-congratulatory reports and constant adulation of the president, including sometimes even his dog.[111] The new media situation along with other important changes implemented by Putin for integrating the regional elites and the oligarchs into a centralized pyramid of power *(vertikal' vlasti)* and propping the political regime with a strong party of power produced a new political context that promoted feelings of greater stability and order among the public.

Of course, several consecutive years of economic growth under Putin were another essential ingredient of Russia's newly found stability. It has been debated whether any of Putin's economic policies contributed to this growth or whether it is associated mostly with the currency devaluation following the August 1998 financial crisis and high oil prices.[112] Indeed, the initial economic growth is likely to have originated from the boost given to the domestic producers by the ruble devaluation in 1998 and supported by high oil prices. Persisting until 2008, high oil prices benefited Russia's economy and society enormously by contributing not only to enlarging the state coffers and enabling new national projects[113] but also to raising personal incomes and bettering the living standards of ordinary people, which, in turn, boosted the retail, construction, and real estate sectors of the economy. At the same time, it seems reasonable to suggest that Putin's early economic policies such as reducing tax levels, increasing fiscal transparency (for regional budgets, for example) and promoting financial sovereignty (paying off the previous debts the country had) could have had a lasting positive effect on the economy as well. Therefore, Putin's popularity might also reflect people's appreciation of this newly found economic prosperity. Indeed, Treisman has argued that public perceptions of economic well-being are the single most important factor explaining presidential popularity in Russia.[114] He claimed that Putin's popularity is a direct reflection of Russia's economic success in the 2000s.[115]

This argument has not withstood the test of the recent economic crisis, which hit Russia hard. Russia's stock market has lost around 70 percent of its peak value, amounting to the worst performance among the emerging markets.[116] The economic crisis has also led to a sharp drop in incomes and rising unemployment levels. The socioeconomic situation became especially dire in Russia's numerous mono-cities (i.e., those built around a single enterprise) as well as the capital city of Moscow, where economic activity (specifically industrial production and construction) fell by around 30 percent in the first nine months of 2009.[117] If anything, it is such a crisis that, according to Treisman's argument, would have tarnished Putin and his successor Medvedev's popularity. But Putin's amazing popularity has not been substantially affected. According to Levada Center reports, Putin's popularity between May 2008 and May 2009 fluctuated between 76 and 88 percent (of those respondents who approve of Putin), and Medvedev's popularity has followed Putin's very closely.[118] These numbers demonstrate very clearly that popular perceptions of the economic situation could not have been the single most important factor in determining presidential popularity in Russia. Rather, I would argue, it is the regime's control of the media and its conditioning effect on public perceptions combined with the absence of publicly available political alternatives to this regime that are responsible for the continuing popularity of Putin and his political formula for Russia.

Conclusion

The analysis of political dynamics under Russia's two presidents provides solid support for the argument advanced in this book about the impact of political competition under crony capitalism. In light of this argument, the authoritarian turn and political consolidation in Putin's Russia are best understood as a reasonable response by the Russian political elite to the problems and challenges that emerged under Yeltsin's competitive crony system. Putin broke away from the vicious cycle of rival elites clashing over state power and undermining the legitimacy of state authorities and political institutions in the process of these clashes. Without publicized elite rivalries being played out during electoral campaigns or over privatization issues, the state could engage in a systematic "convincing and explaining" of the main party line to the public.[119] With full control over the media and in the absence of challenges from outside the political establishment, the authorities could employ propaganda tools effectively and create a deferential public that would not be frustrated with the conflicting information coming from rival information channels.

The elimination of political competition in Russia removed only the fact that cronyism is explicit. Russia remains a crony system and is therefore fundamentally weak and vulnerable. Its longevity hinges, first, on the degree of elite integration and co-optation into the system and, second, on the resuming of the economic success that characterized Putin's presidency. If the regime is not successful in integrating the elites and managing covert conflicts, the cracks and cleavages in the system can lead to an onset of another round of open political competition, repeating the pattern of the 1990s. Similarly, if people feel further impoverished as the economic crisis continues or do not feel appropriate attention from the government to their concerns, propaganda tools employed by the regime are likely to fail, and destabilization of the system becomes more likely. Thus continuing attention to the party of power for uniting the elites as well as national social projects for promoting the people-friendly image of the regime are likely to be crucial for the continuation of Russia's political regime headed, after the 2008 presidential elections, by Putin and Medvedev.

CHAPTER 6

Postcommunist Cronyism and the Choice between Authoritarianism and Democracy

No enduring and viable strategic framework ever emerged to promote the region's development or stability, as the CIS was permanently crippled by its members' lack of common values and vision.
—Mikheil Saakashvili, "The Way Forward"

Democracy under Crony Capitalism: Lessons for Policy Makers

This book views the origins of postcommunist crony capitalism as an inevitable outcome of a historically particular junction of incentives facing economic and political elites. The redistribution of state property and the introduction of the electoral mechanism of power transfer produced the combined effect of encouraging collusive behavior between economic and political elites and producing a state that could not sustain secure property rights. Although some elements of crony capitalism might be present in more developed Western countries, postcommunist crony capitalism in Russia and its regions should be treated as a distinct institutional order. The key difference is the institutionalization of cronyism and its embeddedness in the economic, political, and social fabric of Russia. It is reflected primarily in the degree to which cronyism is taken for granted and has become intersubjective knowledge shared by the population. In more established Western democracies the occasional revelations of cronyism do not threaten the fundamental political and economic institutions, the legitimacy of which has been built up over centuries. If anything, such revelations result in reforms aimed at perfecting those institutions.[1] Cronyism in young and fragile democracies, on the other hand, is much more dangerous as it leads to public skepticism and disillusionment with the basic institutions of democracy and makes the populace open to a radical revision of the entire political and economic system.

Some studies of political corruption in Western democracies have argued that there is an inherent link between corruption scandals and liberal democracy.[2] It has been suggested that "democracies are institutionally predisposed to scandal politics" because of the mechanisms that exist to scrutinize the violation of democratic rules and procedures.[3] Even further, it has been argued that "scandals put in evidence the demand for accountability."[4] This study challenges such benevolent conceptions of scandal-driven politics and backs the recent findings of research on democratic representation in Latin America, in particular, in the countries of the Andean region. Noting the negative impact of political scandals and corruption stories on citizens' perceptions of political institutions and politicians, Mainwaring et al. (2006) suggested, "Ironically, freedom of the press, which is one of the most normatively valued aspects of democracy, may facilitate the denigration of democratic representation."[5] Indeed, more frequently, corruption allegations and scandals represent a political tool for discrediting political opponents rather than a genuine anticorruption stance or policy of particular individuals or political groups. Rather than reflect the demand for accountability, corruption scandals in the competitive politics of the Nizhnii Novgorod region reflected intensifying political competition and rivalries among the main elite groups. They resulted from deliberate elite actions aimed at discrediting political opponents. This pattern was by no means restricted to the Nizhnii Novgorod region. The quantitative analysis discussed in this book has highlighted that public perceptions of corruption in the regions are indeed affected by the degree of political competition. In short, there appear to be only two crucial elements that make scandal politics possible: political competition and a nonmonopolized media representing the interests of specific political forces. These two elements do not always amount to making a liberal democratic system, and, therefore, the link between the public revelation of corruption and democracy is unjustified.

Returning to the questions posed at the outset: what can we learn from this study about the relationships between elections and democracy, between political competition and democracy? What kind of policy recommendations can be made to those interested in supporting and promoting democracy abroad? I have challenged the assumptions of democratic theory as well as the prevailing democracy-promoting efforts, especially in the United States under the Bush administration. The conventional wisdom in democratic theory views elections and political competition not only as beneficial but also as an essential trait of a democratic political system. Elections combined with political competition are expected to encourage elite accountability, give rise to multiple information channels, and ultimately enhance political debate and public engagement in politics. Democracy-promotion policies are also based for the most part on this procedural view of democracy that centers on competitive elections, free press, and political pluralism. My exploration of how competitive elections worked in Russia's regions reveals, however, that in the context of crony capitalism competitive elections can destabilize the political system. This might be a short-term impact of political competition; in the long run, when democratic institutions are more established, competition might indeed work as expected to improve government accountability. But in the short run crony capitalism means that the election outcomes have great impact on the subsequent socioeconomic foundations of the regime. It therefore encourages such forms and methods of political competition that fuel public perceptions of corruption and discredit political elites as well as the electoral process itself. What is most dangerous, the very idea of democracy might be discredited as a result of such politics, thus undermining hopes for any potentially beneficial long-term effects of competitive politics.

One important implication for policy making that emerges from this observation is in regard to the priorities that should be adopted by outside actors promoting democratization in countries undergoing political transformation. The rule of law and secure property rights appear at least as important a condition for democracy as political competition and elections. Democracy building should therefore involve not only the introduction of competitive elections but also the creation of conditions for the development of an impartial state based on the rule of law. Otherwise, in the absence of the rule of law, there are important, if short-term, benefits associated with the noncompetitive political regime in terms of state-society relationships and, therefore, a strong pull toward a noncompetitive system as the population, disgusted with corrupt elite infighting, develops a preference for stronger authoritarian leadership. Alas, a shift of focus from the electoral mechanism and competition to property rights and the rule of law might seem to be a task that is more demanding than outside actors "promoting democracy" might be ready to undertake. Without tackling these prior issues of crony capitalism, however, democratic transitions might be doomed to failure.

The foremost question left unanswered in this story is, then, whether there is a way out of crony capitalism. What factors contribute to the evolution of such a system toward one that is conducive to a democratic state governed by the rule of law?

The Experience of Russia and Its Regions

The cases presented in this study do not give much hope for optimistic scenarios. Although Tatarstan is ostensibly better off in terms of state-society relations than Nizhnii Novgorod, and Putin's Russia appears to have garnered greater popular acceptance than Yeltsin's, in the long run the legitimacy of state authorities, both in Tatarstan and in Russia at large, is shaky at best. The reliance on state propaganda and economic and political centralization could keep the regime going while the economic conditions were favorable and the governments could rely on a variety of socially oriented projects to maintain popular support. In the context of the global economic crisis that has affected Russia's oil-dependent economy especially severely, the survival of the regime built by Putin is not a fore-gone conclusion. A number of analysts of Russian politics suggest that the regime can survive an economic crisis that lasts a year or a little more. A crisis lasting about two or three years, however, is forecasted to be detri-mental to the ruling elite.[6]

The persisting cronyism of political and economic elites corrupts the foundation of the entire system, limits the potential for economic development, and fails to unleash the full potential of human initiative and creativity necessary for social progress. In the end, public opinion cannot be entirely "constructed" by elites seeking new legitimizing strate-gies for their rule. Political instability and uncertainty therefore remain a "congenital" effect of crony capitalist systems, whether competitive or noncompetitive. The authoritarian solution might work in the short and medium term, but it also runs high risks of instability, as discussed in chapter 5. Is Russia's fate sealed? Are there any sources of hope remain-ing? Even a quick look at the patterns of development in the postcommu-nist region at large is instructive.

In the early 1990s crony capitalism or, more accurately, the tendency toward evolving in that direction emerged in all countries that went on the path of democratization and privatization. The fusion of politics and economics reflected in the presence of informal elite networks was evi-dent throughout the postcommunist region.[7] Fifteen years later the pic-ture of this part of the world changed dramatically. The Central European and Baltic states have successfully pursued integration with the Euro-pean Union (EU) and, by the time of their entry into the EU (so far in two stages, in 2004 and 2006), were for the most part considered effec-tive states with well-functioning democratic systems and market econo-mies. Even with many problems remaining in various aspects of their governance, these countries have demonstrated a clear movement away from the most egregious manifestations of crony capitalism toward more secure property rights and a law-governed state. The Russian Federation, Belarus, and most Central Asian countries, on the other hand, evolved in an authoritarian direction, maintaining insecure property rights and arbitrary rule. Still other postcommunist countries, especially Georgia and Ukraine, found themselves in a more volatile situation, undergo-ing the so-called color revolutions during 2003–4. The radical political changes manifested in the overthrow of incumbent governments gave these countries a new promise of success and advancement associated with the West.

These diverging postcommunist experiences provide some hope about possibilities for overcoming crony capitalism. The remaining part of this chapter attempts to place the argument advanced in this book in light of diverging postcommunist trajectories of development by embedding it in the larger historical and geopolitical context.

Two Modes of Postcommunist Development: Positive and Negative Scenarios

The Negative Scenario

Russia

The failure of Russian democratic transition appears by now to be an unquestionable fact of life. Despite the propagandistic attempts by shrewd ideologues in Putin's administration to advocate that Russia is a special type of democracy (especially the idea of "sovereign democracy" promoted by Vladislav Surkov), recent political developments in Russia have shown an unambiguous retreat from democracy. Political pluralism, free press, parties, and elections—all vital signs of a democratic polity vibrant in the 1990s, even when messy and frustrating—were severely curtailed in favor of a centralized system within which every rational participant is compelled to toe the "Putin line" (transformed, after the March 2008 elections, into the "Medvedev-Putin line"). Adding insult to injury, these changes were largely supported by the Russian public, which came to view order and stability as values more precious than pluralism and competition. These developments in the domestic polity were coupled, more recently, by an increasingly assertive foreign policy stance of the Russian Federation that is frequently based on a conscious definition of the Russian path of development as different from that of the West and, more alarmingly, on encouraging anti-Western attitudes. Western attitudes toward Russia have similarly deteriorated, as the country that has turned authoritarian and assertive is being perceived as a growing threat to the West. Taking into account all the domestic developments taking hold under Putin and persisting under his successor, Dmitry Medvedev, and the parallel changes in the relationships between Russia and the West, the unfinished debate of the late 1990s about "who lost Russia" appears to be even more timely today. In current international politics, Russia certainly has been "lost" as a loyal partner of the West and, instead, has evolved into a pole of attraction for other countries in Eurasia asserting their independence and even opposition to the West. There are special relations, for example, between Russia and authoritarian Belarus. There is increasing energy and security cooperation with Central Asian states, frequently in opposition to the West and the projects promoted by Western countries.[8] Even U.S. President Barack Obama's fresh attempt to "reset" relations with Russia does not seem to change fundamentally the opposing disposition of interests between authoritarian Russia and the West.

Attempts to explain the ill fate of Russian democracy abound. Some explanations center on institutionalist or cultural approaches that point to the role of "wrong" institutions (whether super- or patronal presidentialism) or authoritarian political culture embedded in the Russian psyche.[9] Other arguments are structural in nature and look at the role of historical legacies, the strength of civil society, and dependence on raw materials.[10] This book advances a theory of political regime dynamics under a crony capitalist institutional order, pointing out the destabilizing effect of political competition on the political system, including its democratic elements. In accordance with this theory, an understanding of alternative political scenarios playing out in the aftermath of the communist collapse requires a closer look at the impact of political competition played out in the context of crony capitalism. A crony capitalist system characterized by insecure property rights and weak rule of law creates strong incentives for political-economic collusion. When combined with fragmented elites, these incentives lead to an intense, warlike rivalry between elite groups driven by the massive stakes involved in the outcomes of elections and control over the state. The methods used in these political struggles are manipulation of public opinion, real and fabricated compromising materials, and exploitation of legal means and administrative resources. This form of politics differs from ordinary democratic politics, which, even when contentious, is restrained by the rule of law. Its effect on the political system is destabilizing, especially in young, fragile democracies. The heightened public perceptions of corruption resulting from such a form of politics delegitimizes elites and discredits democratic political institutions, thus creating an opening for an authoritarian solution.

The analysis of crony capitalism in two regions of the Russian Federation brought attention to two types of this system: competitive, as in Nizhnii Novgorod, and noncompetitive, as in Tatarstan. These political variants are characterized by different patterns of political and economic change that result from the interaction of cronyism and political competition. One pattern that could be pointed out in the case of Nizhnii Novgorod and Yeltsin's Russia is the growing destabilization of a competitive crony system. While the new institutionalist analysis posits political instability as a variable that precedes and, in fact, determines the emergence of crony capitalism, this study asserts a reverse linkage. Instead of viewing crony capitalism as a response to political instability, it might be more appropriate to view political instability as a *consequence* of cronyism embedded in the institutional tapestry of a country. Cronyism or the absence of the rule of law and the dominance of informal institutions in the political and economic sphere result in public alienation from the political regime and rising demands for political change, especially when interelite fighting plays out in the public sphere. However, a regime change only solves the problem temporarily. Cronyism remains embedded in the system and eventually results in the reemergence of the gap between the elites and the masses and, thus, a political opening for another regime transformation. Hence, a cycle of political instability can *result* from cronyism, not the other way around, as new institutionalists have argued.

The noncompetitive political regimes, of the type described in the case of Tatarstan and Putin's Russia, appear to be more sustainable, at least in the short term. In the case of Tatarstan, one of the threats to regime stability originates from the federal center. The federal authorities represent the strongest external actor that might interfere in the republican political scene and cause major shifts in the balance of power among different actors. More specifically, the integrated power pyramid built in the republic during the 1990s might disintegrate with diminishing economic resources, which might be redistributed in favor of the federal treasury through the tax system or through redistributing republican property to economic elites associated with the federal center.[11] However, the most crucial vulnerability of such noncompetitive political systems is internal in nature and is linked to the personalization of power and relationships that prop up the political regime. Such personalization is inherent in crony systems. After all, the very definition of cronyism involves the predominance of informal institutions and relationships. The carefully constructed power pyramid requires a linchpin that ties all the main tiers of the system together. In Tatarstan it was the president, Shaimiev, whose role in the republican political system has been of outmost importance. He was reelected to the presidency twice (in 1995 and 2000) and then reappointed by Putin in 2005.

The political system that was constructed in Tatarstan in the past two decades was poised to face a critical challenge to its sustainability with Shaimiev's impending departure from power.[12] The rumors about his resignation and potential presidential candidates in Tatarstan became widespread in 2008–9 and created much uncertainty in the republic.[13] People expected his departure to result in an inevitable return to the issue of who can have access to profit-making sectors in the republican economy—an issue that seemed to be resolved under Shaimiev. The uncertainty cleared somewhat in January 2010 when Shaimiev announced that he was stepping down and Medvedev selected Tatarstan's former prime minister, Rustam Minnikhanov, as his successor.[14] Minnikhanov is Shaimiev's preferred successor and will presumably try to maintain continuity in the republic. However, he has big shoes to fill, and his success in maintaining the stability of the political-economic system in Tatarstan is not guaranteed.

The problem of succession poses probably the single most important threat to the stability of all crony systems. Similarly, the linchpin of Russia's political system constructed under Putin is Putin himself. Not surprisingly, "problem 2008"—the next presidential election—loomed over Putin's regime in the last few years of his presidency. Despite careful attempts to institutionalize the system of rule constructed under Putin's administration through various legislative changes and the construction of a durable political party, the personal factor remains the crucial point of the regime's vulnerability. Putin's presidency was characterized by a major reshuffling of property rights in Russia. Many major oligarchs of the Yeltsin era gave way to newly minted oligarchs, including those who control large state corporations. It has been also evident that elite fragmentation in Russia remains. The Russian elite, even at the very top of the political pyramid, is by no means unified. While Putin has been able to coordinate and moderate the conflicts of interest among several powerful groups, no one can guarantee that the interelite divisions will not break open when Putin is no longer in power. Perhaps realizing the stakes involved, Putin's solution to "problem 2008" was an ingenious scenario of creating a "tandemocracy" with Dmitry Medvedev, a person he is personally very close to. By having Medvedev elected president and having himself appointed prime minister, Putin was able to stay in power. This setup has so far enabled the very smooth progression from the Putin regime to the Putin-Medvedev regime and has given Putin an opportunity both to stick to the Russian Constitution, as he has promised, and run for the presidency again in 2012, thus pushing the succession problem farther into the future.

The other major source of vulnerability of the political regime constructed by Putin is its dependence on economic growth driven by high oil prices. Despite the ever-increasing official rhetoric about economic modernization, the reliance of the Russian economy on natural resource exports, specifically, on oil and gas, has been very high.[15] The government did initially undertake the responsible financial policy of accumulating oil profits in the Stabilization Fund rather than spending them and thereby unleashing inflation. Under increasing pressure from various forces in the society and in anticipation of the presidential elections in 2008, the government changed its strategy with regard to oil windfalls and initiated a number of "national priority projects" in housing, agriculture, public health, and education that drew billions of dollars from the Stabilization Fund. These measures were undoubtedly part of the strategy the regime pursued to maintain popular support. Indeed, relying on these measures along with institutional building, such as the strengthening of United Russia and various changes in electoral legislation, Putin was able to enact his plans for succession and bring Medvedev to power.

The onset of the global economic crisis in 2008 undermined not only Russia's economy but also the government's strategy of promoting regime support through reliance on the accumulated resources and high oil prices. It took only a few months for the government to spend almost two-thirds of the Reserve Fund,[16] which had been accumulated over a period of several years.[17] The Reserve Fund will be empty by the end of 2010.[18] The effects of the crisis are felt not only in the dropping GDP[19] and drying reserves but, what is more important politically, in rising unemployment and increasing poverty.[20] The dramatic social impact of this economic crisis undoubtedly reverberates in the political realm. The first incidents of labor protests in Russia started in its mono-cities. While the government has been able to deal with and resolve singular incidents, such as the one in the town of Pikalyovo that required Putin's interference, the spreading of such tactics around the country might prove the personalized methods of conflict resolution by Putin or Medvedev to be ineffective.[21] Various Russian analysts and commentators have predicted and discussed the signs of the impending liberalization and opening of the regime necessitated by new economic realities of the crisis.[22] These signs, however, are not materializing and seem to be rather part of a new political tactic of neutralizing potential unrest among the elites unhappy with "Putinism."

Hope for Russia's future remains, crony capitalism notwithstanding. If Russia is able to recover from this crisis and continue on the path of economic growth, the gradual consolidation of the middle class could be expected to produce the growing demands for accountability and the rule of law and promote popular self-organization in the pursuit of societal interests.[23] The rising middle class can also change the elite calculation regarding democratic institutions by reducing the stakes in a conflict of interests between the elite and the masses.[24] In that sense, then, if Russia's crony capitalism, whether competitive or noncompetitive, allows for economic growth and the development of the middle class, it is likely, in the long run, to undercut the incentives pushing toward cronyism and create conditions for engendering a democratic state ruled by law. After all, democracy has social origins, as Barrington Moore argued so persuasively.[25] Alas, this domestically driven path of change might take much longer than the one enabled by the opportunities derived from international geopolitics. As discussed later, these external opportunities were crucial for successful transformation in the new postcommunist members of the European Union.

Belarus: "An Outpost of Tyranny"

Russia was not alone in turning the wheels of transformation away from democracy while maintaining the crony capitalist foundation of its political-economic system. The path for Putin's policies in Russia was laid a few years earlier by the leader of Belarus, Aleksandr Lukashenka, who in the mid-1990s reversed the country's initial postcommunist trajectory. "An undeniable Soviet success story,"[26] the newly independent Belarus started out in the early 1990s as a parliamentary republic, with a government that, following the developments in neighboring countries, initiated market-oriented reforms.[27] In the first few years after the collapse of the Soviet Union the Belarusian transformation path did not differ significantly from that of Russia or Ukraine, for example. Liberal economic reforms resulted in growing social differentiation based on the rise of a small stratum of super-rich businessmen and an increasingly impoverished majority. The industrial sector went into sharp decline while the banking sector prospered.[28] The political system in this period was competitive, albeit manifesting "pluralism by default" that resulted from a weakly institutionalized state and absence of a dominant leader.[29] Prime Minister Vyachaslau Kebich (1991–94) skillfully divided the powers between the Supreme Soviet and the government: the Supreme Soviet led by Shushkevich played a representative role, responsible for the democratization issues, while the government controlled the economy and the process of market transformation.[30] Kebich, however, did not fully control the security apparatus and had problems controlling district governments and local enterprises.[31] The security services (then closely connected to Russia) engaged in intrigues, collecting loads of compromising materials on key political actors that would later be used by Aleksandr Lukashenka.[32] In short, during the early 1990s no dominant political actor had emerged in Belarus. In the eloquent words of Lukashenka, this meant that "power was lying in the dirt" and waiting for someone to pick it up.[33] The instability and political uncertainty of these first years were soon to be resolved by a former head of the collective farm, a maverick politician named Aleksandr Lukashenka.

The scenario of "picking up" the power was realized in the 1994 presidential election, which was characterized by dirty political technologies and corruption scandals.[34] A vicious article, claimed to be originally published in a Dutch newspaper, discredited Stanislav Shushkevich, the incumbent president. Lukashenka, one of the candidates, was accused of petty theft onboard an airplane. He, in turn, staged an assassination attempt during which his car was shot at. Most important, Lukashenka relied on an anticorruption crusade, promising to eradicate corruption, restore industries, and return Soviet-era prosperity to Belarus. Riding on a wave of popular discontent with the perceived chaos and corruption in the country, Lukashenka easily, if unexpectedly, won the first presidential election.

Shortly after his arrival in office, President Lukashenka reversed governmental policies in a conservative reaction to the processes unleashed by the previous government and set out to consolidate political control over the state and society.[35] Declaring that he came to power "for serious and for long,"[36] Lukashenka started out in 1995 with an "ideological reform" replacing the national symbols of independent Belarus with new ones that resembled the old Soviet symbols.[37] In addition, exploiting the widespread nostalgia for the communist past and appealing to popular sentiments, he positioned himself as a leader who opposed the fall of the Soviet Union and rejected Gorbachev and his perestroika policies.[38] But this was only a part of Lukashenka's strategy. One of the first laws drafted by his administration was concerned with the local government and aimed at building a clear power pyramid that would allow for top-down state control.[39] This reform removed any autonomy possessed by the local governments and made the local administration directly appointed and accountable to the president.[40] Since then, Lukashenka has used the additional tactic of preventing potential threats from arising in the regions. To avoid the emergence of entrenched local interests, he rotated his appointees between regions.[41]

Quickly moving from the symbolic and institutional realm to the economic front, Lukashenka put major brakes on market reforms, halting privatization and renationalizing some banks.[42] According to some estimates, the state in Belarus controls almost 80 percent of the economy.[43] In contrast to Ukraine and Russia, therefore, Belarus did not witness the emergence of oligarchs (at least those visible in the public arena). Instead, the Soviet economic system was largely reconstituted as Lukashenka personally intervened in managing and overseeing the functioning of key enterprises and negotiating with their main suppliers and customers.[44]

By 1996 Lukashenka's actions and policies alienated all the key elites in Belarus. He came into conflict with the Supreme Soviet, the National Bank president, the prime minister, the Constitutional Court, and even the head of his presidential administration.[45] Confronted with these problems, Lukashenka called for another referendum (the first one was organized a year earlier) and, based on its results, dissolved the parliament and amended the Constitution to enlarge the powers of the president. According to the revised Constitution, Lukashenka could appoint the heads of the Constitutional, Supreme, and Supreme Economic Courts, as well as the general procurator and several other key state positions.[46] As Lukashenka's regime strengthened, its tolerance of any independent political activity diminished. Law enforcement agencies cracked down on opposition activists and independent reporting in the newspapers. Many former state officials who found themselves in opposition had to flee the country or face jail sentences. Furthermore, since the late 1990s Lukashenka used the political opposition to create an image of an enemy supported and financed by the West and opposed to the genuine interests of the Belarusian people.[47] This image was strengthened further in the 2000s, as Belarus, branded "the last dictatorship in Europe," found itself increasingly isolated from the international community. Many analysts have commented on Lukashenka's exceptional skills as an autocrat and a dictator. He successfully used the policy of preemption, cracking down on the opposition while it is weak, removing its most popular leaders, and restricting the media coverage of the opposition and the elections.[48] Also notable is his constant adjustment to new political circumstances combining "pressure, slander and sophisticated propaganda" to maintain his grip on power and counter any threats of potential revolutions coming from Serbia in 2000 or Ukraine in 2004.[49]

In brief, Lukashenka constructed a monopolistic regime based on control of the primary sectors in the economy, strong institutional hierarchy of the executive power, and populist appeal to Soviet nostalgia, as well as the anti-oligarchic and anti-elite sentiments of the masses. Given these developments, the Belarusian political system can be usefully compared to the system of systematic corruption that evolved in Putin's Russia. It is almost as if Putin followed the precepts laid out by Lukashenka in constructing a durable political system: reinsert centralized control over regional governments, use the economy to support the political regime, tightly control the media, employ sophisticated propaganda tools for managing public opinion, and, more specifically, develop an image of the West as the enemy.

The systematic corruption and crony capitalism in Lukashenka's Belarus has two main manifestations. On the one hand, most of the economy is still considered state owned and is supposed to work in the fashion of a Soviet-style command economy. Frequently, however, formal state ownership hides the fact that primary financial flows are controlled and appropriated by private firms and individuals connected to the state. The "firm-parasites"—suppliers, marketers, and retailers—are usually hired in accordance with directives from state officials, who in turn get kickbacks *(otkat)* for their services.[50] As noted by the respected parliamentarian and political theorist Gennadii Grushevoi, "Today we witness the development of capitalism that works exclusively for the sake of the authorities."[51] Similar to the new state oligarchs in Putin's Russia, Belarus has nurtured its own state oligarchs, selected according to the principle of loyalty to the regime.[52]

In addition, Belarus has its own equivalent of Tatarstan's TAIF, a uniquely expansive business empire directly connected to the president. The role of TAIF in Belarus is played by the Office of Presidential Affairs (Upravlenie po delam presidenta), which during 1994–99, when headed by Ivan Titenkov, grew into a powerful business structure. The Office of Presidential Affairs controlled some of the most lucrative sectors of the country's economy. All state-owned real estate, natural reserves, tourist and sport facilities, and hotel chains were transferred to the control of this "parallel government."[53] Furthermore, the Office of Presidential Affairs established a network of its own companies, including such trading companies as Torgexpo and BelTechExport. These companies received tax privileges as well as exemptions from custom duties and excises and represented a perfect example of how private and public spheres became merged in Belarus. Torgexpo was involved in export and import of alcohol, tobacco, cars, timber, foodstuff, and other products. It is widely believed to have profited from special deals with the corrupt Russian customs services and made money from selling low-quality alcohol on the Russian market.[54] The state budget did not get any taxes from the profits made by these firms. Instead, profits went to the unofficial and nontransparent special Presidential Fund used arbitrarily by Lukashenka and those close to him. This special fund *(Spetsfond)* also received the proceeds from lucrative arms trade.[55] Several local analysts estimated the size of this fund to be comparable to the official state budget of Belarus.[56]

Therefore, despite the populist pretense of the government that the Belarussian economy approximates the Soviet economic model, in reality there is much private business activity going on, albeit mostly corrupt and nontransparent. Despite the lack of economic freedom, the opportunities for private enrichment are present in Belarus for the selected few who are close to the regime.[57] Although there are no businessmen comparable to the former Russian oligarchs, the private enrichment of businesses close to the regime in Belarus is undeniable, and, if anything, there is a special breed of state oligarchs similar to those currently in Russia. In fact, the limited space for private enrichment in Belarus appears to be controlled by the presidential administration, and, as some analysts suggest, a similar pattern of public-private economic links extends to other levels of government.[58] The publicizing of cronyism and corruption is strictly controlled, however. Because the major information channels and media sources are controlled by the state, the systematically reemerging anticorruption campaigns initiated by Lukashenka in relation to some of his close associates are used as populist tools to enhance support for the political regime and Lukashenka himself.[59]

The Positive Scenario: The New Members of the European Union

The positive scenario of postcommunist development in the post-Soviet space can be illustrated using the case of ten countries in the postcommunist region that in 2004 and 2006 became members of the European Union. In the early 1990s these ten states faced challenges very similar in nature to those in any other postcommunist country: economic reforms, state building, creating and adhering to new political rules of the game. The three Baltic states, Estonia, Latvia, and Lithuania, had to also deal with the burden of Soviet legacies. The incentives facing the elites that promoted crony capitalism elsewhere—the redistribution of state property and the use of electoral mechanism for power transfer—were also present in these countries. Indeed, as in the cases discussed above, these incentives encouraged informal agreements between various elites, the fusion of the political and economic spheres, state capture, and the emergence of oligarchs. Latvia is a good example here. It also witnessed the emergence of a few oligarchs: well-connected businessmen who frequently developed their businesses based on their earlier control of key ministerial seats in the government or using close links to the top state officials. The main profit-generating sectors in the country are related to the transit of oil, food processing, and retail. The control of each sector was for a long time associated by the public with the name of specific individuals: Aivars Lembergs, Andris Skele, and Ainars Slesers. All these individuals have combined administrative posts with extensive business activities, albeit unofficially. Until spring 2007 Lembergs, widely believed to control Ventspils-Nafta, was the mayor of Ventspils. Skele, whose business group for a long time controlled most of the Latvian food processing industry, is Latvia's former prime minister and founder of the influential People's Party. Slesers, who became known as a founder of Latvia's first extensive retail chain, Rimi, was formerly minister of economics and minister of transport and is currently a vice mayor of Riga, Latvia's capital.

An OECD report from 1999 stated unambiguously that "corruption and cronyism are central features of the political/corporate scene in Latvia."[60] Latvia's main parties have been widely believed to have cozy connections with the country's largest businessmen or even to represent directly oligarchic interests. Some secret deals from the 1990s between specific political parties and economic groups are resurfacing. A corruption scandal erupted, for example, in April 2007 concerning Lembergs. According to the recently publicized documents, Lembergs's economic group reached a secret deal with the Latvian Social Democratic Workers' Party on positive media coverage of this party in the newspapers controlled by the Ventspils economic group, and, in return, the business group was expected to "finance" projects initiated by the party.[61] This was not the first corruption scandal associated with Lembergs's name. Just a year earlier, during the general elections in Latvia, he was charged with corruption and money laundering that occurred during 1993–95.[62] Furthermore, some patterns of cronyism are still present in Latvia. In 2006 another scandal, known as "Jurmalagate," implicated Skele and Slesers in election fraud, highlighting that the problems of corruption have not been eradicated.[63] There is a big difference, however, in terms of corruption problems in the 1990s and in the 2000s. Not only has the public tolerance for corruption significantly declined, but the state's capacity to prosecute corrupt officials has increased. Criminal cases are being brought against the worst offenders. The recent arrest of Lembergs is revealing in this regard. In brief, while in the 1990s the problem of corruption and state capture in Latvia and its neigboring countries (especially Lithuania) was not qualitatively different from that of Russia, in the past few years these countries have shown signs of moving in the right direction. The TI scores on corruption perceptions have been improving in these countries. The anticorruption laws were tightened. Other legal initiatives and institutional changes sought to control corruption.[64] What happened? What was different there?

The question of diverging patterns of postcommunist transformation has been extensively debated by scholars. The argument advanced in this book focuses on the domestic determinants of regime change and highlights the role of political competition in the context of crony capitalism. Other scholars have pointed to the role of other domestic factors, including historical legacies, modes of democratic transition, balance of political power among the elites, the strength of civil society, and the types of institutions adopted.[65] Neither of these domestic factor–centered explanations, however, can tell the entire story of postcommunist transformations and explain the tendency toward more successful outcomes in the ten new EU members without taking into account an international factor. No potential problems, including those related to crony capitalism, that could have created obstacles for successful transformation became in the end the determining factor for these countries, which were guided by the pull of the EU. For these countries, the desire to "return to Europe," coupled with the conditionality exercised by the EU in the pre-accession process, played a crucial role in determining the course of their transformation.

As argued by Milada Vachudova, the EU exercised both passive and active leverage over its postcommunist candidates.[66] The westward reorientation was evident in these countries already in the early 1990s, when the issue of membership in the EU still seemed distant. For East Europeans, the EU was closely associated with economic prosperity and democratic stability, and this link created a strong attraction to the EU already in the early years of reforms. The real impact on domestic political change commenced after the conditions for EU membership were worked out, thus opening the possibility for entry into the EU. Known as the Copenhagen criteria, these entry requirements postulated that a candidate country must have "stable institutions guaranteeing democracy, the rule of law, human rights and respect for and protection of minorities" and "a functioning market economy as well as the capacity to cope with competitive pressure and market forces within the Union."[67] In addition, the candidate countries were required to adopt all the EU laws known as the *acquis communautaire.*

Such extensive conditions can only work when the benefits of entering the EU outweigh the costs. Indeed, the rewards were perceived as immeasurable, especially with regard to economic welfare and security dimension. Economically, entry into the EU was associated with a steady flow of transfer payments, expertise, and foreign direct investment, in addition to access to the huge European market. Furthermore, it has been argued that at least for some of the countries that were excluded from the 1997 NATO expansion (such as the Baltic states), EU membership became "a surrogate source of security."[68] Despite such benefits, argues Vachudova, in the early stages of transition during 1989–94 the process of reforms and political change was mainly influenced by domestic factors and depended more on the type of political forces that came to power after the collapse of communism.[69] This "passive leverage" stage later gave way to "active leverage," which the EU exercised during 1995–99, when it was able to interfere directly in the policy-making process of candidate countries.

What were the practical mechanisms through which the EU influenced domestic political change? First, the candidate countries voluntarily subjected their domestic political process to evaluation by the EU. Already prior to the first round of accession negotiations in 1997–98, the EU started to monitor the progress of reforms in countries that expressed their desire for membership. It issued regular progress reports that became the guiding documents that inspired reforms of the judiciary, the civil service, and public administration in the candidate countries. Second, the EU pressured governments through diplomatic channels to change certain policies, especially those related to the provision of ethnic minority rights. This pressure was decisive in changing citizenship laws in Latvia, for example. Perhaps the biggest political impact of the EU was to support democratic forces in these societies. The EU played a key role in promoting democratic attitudes among citizens that aspired for Western integration and therefore in shifting the balance of power in favor of democratic politicians.[70] Moreover, the EU played a crucial role in shaping the preferences of political elites and was especially important in those countries where the original postcommunist governments relied on nationalism and rent seeking rather than liberal reforms. By providing the opposition with a compelling electoral platform—accession into the EU—the European Union effected decisive electoral changes in Romania, Bulgaria, and Slovakia that allowed for pro-Western reformers to come to power in these countries during 1996–98.[71] As suggested by renowned analysts of postcommunist politics, "EU leverage can tip the domestic political balance in favor of liberal democracy."[72] Indeed, that was what happened in Romania, Bulgaria, and Slovakia in the second half of the 1990s. Opposition groups in these countries relied on Western financial support and advice to attack the nationalist ruling elites for "forsaking the country's prospects of a 'return to Europe.'"[73] In light of successful integration steps undertaken by neigboring states, Poland, Hungary, and the Czech Republic, the pro-EU orientation of the opposition forces eventually found greater popular support. Moreover, the accession process allowed the new governments that came to power to use the issue of entry into the EU as a strategy for convincing the electorates to accept difficult economic reforms.

In brief, in the case of East European states that became members of the EU, the international factor—the European Union—played a crucial role in shaping domestic political change. This impact was felt particularly strongly and directly in the second half of the 1990s, when the EU exercised the greatest leverage on policy making of future member states. The earlier incentives that pushed these countries in the direction of crony capitalism were therefore overridden to a certain extent by the incentives presented by EU membership. The earlier informal practices and collusive behavior between economic and political elites therefore were checked and even reversed to a certain degree in favor of adopting the different rules of the "European game" that promised a lot more in return. Although cronyism and corruption have not been completely eradicated in these, more successful countries, from the point of view of public perceptions as well as real institutional and legal changes, the trends are positive. This finding is reassuring in light of the argument advanced in this book as it leaves some countries an escape route from the perils associated with crony capitalism. It is also discomforting, however, as the positive scenario of development appears to be determined by a unique external factor (in this case, the European Union), thus leaving the countries that are not oriented toward the EU or are torn between the European Union and the Russian Federation in the disquieting condition described in this book. The fate of Ukraine, divided between its eastward and westward orientation, is illustrative.

Between Two Power Poles: The Fate of Divided Nations and the Lessons from the Orange Revolution

The transformation experience of Russia, Belarus, and the new postcommunist EU members summarized above reveals two main developmental tendencies of postcommunism. As noted by other analysts in the field, currently the region is "polarized between these two extreme forms of government," democratic and authoritarian, as the formerly semidemocratic regimes progressed toward one of these two, more stable alternatives.[74] As argued above, the process of EU accession dominated domestic politics in Central Europe and the Baltic States and allowed for a strong progressive influence exercised by this powerful international actor. The Russian Federation was not equally affected by the European Union.

Too large and too different, Russia has always represented a geopolitical pole in itself, often viewing its own developmental path as different, "third," conditioned by its location between East and West.[75] These sentiments, manifested in the 1990s in popular Eurasian ideology, have solidified under Putin, along with the growing international assertiveness of Russia and the increasing national-patriotic attitudes of the population.

Under Putin, encouraged by a more active foreign policy, the geopolitical attraction of the Russian pole has grown, as various authoritarian regimes in the post-Soviet region have sought Russia's support and cooperation. Belarus, Uzbekistan, Kazakhstan, and Turkmenistan have all found sought-after validation of their political regimes in growing economic and security cooperation with Russia. Therefore, the EU and Russia have in effect become two main competing poles of power on the European side of Eurasia.[76] Under the influence of these two poles, the number of hybrid regimes in the region has dwindled. But there are still some states that seem to be vacillating between the two alternative scenarios, pulled in opposite directions by these two powerful centers of influence. Ukraine is probably the most dramatic case exhibiting a fluctuation between eastward and westward orientation, between democratic and authoritarian tendencies. Below I review the postcommunist trajectory undertaken by Ukraine.

Ukraine in 1991–2004: Following in Russian Steps

For over a decade after the collapse of the Soviet Union Ukraine's destiny seemed to closely resemble that of Russia. Most economic reforms in Ukraine started under the leadership of Kuchma;[77] however, as in Russia, the new economic actors that emerged under these reforms were closely tied to the state. Ukraine fit the pattern of crony capitalism especially well, as the fusion of economic and political power there was most pronounced.[78] This fusion involved senior government officials and enterprise directors who became private owners using their political connections and privileged status. As reforms advanced in the 1990s, the essence of politics in Ukraine turned into a rivalry between a few major economic-political groups, so that most observers referred to the rise of "clan politics"[79] and privatization of the state by influential financial-economic groupings and bureaucrats.[80] These rival EPNs controlled Ukraine's parliament, the Supreme Rada, and owned major political parties, outstripping Russia, where EPNs only financed political parties.[81] According to some reports, in 2000, 386 deputies in the Supreme Rada controlled 3,954 businesses, which accounted for 25 percent of the country's imports and 10 percent of its exports.[82]

Ukraine also differed from Russia in terms of the basis of major clans, or EPNs. In Russia the major national-level EPNs evolved as a result of the loans-for-shares program and, frequently, of proximity to Yeltsin's immediate family members. Many of the Russian oligarchs are young entrepreneurs who made their fortunes during the uncertain times of transition using both their ingenuity and their proximity to the state. In Ukraine, the political structure and the major clientelist networks are region based. Thus Ukrainian politics had been, for some time, driven and defined by the rivalry between the networks from Dnipropetrovsk and Donetsk that clashed over the course of privatization and control of major industries.[83] President Kuchma became the "Godfather" of the Dnipropetrovsk clan and the second president of Ukraine. The Donetsk clan was organized around the parliament member Volodymyr Scherban.[84] While the EPN based in Donetsk was swept aside with the assassination of the Rada deputy and business magnate Yevhen Scherban in 1996, the interelite rivalries did not wane.[85] In 1997 the Dnipropetrovsk clan split into two, and open warfare broke out between the network led by Kuchma and the network led by Pavlo Lazarenko.[86] Following his dismissal as prime minister in 1997, Lazarenko launched his own political party, Hromada, and challenged Kuchma in the parliamentary elections held in 1998 and in the presidential elections the following year.[87]

It has to be noted that Ukraine is poorer than Russia, especially in terms of natural resources. Therefore, most fortunes in Ukraine have been made by trading imported gas.[88] Whoever had access to licenses allowing for purchase of gas in Russia and selling it on the Ukrainian market found themselves in a very lucrative position. Lazarenko, for example, considered the richest person in Ukraine, followed this path in building his fortune. When he became deputy prime minister, he gave United Energy Systems, the company associated with his clan, an opportunity to benefit from the natural gas market.[89] Metal exports were another important venue for enrichment and thus a central point of interelite contention, which surrounded, for example, the privatization of the Azovstal metallurgical plant.[90] In brief, the saga of the Ukrainian privatization process and struggle for control of crucial resource-generating sectors resembles that of Russia's privatization. Although the economic structure of these two countries differed, the form and methods used in the rivalries for control of major sources of wealth were very similar: they involved patronage, government connections, information wars, threats, and contract killings. In fact, the degree of violence in the Ukrainian transformation has been somewhat higher than that of Russia, especially at the top leadership level.[91]

The intensity of economic conflicts in Ukraine was paralleled by the ferocity of political clashes. Similar to Russia's, Ukrainian politics of the 1990s were extremely competitive. In fact, some analysts referred to Ukraine as an example of "rapacious individualism"—politics dominated by "non-ideological and unstructured competition for power and rents."[92] Political competition played out in several domains: the confrontational relationships between the president and the parliament,[93] within the fragmented and polarized parliament, and during the heated electoral campaigns. The executive-legislative relationships in Ukraine, always very complex, became even more problematic under Kuchma, who had to increasingly use his veto powers to prevent some legislative bills from being enacted into law by the Supreme Rada.[94] At the same time, Kuchma frequently used his presidential powers to issue decrees, thus dominating the policy-making process.[95]

The formal institutional design of Ukraine's political system has contributed to political instability and the continuous tug-of-war between the executive and legislative branches of power. The semipresidential framework defining the Ukrainian political system evolved over the 1990s, culminating in the 1996 Constitution, which practically removed the system of checks and balances between president and parliament while making the government accountable to both.[96] This system vested legitimacy in both the presidency and the parliament, thus making them natural antagonists, especially in countries used to a centralized, undivided power structure.[97] In 2000 Kuchma initiated another round of constitutional changes, seeking greater powers for the president vis-à-vis the parliament. This initiative was supported by the results of the April 2000 referendum on constitutional change (though it was claimed to be fraudulent)[98] but was not approved by the parliament. Ironically, at the end of his presidency in 2004, when faced with the prospect of his candidate losing the presidential election, Kuchma promoted constitutional changes contrary to those he sought earlier. Not surprisingly, Kuchma's 2004 constitutional amendments found parliamentary support as they transformed Ukraine's semipresidentialism into a more parliamentary system.

The formal institutional design of the Ukrainian political system, however, represented only the tip of the political iceberg, most of which remained underwater, inaccessible to public scrutiny. As in Russia, informal institutions and relationships prevailed over formal institutions in Ukraine. Both of the first two presidents of Ukraine, Kravchuk and Kuchma, often resorted to undemocratic means to maintain their power. Kuchma, who stayed in power longer, was especially prone to use informal methods of state control, in effect creating in Ukraine a "blackmail state."[99] It was not only a blackmail state, though; it was also a state dominated by powerful regional oligarchic groups. By 2004 Ukraine had three large economic conglomerates with close ties to the government: (1) Rinat Akhmetov's System Capital Management, a metallurgical industry based in Donetsk; (2) Viktor Pinchuk's Interpipe, specializing in steel products and located in Dnipropetrovsk; and (3) the economic group led by Hrihoryi Surkis and Viktor Medvedchuk, based in Kyiv.[100] Kuchma tried to play the role of arbiter between these groups, although his actions often promoted ever more aggressive competition and lawlessness. This competition involved not only these business groups but also various branches of the state and especially its law enforcement agencies as powerful actors sought recourse for actions initiated against them.[101]

Despite much political ingenuity and unscrupulous methods of governing and remaining in power, Ukrainian presidents were never able to contain serious political opposition and build a consolidated authoritarian regime.[102] In fact, major political challengers of the incumbent regime in Ukraine had often emerged from within the presidential insider group. Thus the notorious Pavlo Lazarenko and the "orange princess" Yulia Timoshenko are both former members of the Dnipropetrovsk regional clan and key government figures who turned into fierce leaders of opposition to Kuchma.[103] The current president, Viktor Yushchenko, had served as prime minister under Kuchma in 1999–2001, highlighting once again the fragmentation tendency within the pro-presidential camp.

In the presence of strong (albeit harassed and abused) political opposition, Ukrainian elections in the postcommunist period had been very competitive and abounded in corruption accusations used to discredit

political opponents. Thus the 1998 parliamentary electoral campaign involved corruption allegations coming from all the major political forces:
the parliamentary faction Hromada led by former Prime Minister Lazarenko charged the new prime minister, Pustovoitenko, and Kyiv's mayor,
Omel'chenko, with corrupt activities involving stealing $40 million dur-
ing renovation of a cultural center in Kyiv. Pustovoitenko, in turn, leveled
charges against Lazarenko himself.[104] Starting in the late 1990s, a pool
of political technologists from Russia worked for various political forces
in Ukrainian elections, creating campaign strategies, setting up fake
or clone parties and other manipulative schemes to steal votes from actual political opponents.[105] The involvement of Russian spin doctors increased in the 2002 parliamentary elections and, finally, culminated in
the 2004 presidential elections, when the key maestros of their profes-
sion, such as Gleb Pavlovsky and Marat Gel'man, became closely allied
with Kuchma's administration advising Yanukovich's electoral campaign
and making themselves at home in Kyiv and in the presidential administration.[106] A massive black PR campaign against Yushchenko depicted
him as an American project, linked to the interests of the West.[107] The
"Bushchenko" campaign, however, was a rather gentle technique compared to the alleged attempt to poison Yushchenko with dioxin that resulted in deep scarring of his face. In brief, many of the methods used in
parliamentary and presidential elections in postcommunist Ukraine resembled or sometimes even outstripped the methods used in competitive gubernatorial and national elections in Russia. The regular black PR
campaigns exposed the elites as corrupt, self-serving, and even criminal.
In this context, the media became one of the crucial tools for making or
breaking candidates.

Similar to Russia of the 1990s, Ukrainian oligarchs control most of
the media that have been used widely for discrediting political opponents.[108] Kuchma's attempts to monopolize or control the media were in
the end ineffective. In fact, his political demise and delegitimization came
about as a result of uncovering the methods used by Kuchma for dealing
with an annoying journalist. Indeed, the biggest political scandal that
caused a major political crisis in Ukraine concerned the kidnapping and
assassination of an opposition journalist, Heorhiy Gongadze. This incident was publicized after the secret tape recordings made in President

Kuchma's office were released,[109] in which Kuchma seems to have authorized the kidnapping.[110] The release of these tapes led to the emergence in November 2000 of the so-called Kuchmagate, a political scandal that spilled over to the international arena when they led to uncovering of information related to the illegal sale to Iraq of four Kolchuha radar systems capable of bringing down U.S. aircraft.[111] Perhaps most important, these tapes uncovered, almost officially, the networks of corruption permeating the highest echelons of power and, even further, revealed how corruption and graft were used by high-ranking state officials to control lower-tier officials.[112]

Cronyism grew during Kuchma's second term in power. In the last two years of his presidency the largest oligarchic groups benefited from discretionary privatization of several large enterprises while facing growing public criticism and competition from other economic groups.[113] The privatization of Kryvorizhstal in 2004, when a group controlled by Akhmetov and Pinchuk bought Ukraine's largest steel mill for $800 million, was the most conspicuous of these cases.[114] This privatization occurred through a rigged auction that involved disqualification of a much higher bid for this enterprise and symbolized the crony nature of Kuchma's regime. In sum, until 2004 Ukraine continued on the path of cronyism that closely resembled Russia's evolution. Unlike Russia and Belarus, however, Ukraine did not turn fully authoritarian. Despite Kuchma's attempts to control the media, manipulate the clan-based factional politics, and rise above ideological differences, he was not able to overcome Ukraine's deep societal cleavage and forge a hegemonic EPN that would allow him to fully dominate the political scene. Therefore, until 2004 Ukraine could be characterized as a competitive authoritarian or hybrid regime. A comparison of the evolution of public attitudes in Ukraine and Belarus is instructive. Various public opinion polls have shown, to the utter surprise of many observers, that by and large Belarusians are more content with the state authorities and the political institutions in their country than Ukrainians. For example, the public opinion polls conducted by the independent Centre for the Study of Public Policy in 2000 demonstrated that people in Belarus are less dissatisfied with their conditions and that of their country than are people in Ukraine.[115] Specifically, the level of satisfaction with the current state of affairs in the country was three times higher in Belarus than in Ukraine, while the level of sharp dissatisfaction was almost three times lower in Belarus than in Ukraine (see Appendix 2).

The perceptions of corruption levels also varied dramatically in these countries. Forty-five percent of respondents in Ukraine thought in 2000 that almost everyone in the national government was corrupt. The comparable figure for Belarus was 20 percent. Sixty-three percent of Ukrainian respondents thought that corruption has increased since the Soviet times; in Belarus, that figure was only 37 percent.[116] The degree of efficacy (perceptions of influence on the government) is also somewhat higher in Belarus. Thirty-five percent of Ukrainian respondents reported that their ability to influence the government has worsened; in Belarus, 23 percent of respondents felt that way. Most ironically, even the level of satisfaction with "the way democracy is working" is twice as high in Belarus, while the level of sharp dissatisfaction is almost two times lower in Belarus than in Ukraine (see Appendix 2). Popular views on the state and the functioning of democracy, political institutions, and the rule of law in Ukraine were, in short, very similar to those in Russia prior to Putin's accession to power and differed from those in Belarus.

The widespread dissatisfaction with the government and the political system in Ukraine, however, did not lead to an authoritarian solution, as could have been expected according to the argument developed in this book. To the contrary, increasing authoritarianism under Kuchma resulted in the Orange Revolution, led by Viktor Yushchenko and Yulia Timoshenko, which mobilized mass support and carried out a radical power shift, shaking up the status quo and removing from power the incumbent president and his designated successor. This scenario of a second wave, pro-democratic revolution that developed in Ukraine diverged from the transformation pattern described in this book. Kuchma did attempt to build a more authoritarian system in the late 1990s: he tried to strengthen control over the parliament,[117] sought to control the media, and established tight control over the regional governments.[118] However, he was not able to create a pocket parliament comparable to the State Duma in Russia; the Supreme Rada maintained its independence from the executive branch. Kuchma also suffered a massive loss of his legitimacy as a result of the 2000 Kuchmagate scandal. The opposition, meanwhile, turned out to be very effective and led a mass revolution against the incumbent regime. In contrast to Russia's authoritarian solution, Ukraine seemed to have established a new pattern that involved changing the leadership and gaining new hope of building a democratic regime based on the dominance of formal institutions. To be more accurate, it was not really new. Such radical reversals occurred earlier in Serbia when its citizens mobilized to throw Slobodan Milosevic out of power in 2000 and in Georgia's Rose Revolution in 2003.[119] Ukraine's Orange Revolution did not automatically resolve the problem of crony capitalism. However, it did reflect a certain degree of pull from the West and create a fresh start for the then-untainted leadership to govern the country.

Ukraine's Orange Revolution: Continuation of Political Instability or the New Promise of Democracy?

In 2004, instead of succumbing to the authoritarian momentum that commenced under the Kuchma presidency, Ukraine faced "a revolution in political consciousness."[120] This revolution was manifested in mass political mobilization against the fraudulent incumbent leadership and the resulting power shift in favor of the political opposition. It inspired great hopes with respect to the country's future. The fulfillment of its promise is, however, conditional on learning the lessons of the past and, perhaps even more important, on the degree to which the European Union can embrace Ukraine and keep it within its sphere of influence. More often than not, the euphoric hopes for Ukraine seem to be linked to assumptions that lack sufficient grounding, while some of the lessons from the past are not being attended to. There are a few major reasons that are usually pointed out as signifying hope for Ukraine's future as a democracy. The first and simplest one is linked to the overthrow in 2004 of corrupt incumbent elites and the assumption of power by new, supposedly noncorrupt opposition leaders, that is, leaders who are pro-West and pro-democratic. Such "black-and-white" thinking assigns the responsibility for Ukraine's problems to particular elites: their views, strategies, and morals. Like any thinking of this type, it is overly simplistic and ignores the multitude of nonpersonal factors that condition political outcomes. Even within the postcommunist world there is an abundance of cases in which the "good" politicians unexpectedly turned into "bad" ones. The gradual negative transformation of Yeltsin and Akayev, for example, is revealing in this respect.

The more serious validation of Ukrainian hopes involved the reference to institutional reform that occurred as a result of the Orange Revolution. Indeed, the power shift in Ukraine was paralleled by constitutional reform that transformed the Ukrainian political system in the direction of a parliamentary-presidential regime, reducing presidential and enlarging parliamentary prerogatives. Many observers placed much stake in this constitutional reform, claiming that it added to the Orange Revolution's credibility and political substance and did not allow for reducing the revolution to a mere elite change.[121] It was hoped that reform of the core political institutions would result in a genuine transformation from a hybrid regime featuring elements of both democracy and autocracy into a true democracy, because this reform was supposed to strengthen horizontal checks and balances and result in a more even distribution of power in the system.[122] Supposedly, this was another case of a "pacted" transition to democracy, when elites, faced with uncertainty and an approximately equal power distribution, opted for political institutions that ensure mutual checks and balances and hinder attempts from any side to usurp power.[123]

This logic has been widely popularized by the transitology literature, which views democratization as the outcome of a strategic elite choice. In the early 1990s such thinking became conventional wisdom, as analysts concentrated on pacted transitions in East Central Europe. The events and processes that followed since then, however, led to rejecting this conventional wisdom and the transition paradigm itself. More important, Ukraine's political evolution since the Orange Revolution has demonstrated that the new, supposedly more equitable distribution of power between the president and the parliament is prone to instability. The balance between the president and the prime minister representing two opposing camps shifted in favor of the prime minister after the 2006 parliamentary elections, and the relationship between these two centers of power—hailed initially as a case of "normal democratic politics"—grew increasingly adversarial. The political crisis that developed in spring 2007 represented the culmination of this growing hostility between the two branches of power. It involved an attempt by the president to dissolve the parliament and led to an escalation of the conflict. The parliament and the government failed to comply with Yushchenko's decree, citing its unconstitutionality, and filed an inquiry with the Constitutional Court to evaluate its legitimacy. This crisis made it clear that the constitutional reforms undertaken after the Orange Revolution and welcomed as a forward-looking shift toward a more democratic system did not live up to their promise.

Ukraine's Orange Revolution has been also hailed as a precedent for holding the elites accountable for their actions and thus representing a major lesson for the postcommunist elites. Since corruption and fraud cannot keep one in power, the elites are expected to *learn* to play by different rules. Thus changing elite perceptions about governance strategies that pay off are expected to change the rules of engagement governing politics. This "learning effect" hypothesis is also linked to a related argument that involves the masses. Arguably, the role of the masses in the Orange Revolution demonstrated to the public that it can play an active role in politics, that it *has* a say and *can* influence the government. Hence there is a mutual "learning effect" that is going on: on the one hand, elites know that they can face punishment for their actions, and the public learns that it can influence the outcome. Supposedly, this should lead to genuine transformation in Ukraine. This last argument is in fact very appealing. Not only does it inspire optimism vis-à-vis Ukraine's future, but, being driven by the agency of elites and the masses, it appears empowering and hopeful with respect to the impact of human volition on social and political outcomes. Its hopefulness and appeal should not, however, divert attention from the need for it to be sufficiently grounded. An agency in any specific time and place is not free from the structures that condition and influence it. The vision of political outcomes as determined solely by elites or the masses appears dismissive of the structural forces that shape those outcomes. The *act* of the Orange Revolution itself is indeed best viewed as a result of the joint agency of elites and the masses, which signified the revolt against the status quo.[124] Whether the revolution will bring about a genuine transformation of the political-economic system in Ukraine will depend on the durability of the structural forces that shaped that status quo. The agents might learn, but if the structures remain the same the effect of learning might be overridden by the old incentives that might prove more resilient.[125]

Crony capitalism is one of the key structural forces that conditioned postcommunist politics in Ukraine. During the 1990s, Ukraine has developed as an outstanding example of a crony capitalist system based on the tight fusion of power and business, with economic-political networks as the main subjects of the political process. Any realistic transformation of such a system would require separation between the political and economic actors and the establishment of a state ruled by law rather than by informal institutions. Therefore, an assessment of Ukraine's future should be based on the potential that the new elites have for propagating a new institutional order and a new state governed by law. What observations could be made with respect to the capacity of the leaders of the Orange Revolution to act on this issue? Have they initiated the process of separation of power and business, or have they replaced the old cronies with new ones?

Viktor Yushchenko always belonged to the camp of progressive reformers and, during his tenure as a prime minister, initiated a set of economic reforms aimed at depriving the previously privileged economic actors of their undue advantages.[126] Such policies earned Yushchenko the reputation of being an effective manager who strengthened the state, leveled the playing field, and, as a result, promoted economic growth while not being personally corrupt or privileging specific businesses. The economic policies of the new government, when Yushchenko became president, however, have raised much concern and criticism. In the first months after the revolution, the government was drawn into an extensive policy debate about reprivatization, threatening to start a new round of property redistribution and thus acting exactly in the manner that would be expected when one crony government replaces another. The actual reprivatization process was not initiated, at least not in any systematic manner. There was only the showcase of the Kryvorizhstal steel mill that was reprivatized and sold to a Dutch company for $4.8 billion. The government led by Timoshenko undertook other populist economic measures, including an increase in social spending (boosting pensions and wages) and instituting price controls on gasoline and meat. Various assessments of the economic policy of the postrevolutionary government therefore point to the lost opportunities to promote a genuine transformation of Ukraine's crony capitalism into a more liberal market-oriented system[127] and blame these policies for worsening macroeconomic indicators.[128] To be fair, Yushchenko instituted serious administrative reform, abolishing a large number of state agencies; but even these reforms received mixed evaluations.[129]

At present, it is still difficult to determine the extent of Ukraine's postrevolutionary transformation from crony capitalism to a state governed by law. The most blatant manifestations of brazen cronyism of the Kuchma era are surely a thing of the past, but building a state based on the rule of law is still a daunting task. What is more evident, though, is that the new government and its members have been subjected to several rounds of public discrediting campaigns that involved charges of corruption, smuggling, and nepotism, all aiming to undermine the support for Yushchenko's team.[130] Despite changes in the leadership, the methods of political struggle that were present under Kuchma were still widely practiced after the Orange Revolution. The return of Yanukovich as president in January 2010 was therefore not surprising.

In the end, learning the lessons of postcommunist transformation means that overcoming crony capitalism in Ukraine would require an international force. If Ukraine would have fully embraced the goal of European integration and if the European Union, in turn, would have fully embraced Ukraine as a potential EU member, then changes similar to those that occurred in the Baltic states and other postcommunist members of the EU would have been possible. The realization of both of these "ifs" at present appears highly doubtful. The identity split between East and West and two different external orientations—Russia and the European Union—are tearing the country apart[131] and making its future uncertain.

Domestic Politics, External Contingencies, and Political Imagination

The foregoing overview of the larger picture of postcommunist development is at once encouraging and disheartening. On the one hand, the geopolitical context in Europe after the collapse of communism was defined by the presence of the European Union, which served as a strong democratic pull for neighboring countries undergoing transformation. To a large degree this geopolitical factor played a crucial role in determining the outcomes of political and economic reforms in the countries that eventually joined the EU. The domestic political-economic dynamics initially pushing toward crony capitalism were in effect overridden by the externally originating force. The postcommunist countries that joined the European Union are therefore well placed now to continue on the path of the evolution of the rule of law and secure property rights combined with other democratic institutions. While beneficial in the case of these ten new members of the EU, this external factor did not work in the case of many other states facing similar challenges. The unique geopolitical configuration favored some countries and disadvantaged others, such as Ukraine, for example, torn between Russia and the West. Even after its Orange Revolution, widely viewed as indicating Ukraine's pro-European and pro-Western choice, Ukraine has not been embraced by the European Union the way its more fortunate neighbors were in the second half of the 1990s. Russia faces even more challenges as it drifts away from the West, using its vast natural resources as the main leverage in international politics and the source of its new assertiveness.

The above observations are also disheartening because the transformation experience from the broader postcommunist region has not so far produced any credible domestic sources of hope. Of course, the amount of time that has passed since the beginning of transformation is too short and limited in the historical sense for making any far-reaching conclusions. A piece of wisdom offered by Isaiah Berlin can provide a source of hope in this story. Reacting to political theorists, who are driven by the aim of searching and understanding patterns in the realm of politics rather than comprehending the particular historical situation in its full uniqueness, Berlin noted, "In the realm of political action, laws are far and few indeed: skills are everything."[132] Indeed, skillful statesmen with sound political judgment and political imagination might provide some unexpected answers for overcoming the difficult predicament of democracy under crony capitalism. What will surely help is the right kind of international engagement that is based on the realization of dangers inherent in crony capitalist systems.

Biographical Information, Nemtsov and Shaimiev

Boris Yefimovich Nemtsov
Born October 9, 1959, in Sochi.

Education:

> 1976–81: physics department, Gorky State University.
>
> 1985: Ph.D. in physics and mathematics.

Employment:

> Until 1990, senior scientist at the Gorky Radio-Physics Research Institute.

Political Career (pre-1991):

> 1986: Organizes protest movement in Nizhnii against the construction of a new nuclear power plant in the region. Attempts to register in the election to the USSR Congress of People's Deputies as an independent candidate but is prevented from running.
>
> 1989: runs for the Soviet Congress of People's Deputies on a reform platform promoting multiparty democracy and private enterprise.
>
> 1990: runs for the Supreme Soviet of the RSFSR (Russian republic) representing Nizhnii Novgorod.

Mintimer Sharipovich Shaimiev*

Born January 1937 in Aktanysh region of the Tatar Autonomous Soviet Socialist Republic (TASSR).

1969–83: Minister of Irrigation and Water Resources of the TASSR.

1983: First Deputy Chairman of the Council of Ministers of the TASSR.

1983–85: Secretary of the Tatar Oblast Committee of the Communist Party of the Soviet Union.

1985–89: Chairman of the Council of Ministers of the Tatar Autonomous Soviet Socialist Republic.

1989–90: First Secretary of the Tatarstan Oblast Committee of the CPSU.

1990–91: Chairman of the Supreme Council of the TASSR.

June 12, 1991: Elected the first president of the Republic of Tatarstan (re-elected in 1996 and 2001; reappointed by Putin in 2005).

March 25, 2010: Resigns from his post and is succeeded by Rustam Minni-khanov.

*Information obtained from the official Web site of the president of Tatarstan: http://president.tatar.ru/eng/biography.

Questionnaire on Popular Level of Satisfaction,

Belarus and Ukraine

	Belarus (%)	Ukraine (%)

1. To what extent are you satisfied with the current state of affairs in this country?

	Belarus (%)	Ukraine (%)
not at all satisfied	23	61
not very satisfied	34	21
neither satisfied or unsatisfied	25	11
somewhat satisfied	15	5
very satisfied	3	2

2. To what extent are you satisfied with how your life is turning out?

not at all satisfied	19	53
not very satisfied	30	20
neither satisfied or unsatisfied	26	10
somewhat satisfied	20	10
very satisfied	5	3

3. Are you satisfied with the way democracy is working in this country?

very satisfied	2	1
fairly satisfied	20	11
not very satisfied	41	42
not at all satisfied	25	46
don't know	12	NA

4. Compared to the old regime before perestroika, would you say today:

People like me can have an influence on government

much better than before	5	6
better	16	10
much the same	48	39
a little worse	11	12
much worse	12	23
don't know	9	10

5. In your opinion, how widespread is bribery and corruption in the national government in Minsk/Kyiv?

hardly anyone is involved	2	1
not a lot	27	11
most officials are involved	37	34
almost every one is corrupt	20	45
don't know	13	10

6. By comparison with Soviet times has the level of bribery and corruption

increased a lot	37	63
increased a little	24	22
has remained much the same	19	13
decreased a little	7	1
decreased a lot	0	1
don't know	14	NA

Source: White and Rose 2001.

NOTES

Introduction

1. See, e.g., Carothers 2006, 2003.

2. One such debate occurred at the U.S. Senate Committee on Foreign Relations (questioning Condoleezza Rice), February 17, 2006 (C-Span channel).

3. For the most recent examples, see Collins 2006; Hale 2006; Smyth 2006; Radnitz 2007; McMann 2006; Way 2006.

4. See, e.g., Fish 2005; Way 2005a; McFaul 2002.

5. The tools of electoral manipulation in post-Soviet states have been described in detail in Wilson 2005.

6. The literature on negative campaigning in American politics scholarship is very extensive. See, e.g., Ansolabehere and Iyengar 1997. For a meta-review of findings from this literature, see Lau et al. 1999. In addition, on the role played by political consultants, see Thurber and Nelson 2000.

7. Ansolabehere and Iyengar 1997.

8. "Rossiiane ob otmene vyborov gubernatorov i deputatov."

9. Konitzer 2005.

10. Colton and McFaul 2001.

11. Schumpeter 1976, 269.

12. Hermet, Rose, and Rouquie, eds., 1978, 197.

13. Weber (1947, 325) advanced one of the most renowned statements about the centrality of legitimacy for understanding social institutions and political order.

14. For a critical discussion of the transition paradigm, see Carothers 2002. For a statement of a cyclical approach, see Hale 2005.

15. Michels 1968, 222, quoted in Cruz 2006, 2.

16. E.g., see Sil and Chen 2004; Reddaway and Glinski 2001; Shevtsova 1999; Van Zon 2000.

17. Lipset 1963, 64.

18. Beetham 1991, 11; cited in Ansell 2001.

19. The famous Orwellian institutions responsible for ensuring loyalty to Big Brother.

20. See, e.g., Reddaway and Glinski 2001.

21. See, e.g., Sil and Chen 2004, 358.

22. For a recent study about Russia that draws attention to the link between people's actual experiences of new political and economic systems and their attitudes toward democracy, see Carnaghan 2008.

23. For a recent example, see the analysis of factors affecting popularity of Russian presidents in Treisman 2007.

24. For an insightful discussion of objectivist vs. constructivist approaches in political economy, see Herrera 2005, 58–94. The overview of mechanisms affecting popular perceptions in this paragraph is based on her narrative. For other recent applications of a constructivist approach to the study of regionalism in Russia, see also Giuliano 2006, 2000.

25. This tactic was offered, e.g., by Snyder 2001, 104.

26. There were 89 regions according to the 1993 Constitution of the Russian Federation. The process of regional mergers initiated under Putin reduced the number of federal units to the current 83.

27. The literature on Russian federalism and regionalism in the 1990s is vast. For some examples, see Herrera 2005; Stoner-Weiss 2006; Lapidus 1999; Stavrakis, DeBardeleben, and Black 1997; Treisman 1997; Solnick 1996; Lapidus and Walker 1994.

28. Woodruff 1999.

29. Moses 1999, 7.

30. Moraski 2006; Gel'man et al. 2003, 2000; Gel'man 2000; Moses 2002, 1999; Matsuzato 2001a, 2000a, 2000b, 1999; Hanson and Bradshaw 2000; Magomedov 2001, 2000; Nechaev 2000; Hale 1999; Kirkow 1998; Khakimov 1998; McAuley 1997; Brie 1997; Farukshin 1994.

31. See, e.g., the discussion of "regionology" in Matsuzato 2000b.

32. For selected studies of Putin's federal reforms, see Reddaway and Orttung 2004, 2005; Slider 2008, 2007; Konitzer and Wegren 2006; Gelman 2006; Goode 2007; Chebankova 2006.

33. The term *network* is used here to indicate a group of individuals connected through various types of ties. It does not follow the quantitative social network analysis developed in sociology (see, e.g., Scott 2000). However, in a broader sense it refers to the same phenomena studied in the social network analyses, i.e., the informal relationships among the members of a group, although the focus here is on the elite groups only.

34. For a similar conceptualization of such a distinct economic-political order, see North, Weingast, and Wallis 2009.

35. *Institutionalization* is used here in the sociological sense, as elaborated in March and Olsen 1984.

36. Sharafutdinova 2006.

37. For an excellent and recent analysis of this role, see Graney 2009.

38. Przeworski and Teune 1970.

39. In the 1990s this was usually a group of twelve to fourteen regions. Nizhnii Novgorod dropped out of that group in 1997.

40. For the latest reassessment of modernization theory, see Przeworski 2000.

41. Kitschelt 1999.

42. For a recent study of distinct political-economic orders, see North, Weingast, and Wallis 2009.

Chapter 1. **Postcommunist Crony Capitalism**

1. Hoffman 2002, 358.

2. This is a play on the word *semiboyarschina,* referring to the rule by seven prominent boyars in the early seventeenth century. In addition to himself, Berezovsky mentioned Mikhail Fridman, Pyotr Aven, Mikhail Khodorkovsky, Alexander Smolenski, Vladimir Potanin, and Vladimir Gusinsky.

3. This story has been told by many analysts; see, e.g., Klebnikov 2000; Hoffman 2002; Shevtsova 2003.

4. Hellman, Jones, and Kaufmann 2000.

5. Stiglitz 2002.

6. Haber et al. 2002.

7. Kang 2003, 2002; Gomez 2002.

8. See, e.g., Hutchcroft 1998; Hellman 1998; Rose-Ackerman 1999.

9. Weber 1950, 277.

10. Ibid., 339.

11. Locke 1980, 51.

12. Weber 1950, 275.

13. See, e.g., the conceptualization of different social orders in North, Wallis, and Weingast 2009. Crony capitalism approximates their category "limited access order."

14. For an illuminating study of a powerful Chubais clan, see Wedel 1998.

15. Gubernatorial elections were held on a regular basis in Russia starting in 1996. Previously only selected regions and ethnic republics held elections for their top executive posts.

16. See, e.g., Zubarevich 2005; Turovskii 2002; Barsukova and Zviagintsev 2006.

17. Graham 1995.

18. Kryshtanovskaia 1996.

19. Camdessus 1998.

20. Hagopian 1996; Collins 2006.

21. Haber et al. 2002.

22. Ibid., xiii.

23. Grzymala-Busse 2006, 2003.

24. Grzymala-Busse 2006.

25. Chavez 2003.

26. Beer 2003.

27. Levitsky and Way 2002.

28. Ledeneva 2006, 91–114.

29. Such an argument has been advanced in regard to the pervasiveness of clientelism in Southeast Asia and Latin America; see, e.g., Scott 1972; Hagopian 1996.

30. Coulloudon 2002; Verdery 1999. For a slightly different exposition of the logic of the culturalist approach to informal institutions, see Gel'man 2003, 2004; Afanas'ev 1998.

31. Kliamkin and Timofeev 2000; Ledeneva 2006.

32. See studies of corruption by the INDEM foundation at www.indem.org.

33. Haber et al. 2002.

34. Weingast 1997, 262; Shepsle 1991, 254. See also Olson 2000; North, Summerhill, and Weingast 2000.

35. The relatively recent Enron scandal and the Jack Abramoff case have raised plenty of questions in regard to the presence of "cronyism" in the United States. See Heilbrunn 2003.

36. For the transaction-costs-based argument, see Kang 2003, 2002.

37. North, Wallis, and Weingast 2009.

38. Ibid.

39. Ibid.

40. Steinmo, Thelen, and Longstreth 2002.

41. For an excellent comprehensive analysis of privatization process in Russia, see Barnes 2006.

42. While Tilly (1985) examined the experience of state building in Western Europe as driven by the elite project of war making, Ganev (2005) used Tilly's concept of the "dominant elite project" to explore the weakening of postcommunist states. He posited that "extraction from the state" was a new predatory elite project that damaged the institutional capacity of the state after the collapse of communism.

43. Ganev 2006, 2005.

44. Feigenbaum, Henig, and Hamnett 1998. Their typology included the categories of tactical, pragmatic, and systemic privatization, differentiated according to the motivating forces behind privatization policies and, subsequently, its impact on society (42–43).

45. Feigenbaum, Henig, and Hamnett 1998, 52.

46. For adaptation of this Tillyan term to the postcommunist period, see Ganev 2005.

47. For the discussion of the ideological underpinnings of privatization process in Eastern Europe, see Appel 2004.

48. Woodruff 2004.

49. Goldman 2003.

50. Barnes 2006.

51. Among the best-known studies are Goldman 2003; Hoffman 2002; Freeland 2002; Blasi et al. 1997; Hellman, Jones and Kaufmann 2000; Klebnikov 2000.

52. For a discussion of state-business relationships under Putin, see Tompson 2005; OECD Economic Survey of the Russian Federation 2006; Peregudov 2001; Zudin 2001; Turovskii 2002.

53. For an analysis of the Third Wave, see Huntington 1991.

54. Smyth 2006, 1.

55. Ibid., 2.

56. Ibid.

57. Hale 2006.

58. Barnes 2006.

59. For rough estimates of campaign costs, see Barsukova 2006.

60. The term *network* is used here to indicate a group of individuals connected through various types of ties.

61. For some excellent examples of such research, see Hale 2006; Smyth 2006; Remington 2001; Breslauer 2002.

62. Hoffman 2002; Freeland 2002.

63. Collins 2006; Schatz 2004, 2005. For exceptions on Russia, see Goldman 2003; Wedel 1998; on Russian regions, see Moses 2002, 1999.

64. Moses (1999) adheres to a similar conception of political pluralism in Russia. Thomas Graham, who worked in Russia from 1994 to 1997, advanced a similar conceptualization of Russian national-level politics (see n. 73). Many Russian observers follow this view as well; see, e.g., Badovskii and Shutov 1997; Brovkin 1998.

65. Rigby 1981; Jowitt 1983.

66. Easter 2000; Willerton 1992.

67. Rigby 1981, 25.

68. Easter 2000, 11.

69. Willerton 1992, 77.

70. Shlapentokh 1996.

71. Haber et al. 2002.

72. Ledeneva 1998, 184.

73. Ibid., 186–87.

74. For more on clans, see Collins 2006, 2004; Schatz 2005a, 2005b. Although in Russia the term *clan* is commonly used to refer to such networks, this usage appears unwarranted as it implies the existence of very strong ties between group members.

75. Mann 1986.

76. Giddens 1981.

77. For more on protection rackets, see Volkov 2002, 1999. For the role of krysha, see also Shlapentokh 1996.

78. Breslauer 2001.

79. Hale 2006.

80. United Russia and Just Russia are the most significant Kremlin-sponsored party projects so far.

81. Smyth 2006.

Chapter 2. **Fragmented Cronyism**

1. For references, see introduction, notes 27 and 30.

2. For an especially clear exposition of this view, see Moses 2002, 1999.

3. Nizhnii Novgorod region is often referred to informally as Nizhnii. Hereafter I use Nizhnii Novgorod and Nizhnii interchangeably to refer mostly to the region rather than to the capital city.

4. Borisov 1999b, 19.

5. Ibid., 27.

6. Fomenko 1992.

7. Personal ties between Nemtsov and Yeltsin originated in 1990, when Nemtsov, elected people's deputy of the Russian Federation, backed Yeltsin's candidacy for the chairmanship of the Supreme Soviet of the Russian Federation. Nemtsov was also among the active supporters of Yeltsin's camp during the August 1991 putsch.

8. This bargaining resulted in bringing Ivan Skliarov, former first secretary of the Arzamas party committee, into his team.

9. I differ in this view from other political analysts, such as Gel'man (1999), who argued that the Nizhnii Novgorod region fits the model of a "pacted" transition and features the emergence of an elite settlement based on the exchange of resources and political support among the major political actors in the region. Nemtsov's personal ties with Yeltsin appear to be a more important factor underlying Nemtsov's authority in the region than the elite settlement. A view similar to that advocated here is also held by local observers (see, e.g., Borisov 1999a).

10. In fact, Nizhnii Novgorod was the only region in Russia that lacked a separate presidential representative in the early 1990s because Nemtsov combined both the positions of the governor and the presidential representative.

11. Orttung 2000, 368–69.

12. This fund was based partly on the tax money that enterprises paid to the federal budget.

13. Borisov 1999b, 15. Because of the large defense sector, until 1991 the city of Nizhnii Novgorod was closed to foreigners.

14. For a serious discussion of the role of Soviet state enterprises, see Brie 2000.

15. Borisov 1999a, 113.

16. In this view, Nikolai Pugin, who replaced Vidiaev as GAZ's president and became Nemtsov's ally, is an exception.

17. Fomenko 1992.

18. From an August 2000 interview with Vasilii Sarychev, who worked in the public relations office of the three consecutive governors in Nizhnii Novgorod.

19. *Birzha,* no. 7, February 21, 1994, 2.

20. *Birzha,* no. 4, January 31, 1994, 7.

21. In fact, the post of director general was replaced by the post of president.

22. Soon after that Vidiaev retired.

23. Boycko et al. 1995.

24. With the support of Russia's deputy prime minister at that time, Oleg Soskovets, who in 1995 became head of the association of financial-industrial groups.

25. Braun 1996.

26. Ibid.

27. The particular grudge of municipal authorities might have been related to the fact that they were distanced from the sales of the companies' products and thus from the profits.

28. Semeniuk and Shukov 1997.

29. In 1993 some regional experts wrote articles warning of the need to develop a protectionist strategy of privatization that would take into account the interests of the regional economy and allow for the regional authorities to maintain control over a large share of the regional enterprises. However, as later developments revealed, these ideas were not taken seriously into account (see Inkin 1993a, 1993b).

30. "Otchet po resul'tatam otsenki pravil'nosti otsenki velichiny ustavnogo kapitala pri privatizatsii tselliulozno-bumazhnogo kombinata v g. Balakhne Nizhegorodskoi oblasti (Aktsionernoe obshchestvo 'Volga')."

31. It has to be noted also that CS First Boston Bank was represented by Gretchen Wilson, who had good relations with Nemtsov. She later married Nemtsov's close associate, Boris Brevnov, chairman of NBD bank.

32. Lugovoi 1997.

33. Lysov 1997b.

34. Anisimov 2000.

35. *Politicheskoe razvitie Nizhegorodskoi oblasti v predstavleniakh regional'noi elity: nastoiashchee i budushchee,* 2001, 28.

36. This company was considered strategically important as one of the important suppliers to the automobile maker GAZ.

37. *Politicheskoe razvitie Nizhegorodskoi oblasti v predstavleniakh regional'noi elity: nastoiashchee I budushchee,* 2001, 28.

38. Ekonomicheskii kurs, September 12, 2003 (ezhenedel'nik). www.kurs-n.nnov.ru/12.09.2003/36-12-1.html.

39. Ibid.

40. Ibid.

41. Barnes 2006, 145.

42. Ibid.

43. For the most elaborate discussion of economic transformation in the agricultural sector in Russia, see Wegren 2000, 1998, 1997, 1994a, 1994b.

44. The region's external debt amounted to over 5 billion rubles in 2001 (Anisimov 2002), while in 2002 the reported debt of the regional budget amounted to 11 billion rubles (Noskov 2002).

45. Anisimov 2002.

46. Fomenko 1992.

47. Nemtsov managed to persuade the federal government to contribute half of the taxes paid by defense enterprises to this conversion fund (see Fomenko 1992).

48. Petelina 1997.

49. Lysov 1997a.

50. The major regional newspaper *Birzha* had published countless articles and interviews with Kliment'ev in 1994–96.

51. Lysov 1998.

52. *Birzha,* no. 4, January 30, 1993, 1.

53. Interview with Vasilii Sarychev (he recounted his personal experience), August 2002.

54. This was not the first criminal investigation against Kliment'ev. The businessman had already served time in jail in the 1980s for the distribution of video pornography (apparently he was later acquitted as the business for which he was sentenced became legalized).

55. He was paroled in 2000.

56. Matsuzato and Shatilov 1999, 99.

57. Nizhnii Novgorod's $100 million Eurobond was issued in 1997, under Nemtsov, and was considered a very successful deal for the region.

58. Makarychev 1999.

59. *Russian Federation Report,* vol. 1, no. 42, Radio Free Europe/Radio Liberty, December 15, 1999.

60. For more on the 1998 financial crisis in Russia, see Woodruff 2005; Aslund 1998.

61. I differ in this assessment from a local expert, Raspopov, who suggested that Skliarov in 1999 led a strong political-economic network (interview with Raspopov, September 1999).

62. Makarychev 2002, 128.

63. The saying "Letiashchii lom ne ostanovish'" (You cannot stop the flying crowbar) was applied to him.

64. *Russian Regional Report,* vol. 3, no. 41, October 15, 1998.

65. Makarychev 2001a.

66. Ultimately, because of problems with signatures, Lebedev was not registered as a candidate and instead supported Dmitrii Savel'ev.

67. See Reddaway and Orttung 2004, 2005 for an elaborate analysis of what the federal reforms were and what they have achieved.

68. For a thorough analysis of the impact of federal reforms on the regions, see Reddaway and Orttung 2004.

69. For example, in the 2001 gubernatorial elections Kirienko supported Skliarov's candidacy, while Nemtsov afterward expressed his support for Khodyrev.

70. In 1999 the main project advanced by Kirienko was to integrate all the Dzerzhinsk enterprises into a holding company, Volzhskaia Neftekhimicheskaia kompania (VNKhK) (see Raspopov 1999).

71. Reddaway and Orttung 2004, 158.

72. The institution of presidential envoy is an extension of the presidential administration.

73. Chief federal inspectors are part of the presidential envoy's staff.

74. Burg 2002; Galkin and Nagornykh 2001.

75. In June 1999, for example, Nizhnovenergo took one of the Dzerzhinsk plants, Orgsteklo, to court (Raspopov 1999).

76. For a case study of a hostile takeover using bankruptcy law, see Woodruff 2003.

77. Gubenko 2000; Trifonova 2001.

78. Reddaway and Orttung 2004, 158.

79. He used to work in the staff and later became a deputy director of Kirovenergo.

80. One of the most famous Russian oligarchs, who controlled, among other assets, numerous media sources.

81. Viktiukov 2000.

82. Glikin 2001.

83. Buzmakova 2003.

84. Ibid.

85. Another contender, the State Duma deputy Bulavinov, also had extensive influence over some media outlets, such as the television company Seti-NN; he lacked an independent economic base, however, so was not clearly associated with a particular EPN. His was more of a potential EPN.

86. Interview with Denis Akhmadullin, federal inspector in Tatarstan, July 2002.

87. For an excellent discussion of the role of force in Russian capitalism, see Volkov 2002; Varese 2001.

Chapter 3. **Centralized Cronyism**

1. Sharafutdinova 2006; Hale 2003.

2. See Gravingholt 2002; Alexander and Gravingholt 2002.

3. As a result of recent regional mergers under Putin, the number of units decreased to 83 by 2007.

4. This idea is recognized formally in the 1993 Constitution of the Russian Federation.

5. This structure came into being in 1991. Before 1991, the federation consisted of 49 oblasts, 6 krais, 16 autonomous republics, 5 autonomous oblasts, and 10 autonomous okrugs. In 1991 the 16 autonomous republics and 4 of the 5 autonomous oblasts were given the status of republics.

6. There has developed a new trend under Putin of merging the autonomous okrugs with the larger region in which they are situated. By 2007 five autonomous okrugs—Komi-Permyatskii, Taimyrskii, Evenkiiskii, Koryakskii, and Ust-Ordynskii (Buryatskii)—had been united with their "host" regions. For a general discussion of relations between the autonomous okrugs and the regions they were a part of under Yeltsin, see Dobrynin 1998, 46–50. For a case study of interregional relations involving autonomous okrugs with their host region, see Pryadilnikov 2001.

7. Lapidus and Walker 1994.

8. Mukhariamov 2000, 51.

9. The text of the treaty is available in Khakimov 1996.

10. These treaties were abrogated under Putin, with the exception of Tatarstan and Chechnya. Tatarstan has prepared a new (heavily watered down) version of the treaty and has been trying to get approval of the Russian parliament for the treaty. Chechnya, on the other hand, is expected to sign such a treaty in the near future.

11. If these local chief executives lose elections, they lose their executive positions as well.

12. Matsuzato 2001a, 54.

13. Evans and Gel'man 2004; Lankina 2002.

14. Moses 2002, 910.

15. Although most state officials deny the occurrence of such a revolt and consider the discussions surrounding that parliamentary session an exaggeration promoted by the press.

16. In the end, Altynbaev refused to officially join the presidential campaign of 2001, although he participated in its preliminary stages. His refusal to participate was a big blow to the elites who supported him in Tatarstan

(interview with former prime minister of Tatarstan, Mukhammat Sabirov, July 2002).

17. Ekzam Gubaidullin was invited from Elabuga to head the presidential apparatus.

18. For example, Ruslan Aushev's regime in Ingushetia that collapsed in 2002 after federal interference in the republican presidential elections.

19. Lapidus and Walker 1994; Treisman 1997; Solnick 1996.

20. Abdulatipov and Boltenkova 1992.

21. For example, in the Sakha republic; see Young 2000, 184.

22. Farukshin 1994.

23. Ibid.

24. Declaration of Sovereignty 1990: "Deklaratsiya o gosudarstvennom suverenitete Tatarskoi Sovetskoi Sotsialisticheskoi Respubliki," August 30, 1990, Special publication of Tatarstan-related documents (Kazan: Obrazovanie, 1998), 7–8.

25. Matsuzato 2000a, 33.

26. Not everybody complied; Nikolai Bekh, a well-connected director of KamAZ (the truck-making plant), refused to reregister and considered the company under Moscow's jurisdiction. The Tatarstani government was able to obtain control of KamAZ only in 1997, when the company faced bankruptcy.

27. Matsuzato 2000a, 33.

28. Farukshin 1994, 67–79.

29. Interview with Lilia Sagitova, June 2001.

30. For example, the enterprises of very successful brothers Khairullin (including the brewery "Krasnyi Vostok" which was sold in 2005 to an outsider) enjoyed the strong support of the mayor of Kazan.

31. Egor Gaidar was Yeltsin's first acting prime minister (1992) and is known as the architect of "shock therapy" reform in Russia.

32. Galeev 1993.

33. Kuznetsov 1997; Fatullaev 2001.

34. Khakimov 1997; Thornhill 1996.

35. Pechilina and Ptichii 1998; "Pravitel'stvo Tatarstana reshilo zagruzit' neftekhimicheskie predpriiatiia syr'em v dobrovol'no-prinuditel'nom poriadke" (http://elemte.bancorp.ru/koi/press/press00567).

36. Ivanov 1998.

37. Along with a few other regional utility companies, Tatenergo operated independently of Russia's United Energy Systems (UES).

38. "Dolgozhdannaia aktsiia"; "Electroenergetics."

39. Rost 1996.

40. Ibid.
41. Sapozhnikov and Khannanova 1998.
42. 2005 annual report, www.tatneft.ru.
43. www.tatneft.ru.
44. Idiatullin 2001, 55; Garifullina 2000.
45. Akopov 2001.
46. For the company's structure, see www.tatneft.ru.
47. Sharafutdinova 2001.
48. "Neft—vsemu golova," 2001.
49. Alaev 2002.
50. Chernobrovkina 1997a.
51. "Regional'nyi egoizm ekonomicheski tselesoobrazen. Eksperimenty Tatarstana v ozhidanii effektivnogo sobstvennika," 2000.
52. Andreeva 1997.
53. Chernobrovkina 1997b.
54. Farukshin 1999.
55. Grammatchikov 2007.
56. "Rostekhnologii ruliat," 2009.
57. Minnikhanov 2001, 14.
58. Indeed, in the 1990s the Russian Aeroflot was mostly buying Boeings and Airbuses.
59. "O polozhenii v respublike i osnovnykh napravleniiakh sotsial'no-ekonomicheskoi politiki v 2002 godu," 2002.
60. "OAK razvorachivaetsia," 2009; "'Rosoboronexport' garantiroval," 2007.
61. Faizullina 2000.
62. Only the Saratov region adopted a land code earlier, in 1997. In Russia the land code was adopted in October 2001.
63. The government has gradually accomplished its plan to supply gas to the population throughout the rural areas of the republic.
64. See, e.g., Shaimiev 2002, 11.
65. Fatullaev 2001.
66. Gogolev and Volynets 1997.
67. Lazarev 2001.
68. Malikov 2001.
69. "Pribavlenie v semeistve bankov," 2003.
70. It is considered *"upolnomochennyi,"* a government-delegated bank in the republic.
71. Radio Free Europe/Radio Liberty, January 16, 2004.

72. Minnikhanov 2002.

73. The bridge of almost fourteen kilometers in length has been opened to traffic in 2002. It creates a shorter way from Kazan to Samara and Orenburg.

74. Over 40,000 people moved to the new apartments (Fatullaev 2001).

75. A week before the court's decision the republican parliament created a special fund to maintain this project. From then on, the financial contributions from economic entities were considered voluntary, though an unspoken agreement between the authorities and the businesses made it fairly obligatory (Prokof'ev 2002).

76. This term has been abused somewhat. It was first used to indicate the peaceful process of power division between Tatarstan and Moscow (in contrast to the "Chechen model"); however, it is now being applied to other spheres of the republican development as well. See, e.g., Fatullaev 2001.

77. In Russia overall economic growth resumed only in 1997.

78. In 2000, for example, Tatarstan ranked fourth among Russia's regions in the volume of industrial production.

79. www.tatar.ru/index.php?DNSID=cbaf532b2fc8de1e89db9fa8825-fa0c9&node_id=1088.

80. See, e.g., McCann 2005; Farukshin 2005.

81. Farukshin 1994.

82. McCann 2005, 71.

83. Ibid., 63.

84. See, e.g., Ledeneva 2006.

85. McCann 2005, 51.

86. "Vnedrenie vysokikh tekhnologii—osnova dinamichnogo razvitiia ekonomiki Tatarstana," 2001.

87. Ibid.

88. "Tatneft' sdala neftepererabotku," 2005.

89. Gazizova 2006.

90. www.taif.ru.

91. "TAIF budet opredeliat' ekonomichskuiu strategiiu Nizhnekam-skneftekhima," 2005.

92. In 2003, though under increasing pressure from national mobile phone operators, TAIF sold Santel to Mobil'nye telefonnye sistemy (MTS).

93. Taran 1998.

94. Ibid.

95. "Goskomsviazi ulichen v narushenii zakona," 1998.

96. Filippova 2002.

97. Ibid.

98. Ibid.

99. Vnedrenie vysokikh tekhnologii—osnova dinamichnogo razvitiia ekonomiki Tatarstana," 2001.

100. Postnova 1999.

101. In 1998 Radik Shaimiev was also chair of the company's board of directors.

102. Mukhamadiev 2001, 2.

103. Postnova 1999.

104. Ibid., 2.

105. Author's interviews with Rashit Akhmetov and Damir Iskhakov, July 2001.

106. Makarkin 2001, 4.

107. Chernobrovkina 1997c. It should be noted that this is not a common hobby in Tatarstan.

108. "Potomki detei leitenanta Shmidta," 2001.

109. Khairullin 2002.

110. Krasnyi Vostok was sold to Turkish brewers in 2006.

111. Reddaway and Orttung 2005; Alexander 2003.

112. "Ob obshchikh printsipakh organizatsii mestnogo samoupravleniia v Rossiiskoi Federatsii," 2003.

113. "O polozhenii v respublike i osnovnykh napravleniiakh sotsialno-ekonomicheskoi politiki v 2004 godu," 2004.

114. Putin appointed Iskhakov a presidential envoy to the Far Eastern Federal District.

115. This issue was brought to court by Irek Murtazin as illegal.

116. Akopov 2001.

117. Gaddy and Ikes 1998.

118. It happened, for example, in the case of Ulyanovsk oblast, whose "red" governor, Yuri Goryachev, was replaced in 2000 with the Kremlin's interference.

119. From an interview with Rashit Akhmetov, editor of *Zvezda Povolzhia*, Kazan, July 2002.

120. Rafgat Altynbaev was the potential candidate, supported by the Kremlin. His campaign was suddenly stopped in its very initial stages (which resulted in the bitter disappointment of some of the forces in the republic that counted on Altynbaev). From an interview with Mukhammat Sabirov, Kazan, July 2002.

121. Hanson and Bradshaw 2000; Van Selm 1998.

122. Van Selm 1998.

123. For a detailed analysis of political regime evolution in Ulyanovsk, see Konitzer-Smirnov 2005.

124. These joint ventures involved some Western businessmen known for their fraudulent activities in other countries. Marc Rich was, for example, sought by the U.S. authorities for tax evasion; Johan Bonde-Nilsen was known for financial fraud in Europe. As a result, Komineft' experienced a drastic decline and eventually went bankrupt, while the joint ventures increased their production from 815,000 tons in 1992 to more than 4.5 million tons in 1997 (Krotov 2001).

125. Khodorkovsky's case in Russia is very revealing in this regard.

126. For more on ethnic mobilization in Russia's regions, see Gorenburg 2001, 2000, 1999; Giuliano 2006, 2000; Mandelstam-Balzer 1994. For projecting nationness and statehood in Tatarstan, see Graney 1999. For using economy and ethnicity in building regional political machines in Russia, see Hale 2003.

127. Sharafutdinova 2006.

128. Brie 1997.

129. "The Democratic Audit of Russia's Regions" accomplished by several reputable think tanks in Moscow, for example, listed these two regions in the group of the least democratic regions of Russia. www.freepress/ru/publish/publish043.shtml; last accessed September 10, 2007.

Chapter 4. **Regional Lessons of Electoral Competition**

1. Haber et al. 2002, 25–27.

2. Ibid., 26.

3. Kotkin and Sajo 2002, 1.

4. This term, widely used in Russia, refers to a variety of techniques designed by political consultants to achieve the desired election result.

5. Bikmetov 2002, 137.

6. Borisov 1999b, 44.

7. Moses 2002.

8. The decree did not elaborate on what that violation was (Presidential decree #598, March 29, 1994). Interestingly, the story did not end at that. In 1997 Nemtsov once again lobbied Yeltsin to issue another decree that would "rehabilitate" Bedniakov. Thus Bedniakov is the only person in Russia whose name became the focus of two personal presidential decrees.

9. See, e.g., an interpretation by a regional observer in one of the respected newspapers in Nizhnii Novgorod (Makarychev 1994, 2).

10. In October 1993 Yeltsin postponed the regional gubernatorial elections; therefore, in most oblasts and krais elections occurred only in 1996–97. Nizhnii Novgorod received special permission to hold gubernatorial elections in 1995.

11. The gubernatorial and mayoral elections were set for the same day.

12. Matsuzato and Shatilov 1999, 75.

13. Ibid.

14. Ibid., 76.

15. Ibid., 77.

16. Raspopov 1997 (February).

17. He was appointed first deputy prime minister of the Russian Federation.

18. In the first round, he received 40.9 percent of the votes, while his main opponent, Gennadii Khodyrev, won 37.8 percent. In the second round Skliarov received 52 percent of the votes, while Khodyrev received 42 percent. The overall turnout rate in the first round amounted to 40.1 percent. The second round attracted more attention: 48.9 percent came to the voting booths.

19. Raspopov 1998 (May).

20. Raspopov 1997 (June–July).

21. Kliment'ev received 34 percent of the vote; Gorin, 31 percent; and Bedniakov, 24 percent.

22. Raspopov 1998 (January).

23. Raspopov 1998 (March–April).

24. Radio Free Europe/Radio Liberty Russia Newsline, August 4, 1997.

25. Raspopov 1998 (March–April).

26. He was paroled in 2000.

27. Raspopov 1998 (June).

28. The main contenders were Lebedev, Bedniakov, and Semago. Lebedev received 33.8 percent of the vote in the first round, followed by Bedniakov with 25.1 percent. Lebedev won in the second round; however, this time the gap between him and Bedniakov was reduced to 3 percent. The turnout rate in the first round amounted to 37.2 percent (with 10.1 percent voting against all candidates) and in the run-off elections, 36.1 percent (with 12.8% voting against all candidates).

29. Semago was a State Duma deputy associated with Kliment'ev.

30. Bedniakov really was the only choice Skliarov had at that time. Lebedev always was his opponent, and Semago entered the race based on Kliment'ev's support and hoping to capture the protest electorate.

31. Matsuzato and Shatilov 1999, 125–26.

32. Raspopov 1998 (October).

33. Ibid.

34. Ibid.

35. Kliment'ev was released from prison in fall 2000.

36. Bikmetov 2002.

37. Ibid., 137.

38. Ibid., 138.

39. Some analysts have argued that it was an attempt to replay the famous incident with the Ukrainian journalist Gongadze, whose murder was allegedly authorized by the president of Ukraine.

40. Bikmetov 2002.

41. Most analytic forecasts focused on Skliarov and one of the candidates (except Khodyrev) as the challengers likely to meet in the second round.

42. Migacheva 2001.

43. Mikhail Dikin, a deputy of the regional legislative assembly. His candidacy was supported by the regional branch of the Union of Rightist Forces (SPS).

44. Yurii Sentiurin was invited to Nizhnii Novgorod from Moscow by the new governor, Khodyrev, to serve as deputy governor.

45. Bulavinov's and Dikin's names were associated with Kirienko, while Sentiurin was Khodyrev's protégé.

46. Candidate cloning has since become a widespread electoral trick in elections across Russia.

47. "Reiting," 2002.

48. Each of the companies owed Nizhnovenergo over 300 million rubles (Chesnokov 2002).

49. This is the way it was interpreted by many observers in and outside the region (Dolgodvorov 2002; Orlova 2002).

50. Chesnokov 2002.

51. Ionov 2002.

52. Migacheva 2002.

53. Ibid.

54. Actually, the ballots had the names of eighteen candidates. Six candidates' names were crossed out, thus leaving a choice among twelve candidates. Publishing of clean ballots, though requested by a number of political actors in the region, was considered too expensive by the *gorizbirkom* (electoral commission), especially given the possibility of more changes.

55. Bulavinov's 30.9 percent against Lebedev's 31.5 percent in the first round and Bulavinov's 35.1 percent against Lebedev's 34.5 percent in the second round.

56. In fact, some regional observers noted that the real winner might have actually been the option "against all" (Kliment'ev was also actively advancing this idea). And it might not be too far from the truth since the gap between the three front-runners is very narrow and even the official results show that, in some districts, a majority of people voted against all candidates. Ballot counting falsification is not new in Russian elections and has been occurring in regional elections as well.

57. It appears that the party of power was either concerned about Lebedev's influence on city election commissions and the possibility of fraud or wanted to make certain that Bulavinov would win in a situation of very close proximity of the three front-runners (Bulavinov, Lebedev, and "against all").

58. Okmianskii 2002.

59. Ibid.

60. Ionov 2001; Vitebskaia 2002.

61. Iudin et al. 2001, 201–8.

62. The full version of Putin's press conference held on June 24, 2002, can be found at www.strana.ru/stories/02/06/21/3083/150299.html.

63. This reform abolishing gubernatorial elections in Russia was announced after the Beslan tragedy in September 2004.

64. There are no mayoral elections in Tatarstan. Until 2006 the mayor of Kazan was appointed by the republican president; and after 2006, elected by the city council.

65. Mukhariamov 2000, 32.

66. From 213 deputies elected to the Supreme Soviet in March 1991, about 190 deputies were directly dependent and responsible to the republican leaders (including all the first party secretaries in the districts, directors of major enterprises, and other members of nomenklatura). From communication with Valentin Mikhailov, a member of the democratic opposition in Tatarstan, May 2003.

67. From communication with Valentin Mikhailov, May 2003.

68. Russia's ethnic republics are considered as states *(gosudarstvo)* by the Constitution.

69. Ramil' Gabdrakhmanov, the director of a vinegar plant.

70. Vasil'ev, vice president of the Foundation for the Defense of Motherhood and Childhood, and Minnekaev, director of the cultural center Vozrozhdenie planety (Planet's Revival).

71. As was the case with the later bilateral treaties signed by the center and the federal units, all the practical issues, such as tax sharing arrangements and control over economic assets in the regions, were left for elaboration in

the special attachment sections of the treaty, which were usually not made public.

72. Elections without alternative candidates are not legal according to the federal legislation.

73. The center for economic and sociological research in the republican government, for example, produced a document describing the major elements of economic and social transformation in Tatarstan (under the authorship of Artem Karapetian).

74. To ensure the necessary "alternativeness" of the election if all others would withdraw from the race to invalidate it.

75. Farukshin and Mikhailov 2002; Mikhailov, Bazhanov, and Farukshin 2000.

76. Based on face-to-face confidential interviews with anonymous interviewees holding managerial positions in the republic and involved in the electoral process.

77. The population of Kazan is about 1.16 million.

78. Bronshtein 2001.

79. Azfar and Murrell 2009.

80. This conclusion is corroborated by studies that show a positive link between political and economic stability and popular support for authoritarianism in other settings, such as Ukraine. See, e.g., Person 2009.

81. Mikhailov and Farukshin 2002.

82. Magomedov 2001, 2000; Makarychev 2001a, 2001b.

83. Przeworski 1991, 12.

84. Hale 2006.

85. Haber et al. 2002; Grzymala-Busse 2006.

86. "Administrative resources" refers here to the resources possessed by virtue of controlling some parts of the state apparatus, such as the police, courts, and tax authorities.

87. Moses 2002.

88. Konitzer-Smirnov 2005, 198.

89. For candidate and party cloning in Ukraine, see Wilson 2005, 162–64.

90. See, e.g., the discussion of various cases of the Kremlin's intervention in regional elections, channeled through presidential envoys, in Reddaway and Orttung 2004.

91. Especially in Mordovia in 1998 and the Rostov region in 2001.

92. Ledeneva 2006, 53.

93. For an excellent analysis of the use of kompromat in Russia, see Ledeneva 2006. Most of the discussion in this paragraph is based on Ledeneva's analysis.

94. Ledeneva 2006, 77.
95. Ibid., 73.
96. Colton 2000, 61.
97. www.levada.ru/press/2004092702.html; last accessed May 14, 2007.
98. Until 1988 a single candidate was nominated for single-member district elections.
99. For a discussion of the origins of this option, see Oversloot, van Holsteyn, and van der Berg 2002.
100. Hutcheson 2004, 106.
101. Such campaigning was only allowed for registered candidates.
102. Hutcheson 2004; Akhremenko 2004; Anokhina and Meleshkina 2004; Liubarev 2003; Oversloot, van Holsteyn, and van der Berg 2002.
103. Hutcheson 2004, 100.
104. Ibid., 117.
105. Sharafutdinova 2006.
106. Both Levada polls and the Public Opinion Foundation (FOM) produced similar results (Konitzer-Smirnov 2005, 7).
107. "Election Reform: What Will Russian Political Spin Doctors Do?" 2004.
108. For the best-argued study, see Konitzer-Smirnov 2005.
109. www.ftp.carnegie/seminars.
110. This section borrows heavily from my article "What Explains Corruption Perceptions? The Dark Side of Political Competition in Russia."
111. Dininio and Orttung 2005.
112. The INDEM data are representative of Russia's regions: it includes regions from each of the seven federal districts and accounts for differences in federal status and levels of economic development. The data set is based on a stratified random sample drawn from the regional population. The sample size is more than 7,500 households and business representatives. The conceptualization of corruption that the analysts relied on in this study included two aspects: *everyday corruption* (viewed mostly as bribes paid to officials) and *business corruption* (involving state capture, business capture, and administrative corruption). The description of the project's methodology is available at www.transparency.org.ru/proj_index.asp (last accessed March 12, 2007).
113. www.freepress.ru/publish/publish043.shtml (last accessed December 12, 2006).
114. For alternative indicators, see McMann and Petrov 2000; Marsh 2000; Moraski and Reisinger 2003.
115. Petrov 2003.

116. These indicators included the measures of political competition, length of incumbency, the degree to which the legislatures are monopolized by one party, the use of administrative resources, adherence to the principle "one person, one vote," and the proportion of people voting "against all" (www.freepress.ru/publish/publish043.shtml).

117. This project was a result of collaboration of three respected Russian think tanks (INDEM, Obshchestvennaia Expertiza [Public Expertise], and Merkator) and is, arguably, one of the most accurate systematic assessments of regional-level democracy in Russia under Putin.

118. For more elaborate discussion of these factors, see Sharafutdinova 2010.

119. The data on press freedom was produced by the nongovernmental think tank Obshchestvennaia Expertiza. There is also a regional press freedom rating produced by the Glasnost Defense Foundation (www.gdf.ru/content/2006/11/14112006.shtml). Its indicator is a categorical variable, taking values from 1 (least free) to 4 (most free). I tested the model also using this indicator, and the results were generally consistent with those presented below.

120. The economic development variable was constructed using the data on gross regional product per capita, also produced by Goskomstat (State Statistics Committee of the Russian Federation).

121. The data on age and the percentage of retired people as well as the unemployment data were taken from Goskomstat (www.gks.ru).

122. To even the measurement scales, I used the logarithms of gross regional product indicator.

123. Dininio and Orttung 2005.

124. For excellent studies of the press and media in Russia, see Mickiewicz 2008; Zassoursky 2004.

125. The democracy indicator is a categorical variable ranging from 1 to 5. Because the ranges between the categories are arbitrary, to avoid the bias in model specification I decomposed this variable into dummy variables and used them in the regression.

126. McFaul 2006.

127. Silitski 2006, 2005; Way 2005a.

128. Bikmetov 2002; Moses 2002.

129. Grzymala-Busse 2003, 2006; Chavez 2003; Geddes and Neto 1992; Beer 2003.

130. Belin 2001; Zassoursky 2004.

131. Roudakova 2007.

Chapter 5. **Corruption and Democracy under Yeltsin and Putin**

1. "Diagnostics of Corruption in Russia: 2001–2005."
2. For selected references, see chapter 1, notes 51–52.
3. Hellman et al. 2000.
4. Reddaway and Glinski 2001, 408.
5. For an excellent exposure of interpersonal relations between the oligarchs and Yeltsin's government, see Hoffman 2002.
6. Most of these cases occurred during Putin's presidency. The most famous campaigns during 2000–3 were waged by the state authorities against Berezovsky, Gusinsky, and Khodorkovsky.
7. Wallis 2006.
8. Ibid., 23.
9. Ibid.
10. Ibid.
11. Ibid.
12. For a detailed analysis of the Yukos case, see Sakwa 2009.
13. "'Sibneft' and Production Control," *Kommersant,* September 29, 2005.
14. "Gutseriev Says Goodbye to It All," *Kommersant,* July 31, 2007.
15. Orttung 2006.
16. Ibid.
17. As reported by the *Global Competitiveness Report 2006–2007,* prepared by the World Economic Forum (see Orttung 2006).
18. Markus 2007.
19. For a similar view, see Easter 2008, who uses the concept of concessions capitalism to characterize Russia's political economic system.
20. As, for example, the merger of two aluminum-producing giants, Rusal and Sual, that occurred in 2006.
21. Mechel is the Russian mining and steel firm that was accused by Putin in coarse language of holding artificially high prices. In response, Mechel's shares dropped by 20 percent.
22. For Putin's regional reforms, see Orttung and Reddaway 2004, 2005.
23. Ismailov poslushalsya "prem'era." http://gazeta.ru/business/2010/04/03/3346949.shtml. Last accessed April 26, 2010.
24. This view of the system created under Putin is supported by other political analysts. See, e.g., Shevtsova 2007a, 2007b.
25. Easter 2008, 213.
26. For the most scrupulous analysis of Russia's politics under Yeltsin, see Reddaway and Glinski 2001; see also Sakwa 2002; Shevtsova 1999.

27. For an excellent analysis of this episode, see Reddaway and Glinski 2001, 370–434.

28. This vote, held in June 1995, was precipitated by the hostage crisis in Budennovsk.

29. In 1998 Yeltsin had to withdraw Chernomyrdin's nomination, for example.

30. Reddaway and Glinski 2001, 512.

31. Although vote falsification was clear in some regions, Zyuganov did not challenge the election results, and most observers concluded that the vote was relatively free and fair (see McFaul 1997, x).

32. Most notoriously, over privatizing the giant telecommunication company Svyazinvest. See Hoffman 2002, esp. chap. 14 (pp. 365–96).

33. Rutland 2001, 4, quoting Pinsker 1997.

34. "Russian Elections," 1999.

35. For the origins of Unity, which later became United Russia, see Hale 2004.

36. Sigelman and Shiraev 1997.

37. For selected works on politics under Putin, see Herspring 2007; Sakwa 2004; Shevtsova 2005; Jack 2004; Ross 2004.

38. After a series of regional mergers, the number of federal units decreased to eighty-three.

39. Reddaway and Orttung 2004, 21–22.

40. For more detail, see Reddaway and Orttung 2004, 19–52.

41. For further analysis of curtailing regional sovereignty in Russia, see Sharafutdinova and Makarychev 2009; Gel'man 2006; Bahry 2005; Hahn 2003.

42. For further discussion of this reform, see Goode 2007; Chebankova 2006.

43. He is now a political refugee in the United Kingdom.

44. See, e.g., Sakwa 2009; Pazderka 2005.

45. Pazderka 2005.

46. Tompson 2005.

47. The text of Putin's 2007 address to the Federal Assembly can be found at http://kremlin.ru/mainpage.shtml; last accessed May 3, 2007.

48. Bremmer and Charap 2006–7; Kryshtanovskaya and White 2005, 2003; Baev 2004; Rivera and Rivera 2006.

49. See, e.g., Bremmer and Charap 2006–7; Salin 2007.

50. Treisman 2008.

51. For more on Putin's biography, see Jack 2004, 42–87.

52. For an explicit argument linking Putin's policies on the press to Soviet-style propaganda, see Panfilov 2005.

53. Belin 2004, 134.
54. Ibid., 136.
55. Ibid., 138–42.
56. Ibid., 140.
57. Ibid., 141.
58. Yasmann 2005.
59. Ibid.
60. Panfilov 2005, 7.
61. Ibid.; see also Politkovskaya's last piece, "What Did I Do That Was So Wrong?" published in the special issue of *Novaya Gazeta* dedicated to her death; it can be found at http://casnov1.cas.muohio.edu/havighurstcenter/Russian%20Journalism/Politkovskaya%20translation.pdf.
62. Belin 2001, 326.
63. Panfilov 2005, 13.
64. Smyth 2002.
65. See, e.g., Way and Levitsky 2006; Brownlee 2007, 2003; Geddes 1999; Smith 2005.
66. Way and Levitsky 2006, 15–17; see also Reuter and Remington 2009.
67. For this insightful observation, see Hale 2004.
68. For a detailed discussion of the 1999–2000 electoral campaign, see Colton and McFaul 2003.
69. Hale 2004, 181.
70. Smyth 2002.
71. Reuter and Remington 2009, 502.
72. Ibid., 508.
73. Ibid., 502.
74. Personal interviews in Tatarstan, July 2005, 2006.
75. Colton and McFaul 2003; the term *managed pluralism* is also used (Balzer 2003).
76. Shevtsova 2004.
77. Fak 2004.
78. An investment fund that has been working in Russia for over ten years.
79. www.gateway2russia.com/artr.php?artid=162259&srcid=1241,821&parent=FT.COM%20News.
80. Mishler and Willerton 2004, 10; see also Treisman 2008.
81. Mishler and Willerton 2004, 9–10.
82. "Dosrochnaia otstavka Borisa Yeltsina."
83. Sal'nikova 2004.
84. Treisman 2008.

85. Rose, Munro, and Mishler 2004, 12.

86. Ibid.

87. Rose and Munro 2002, 123.

88. Ibid., 226.

89. Reuter and Remington 2009; Konitzer and Wegren 2006.

90. Wilson 2005.

91. Fleron, Hahn, and Reisinger 1997.

92. Ibid., 3.

93. Polikanov 2005; see also Levada polls.

94. See, e.g., Kertman 2006.

95. Rose, Munro, and Mishler 2004, 16; Fleron, Hahn, and Reisinger 1997.

96. "Where would you personally like our country to be placed" (on a scale of 1 to 10, where 1 means complete dictatorship and 10 means complete democracy).

97. Rose and Munro 2002, 76 (1998 survey); only 15 percent preferred dictatorship.

98. "To li Lukashenko, to li Nazarbayev," 2005.

99. Ibid.

100. Rose 2004, 24–25; Rose, Munro, and Mishler 2004, 9.

101. Rose and Munro 2002, 75 (1998 survey).

102. Rose, Munro, and Mishler 2004, 9.

103. The range is from 10 (highly clean) to 0 (highly corrupt).

104. The Russian version of the report can be found at www.anti-corr .ru/indem/2005diagnost/2005diag_press.doc; last accessed May 4, 2007.

105. Bentley 2008; Myers 2005.

106. Stephen White and Ian McAllister, unpublished manuscript presented at BASEES annual conference, Cambridge, U. K., April 2009.

107. Rose and Munro 2002, 220.

108. See Treisman 2008; Mishler and Willerton 2004.

109. Rutland 2003; Beliaev 2004.

110. The most important incidents in the process of establishing state control of the mass media were concerned with getting rid of Berezovsky's influence on the ORT channel and forcefully transferring Gusinsky's NTV channel to the state-controlled Gazprom.

111. Panfilov 2005; see also O'Flynn 2005.

112. More skeptical analysts relate Russia's economic growth to these external factors with the ruble devaluation encouraging import-substitution and high oil prices replenishing the federal budget (Beliaev 2004).

113. Initiated by Putin in 2005, national priority projects involved additional allocations of state funds for reforms and increasing salaries in education, public health, housing, and agriculture.

114. Treisman 2008.

115. Ibid.

116. Kuchins 2009.

117. www.lenta.ru/story/monocities/; http://www.lenta.ru/news/2009/08/13/moscow/.

118. www.levada.ru/press/2009082001.html.

119. See chapter epigraph above from Surkov.

Chapter 6. **Postcommunist Cronyism and the Choice between Authoritarianism and Democracy**

1. Note, for example, how the Enron scandal in the United States resulted in sweeping anti-fraud legislation (Milhaupt and Pistor 2008; Iwata 2006).

2. Markovits and Silverstein 1988.

3. Tumber and Waisbord 2004, 1035.

4. Ibid.

5. Mainwairing et al. 2006, 312.

6. Personal interviews with Natalya Zubarevich, June 2009; and Vladimir Gel'man, March 2009.

7. On East Central Europe, see Borosz 2000; Stark and Bruszt 1998; Wedel 1998. On Bulgaria, see Ganev 2006; Peev 2002. On the Baltic states, see Allnutt et al. 2001. There are also numerous World Bank studies on state capture and corruption in transition economies (e.g., Gray, Hellman, and Ryterman 2004; Hellman, Jones, and Kaufmann 2000).

8. "The Big Chill."

9. Fish 2005; Hale 2006; Pipes 2005.

10. Pop-Eleches 2007; Howard 2002; Fish 2005.

11. Indeed, such policies of weakening the regional elites while strengthening the federal center have been undertaken under Putin. The tax code adopted in 2001 introduced a major change in the tax system that benefited the center at the expense of the regions. Furthermore, a recent case of the ruling elite in Bashkortostan losing its economic assets alerts us to such possibilities in the case of Tatarstan as well.

12. Shaimiev turned seventy years old in 2007 and has announced several times that this will be his last term in office.

13. Based on personal interviews with journalists and local political experts in Tatarstan, summer 2008 and summer 2009.

14. "Tatarstan's New President Sworn In," March 25, 2010; www.rferl.org/content/Tatarstans_New_President_Sworn_In/1993656.html.

15. In 2001–4, 40 to 50 percent of Russia's economic growth was due to oil production (OECD reports on the Russian economy).

16. Created in 2008 by splitting the Stabilization Fund into two funds.

17. The *Economist*, July 24, 2009, reported that Russia's Reserve Fund had fallen from a peak of US$137 billion in March to $54 billion in the third quarter of 2009.

18. *Economist*, July 24, 2009.

19. Amounting to 7.9 percent in 2009.

20. See, e.g., the World Bank's "Russian Economic Report 19: From Crisis to Recovery" (available at http://go.worldbank.org/Z61KG4EK20).

21. Indeed, trying to avoid such developments, Medvedev has warned the governors about their personal responsibility for preventing protests such as occurred in Pikalyovo.

22. See Vladimir Milov, "Phantomy Liberalizatsii," gazeta.ru/column/milov/2976296.shtml, April 20, 2009.

23. For a classical statement of the argument linking democracy to economic development and the emergence of the middle class, see Lipset 1959.

24. Acemoglu and Robinson 2006.

25. Moore 1966.

26. Belarus demonstrated great accomplishments in term of social and economic development during the Soviet era (Ioffe 2004).

27. Prices were liberalized in 1992, though some prices for essential products remained fixed. Privatization started according to the temporary rules adopted by the Council of Ministers because the conservative parliament did not pass the law on privatization.

28. Feduta 2005, 126.

29. Way and Levitsky 2006, 35–36.

30. Feduta 2005, 67.

31. Way and Levitsky 2006, 36.

32. Feduta 2005, 67.

33. Ibid., 105.

34. The following details come from Feduta 2005, 151–55.

35. There is some evidence that initially Lukashenka intended to continue economic reforms. These ideas, however, were quickly abandoned in favor of the restoration of the planned economy (Feduta 2005, 193–96).
36. Feduta 2005, 205.
37. Popov 2002, 25.
38. Marples 2004, 32–33; Feduta 2005.
39. Feduta 2005, 207.
40. Ibid., 207–9; Popov 2002, 25.
41. Matsuzato 2004, 250–51.
42. Zlotnikov 2002.
43. Silitski 2006.
44. "Belarus Inc.: Cooking the Books," 2007.
45. Matsuzato 2004, 244.
46. Ibid., 246.
47. Ibid., 255.
48. Silitski 2005, 85–86.
49. Ibid., 89–90, 94.
50. Feduta 2005, 422–23.
51. Ibid., 423.
52. Ibid., 422.
53. Silitski 2005, 15–16.
54. Ibid.; Feduta 2005, 578–82.
55. Feduta 2005, 402–14.
56. Ibid., 402; Silitski 2005, 16.
57. See also Shukan 2004.
58. Communication with Vitali Silitski, May 25, 2007.
59. For details on such campaigns, see Feduta 2005.
60. Vanags and Stripiss 1999, 12.
61. "Power and Money Rule Latvian Politics."
62. "General Elections in Latvia, 7th October 2006."
63. Ibid.
64. See, e.g., the discussion on corruption issues in Freedom House country report, "Latvia (2006)."
65. See, e.g., Linz and Stepan 1996; Ekiert and Hanson 2003; McFaul 2002; Ekiert, Kubik, and Vachudova 2007; Howard 2002.
66. Vachudova 2001, 4.
67. This can be found at http://europa.eu/pol/enlarg/index_en.htm.
68. Vachudova 2001, 10.
69. Ibid., 23–24.

70. Ekiert et al. 2007, 23.
71. Vachudova 2001, 5.
72. Ekiert et al. 2007, 23.
73. Vachudova 2001, 28.
74. McFaul 2006, 45.
75. For more on Russian national identity, see Tolz 2004, 2001.
76. Not to complicate the discussion, I omit here the very important and ever-growing influence of China, a country that represents an especially important factor for Central Asia.
77. Aslund and Menil 2000.
78. Puglisi 2003a, 2003b.
79. Van Zon 2000; Kubichek 2000; Oosterbaan 1997.
80. Van Zon 2000, 39.
81. Aslund and Menil 2000, 267.
82. Way 2005b, 196.
83. Oosterbaan 1997.
84. For the origins of the Donetsk clan, see Kovaleva 2001.
85. In May 2000 the Prosecutor General's Office launched criminal proceedings against former premier Pavlo Lazarenko, who was suspected of having a hand in this murder and arranging for others. Of course, these proceedings have to be analyzed in light of his rivalry with President Kuchma.
86. Lazarenko was appointed deputy prime minister by President Kuchma in 1995.
87. In addition to facing charges in Ukraine, Lazarenko was convicted of money laundering in Switzerland and in a San Francisco, California, court.
88. On the political economy of gas trading in Ukraine, see Shinkichi 2004.
89. Van Zon 2000, 45; Banaian 1999, 121–22.
90. Banaian 1999, 123–24.
91. "Constitutional Watch: A country-by-country update on constitutional politics in Eastern Europe and the ex-USSR," 1999; also see www.ukar .org/kuchma16.html for information gathered by the U.S. Department of State on contract killings (www.state.gov/www/global/human_rights/1997 _hrp_report/ukraine.html).
92. Way 2005b, 192.
93. Protsyk 2005.
94. Ibid., 25.
95. Ibid., 28–30.

96. Matsuzato 2005; Protsyk 2005, 24.

97. For more on semi-presidentialism in Central and Eastern Europe, see Elgie and Moestrup 2006.

98. Wilson 2005, 270.

99. Darden 2001, 2003.

100. Aslund 2005, 335.

101. Ibid., 336.

102. Way 2005b, 193.

103. Ibid., 196.

104. "Ukraine's Parliamentary Elections: March 29, 1998," 1998.

105. Wilson 2005, 87.

106. Ibid., 87–88.

107. Ibid., 95–96.

108. Ibid., 42; Van Zon 2000, 46.

109. The tapes were made by Mykola Melnichenko, a security officer and Kuchma's former bodyguard, who handed them in to Oleksandr Moroz, leader of the Socialist Party of Ukraine (see Kuzio 2003).

110. The U.S. Department of Justice has authenticated some sections of the tape; furthermore, most of the Ukrainian elites have accepted that the tapes were genuine.

111. Kuzio 2002.

112. Darden 2003, 2001.

113. Aslund 2005, 337.

114. Ibid., 341.

115. White and Rose 2001.

116. Ibid., 96.

117. Way 2005c.

118. Matsuzato 2001b.

119. Bunce and Wolchik 2006.

120. "One Year after the Orange Revolution: An Assessment" (Carnegie panel).

121. D'Anieri 2007.

122. Beichelt and Pavlenko 2005, 52.

123. This logic of democratic transition is central to the transition paradigm, which focuses on democratization as a result of strategic elite choice. It was most clearly depicted in Przeworski 1986.

124. For an excellent analysis of mass mobilization during the color revolutions that integrates the role of elites, masses, and structural preconditions, see Radnitz 2010.

125. North, Weingast, and Wallis 2009 also points to the stickiness of economic-political structures.

126. Aslund 2005, 328; Sushko and Lisnychuk 2005, 103.

127. Aslund 2005; Maksymiuk 2005.

128. By April 2005, GPD growth had fallen to 3.9 percent relative to 12 percent in 2004, while inflation had increased from 8 percent in 2003 to 15 percent by April 2005.

129. Aslund 2005, 339.

130. Petr Poroshenko, a former oligarch and one of the closest associates of Yushchenko, has been subjected to an especially dirty discrediting campaign.

131. A clear manifestation of such a split is the gap between popular support for NATO and EU membership in Ukraine. The support for NATO membership has hovered only around 20 percent in the past few years, while the degree of support for the EU membership is much higher (Mite 2005).

132. Berlin 1996, 45.

BIBLIOGRAPHY

Abdulatipov, Ramazan G., and Liubov F. Boltenkova, eds. 1992. *Federativnyi dogovor: Dokumenty. Kommentarii.* Moscow: Respublika.

Acemoglu, Daron, and James Robinson. 2006. *The Economic Origins of Democracy.* Cambridge: Cambridge University Press.

Afanas'ev, Mikhail. 2000. *Klientelizm i Rossiiskaia gosudarstvennost': issledovanie klientarnykh otnoshenii.* Moscow: MONF.

———. 1998. "Ot vol'nykh ord do khanskoi stavki." *Pro et Contra* 3 (3): 5–20.

Ahrend, Rudiger. 2002. "Press Freedom, Human Capital and Corruption." *DELTA Working Paper 2002–11.* http://ideas.repec.org/p/del/abcdef/2002-11.html.

Akhremenko, Andrei S. 2004. "Golosovanie 'protiv vsekh' v 1995–2003 gg.: rezul'taty empiricheskogo issledovaniia." *Vestnik moskovskogo universiteta,* series 12, *Political Science* (6): 60–75.

Akopov, Petr. 2001. "Nado delat stavku na interesy regionov. Respublika Tatarstan." *Izvestiia,* January 24, 8.

Alaev, Iurii. 2002. "Tatneft"—ekspansiia po vsem napravleniiam." January 4. www.tatnews.ru/articles/asrticle.php3?id=2043.

Alexander, James. 2003. "Federal Reforms in Russia: Putin's Challenge to the Republics." http://arapaho.nsuok.edu/~alexa001/Fedreforms03.pdf.

Alexander, James, and Joern Gravingholt. 2002. "Evaluating Democratic Progress inside Russia: The Komi Republic and the Republic of Bashkortostan." *Democratization* 9 (4): 77–105.

Allnutt, Luke, Jeremy Druker, and Jen Tracy. 2001. "Central Europe, Southeast Europe and Baltic States." *Transparency International Global Corruption Report 2001.* www.transparency.org/content/download/4291/26278/file/rr_ceseb.pdf.

Andreeva, Iuliia. 1997. "KamAZ doili kak mogli." *Vecherniaia Kazan,* November 1.

Anisimov, Sergei. 2002. "Khochesh zhit'—ne spor' s Minfinom." *Nezavisimaia gazeta,* April 9.

———. 2000. "Bumazhnaia pravda. Ubytochnyi kombinat vyshel na mirovoi rynok." *Nezavisimaia gazeta,* February 19.

Anokhin, N.V., and Elena Y. Meleshkina. 2004. "Golosovanie 'protiv vsekh' na regional'nykh vyborakh." *Rossiia i sovremenyi mir* (2).

Ansell, Christopher K. 2001. "Political Legitimacy." In *International Encyclopedia of the Social and Behavioral Sciences,* ed. N.J. Smelser and Paul Bates, 8704–6. Oxford: Pergamon Press.

Ansolabehere, Stephen, and Shanto Iyengar. 1997. *Going Negative: How Political Advertisements Shrink and Polarize the Electorate.* New York: Free Press.

Appel, Hilary. 2004. *A New Capitalist Order: Privatization and Ideology in Russia and Eastern Europe.* Pittsburgh: University of Pittsburgh Press.

Aslund, Anders. 2005. "The Economic Policy of Ukraine after the Orange Revolution." *Eurasian Geography and Economics* 46 (5): 327–53.

———. 1998. "Russia's Financial Crisis." Briefing on the Russian Economy, Carnegie Endowment for International Peace. www.carnegieendowment.org/programs/russia/index.cfm?fa=viewAuthor&pID=2.

Aslund, Anders, and Georges de Menil, eds. 2000. *Economic Reform in Ukraine: An Unfinished Agenda.* Armonk, NY: M.E. Sharpe.

Badovskii, Dmitry V., and J. Iu. Shutov. 1997. "Regional Elites in Post-Communist Russia." *Russian Social Science Review* 38 (May–June): 32–55.

Baev, Pavel K. 2004. "The Evolution of Putin's Regime: Inner Circles and Outer Walls." *Problems of Post-Communism* 51 (6): 3–13.

Bahry, Donna. 2005. "The New Federalism and the Paradoxes of Regional Sovereignty in Russia." *Comparative Politics* 37 (2): 127–46.

Balzer, Harley. 2003. "Managed Pluralism: Vladimir Putin's Emerging Regime." *Post-Soviet Affairs* 19 (3): 189–227.

Banaian, King. 1999. *The Ukrainian Economy since Independence.* Cheltenham, UK: Edward Elgar.

Barnes, Andrew. 2006. *Owning Russia: The Struggle over Factories, Farms, and Power.* Ithaca: Cornell University Press.

Barsukova, Svetlana. 2006. "Uchastie biznesa v politike: izmenenie pravil (na primere finansirovaniia izbiratel'nykh kampanii i deiatel'nosti politicheskikh partii)." www.ecsocman.edu.ru/db/msg/293974.html). Last accessed September 9, 2007.

Barsukova, Svetlana, and Vasilii Zviagintsev. 2006. "Mekhanizm 'politicheskogo investirovaniia,' ili Kak i zachem biznes uchastvuet v vyborakh i oplachivaet partiinuiu zhizn." *Ekonomicheskaia sotsiologia* 7 (2): 8–22.

Beer, Caroline C. 2003. *Political Competition and Institutional Change in Mexico.* Notre Dame, IN: University of Notre Dame Press.

Beetham, D. 1991. *The Legitimation of Power.* Atlantic Highlands, NJ: Humanities Press International.

Beichelt, Timm, and Rostyslav Pavlenko. 2005. "The Presidential Election and Constitutional Reform." In *Presidencial Elections and Orange Revolution Implications for Ukraine's Transition,* ed. Helmut Kurth and Iris Kemke. Munich: Center for Applied Policy Research, University of Munich. www .cap.lmu.de/download/2005/2005_ukraine.pdf.

"Belarus Inc.: Cooking the Books." 2007. *Belarusian Review* 19 (1). www.bel-review.cz/articles/3074.html.

Beliaev, Mikhail. 2004. "Putin's Russia: Is It a Doable Project?" *Demokratizatsiya* 12 (1): 13–40.

Belin, Laura. 2004. "Politics and the Mass Media under Putin." In *Russian Politics under Putin,* ed. Cameron Ross, 133–52. Manchester: Manchester University Press.

———. 2001. "Political Bias and Self-Censorship in the Russian Media." In *Contemporary Russian Politics: A Reader,* ed. Archie Brown, 323–42. New York: Oxford University Press.

Bellamy, Edward. 1982. *Looking Backward: 2000–1887.* New York: Penguin Books.

Berlin, Isaiah. 1996. *The Sense of Reality: Studies in Ideas and Their History.* New York: Farrar, Straus and Giroux.

"The Big Chill." 2007. *Economist,* May 19–25, 55–56.

Bigg, Clair. 2006. "Russia: Are Mayors Next 'Power Vertical' Victim?" Radio Free Europe/Radio Liberty, November 8. www.RFERL.org/content/article/1072597.html.

Bikmetov, Rustem. 2002. "Rol' sredstv massovoi informatsii v vyborakh gubernatora Nizhegorodskoi oblasti 2001." In *Regionalnye vybory i problemy grazhdanskogo obshchestva v Povolzhie.* Carnegie Moscow Center, Working Papers (3): 137.

Blasi, Joseph R., Maya Kroumova, and Douglas Kruse. 1997. *Kremlin Capitalism: The Privatization of the Russian Economy.* Ithaca: Cornell University Press.

Borisov, Sergei. 1999a. "Aktual'nyi politicheskii rezhim v Nizhegorodskoi oblasti: Stanovlenie v 1990-e gody," *Polis* (1): 98–115.

———. 1999b. "Politicheskaia istoriia Nizhegorodskoi oblasti (1989–1994)." In *Regiony Rossii: Khronika i rukovoditeli,* vol. 6, ed. Kimitako Matsuzato, 13–69.

Borosz, Jozsef. 2000. "Informality Rules." *East European Politics & Societies* 14 (2): 348–80.

Boycko, Maxim, Andrei Shleifer, and Robert Vishny. 1995. *Privatizing Russia.* Cambridge, MA: MIT Press.

Bradshaw, Michael, and Stephen Hanson, eds. 2000. *Regional Economic Change in Russia.* Cheltenham, UK: Edward Elgar.

Braun, Valerii. 1996. "Khimicheskii uzel pridetsia rubit." *Birzha,* no. 35.

Breiner, Peter. 1995. *Max Weber and Democratic Politics.* Ithaca: Cornell University Press.

Breslauer, George. 2001. "Personalism or Proceduralism." In *Russia in the New Century: Stability or Disorder?* ed. George Breslauer and Victoria E. Bonnell, 35–58. Boulder, CO: Westview Press.

Brie, Michael. 2000. "Regional'nye politicheskie rezhimy i sistemy upravleniia." In *Rossiia Regionov: Transformatsiia politcheskikh rezhimov,* ed. Vladimir Gel'man, Sergei Ryzhenkov, and Michael Brie, 61–108. Moscow: Ves' Mir.

———. 1997. "The Political Regime of Moscow—Creation of a New Urban Machine?" Discussion Paper P 97-002. Wissenschaftszentrum, Berlin.

Bronshtein, Boris. 2001. "Vybory pod flagami." *Vecherniaia Kazan* 42, March 21.

Brovkin, Vladimir. 1998. "Fragmentation of Authority and Privatization of the State: From Gorbachev to Yeltsin." *Demokratizatsiya* 6 (3): 504–17.

Brown, David J., John S. Earle, Vladimir Gimpelson et al. 2006. "Nonstandard Forms and Measures of Employment and Unemployment in Transition: A Comparative Study of Estonia, Romania, and Russia." W. E. Upjohn Institute for Employment Research, Staff Working Paper 06-127. http://ideas.repec.org/p/upj/weupjo/06-127.html.

Brownlee, Jason. 2007. *Authoritarianism in the Age of Democratization.* New York: Cambridge University Press.

———. 2003. "The Party Rules: Durable Authoritarianism in the Middle East and Southeast Asia." Ph.D. diss., Princeton University.

Brunetti, Aymo, and Beatrice Weder. 2003. "A Free Press Is Bad News for Corruption," *Journal of Public Economics* 87 (7–8): 1801–24.

Bryane, Michael. 2004. "The Rapid Rise of the Anticorruption Industry: Toward Second Generation Anticorruption Reforms in Central and Eastern Europe?" http://users.ox.ac.uk/~scat1663/Publications/Papers/Soros%20Article.pdf. Last accessed May 14, 2007.

Bunce, Valerie J., and Sharon L. Wolchik. 2006. "Favorable Conditions and Electoral Revolutions." *Journal of Democracy* 17 (October): 5–18.

Burg, Ekaterina. 2002. "PFO—zolotoi kadrovyi rezerv Sovfeda." *Monitor,* no. 2, January 21–27.

Buzmakova, Valentina. 2003. "Imperii Dmitriia Savel'eva nanesen ocherednoi udar." www.politkuhnya.ru/index.php?IDobj=309.

Čabelkova, Inna. "Perceptions of Corruption in Ukraine: Are They Correct?" www.cerge-ei.cz/pdf/wp/Wp176.pdf.

Camdessus, Michel. 1998. "Russia and the IMF: Meeting the Challenges of an Emerging Market and Transition Economy." Address to the U.S.-Russia Business Council,Washington, DC, April. www.imf.org/external/np/speeches/1998/040198.htm.

Carothers, Thomas. 2006. "The Backlash against Democracy Promotion." *Foreign Affairs* 85, no. 2 (March–April): 55–68.

———. 2003. "Promoting Democracy and Fighting Terror." *Foreign Affairs* 82, no. 1 (January–February): 84–97.

———. 2002. "The End of the Transition Paradigm." *Journal of Democracy* 13 (1): 5–21.

Chavez, Rebecca Bill. 2003. "The Construction of the Rule of Law in Argentina: A Tale of Two Provinces." *Comparative Politics* 35 (4): 417–37.

Chebankova, Elena. 2006. "The Unintended Consequences of Gubernatorial Appointments in Russia." *Journal of Communist Studies and Transition Politics* 22 (4): 457–84.

Chernobrovkina, Elena. 1997a. "Gde potainye scheta s valiutoi." *Vecherniaia Kazan,* March 19.

———. 1997b. "Vid na KamAZ s 42-go etazha: vyrulit?" *Vecherniaia Kazan,* November 4.

———. 1997c. "Syn prezidenta vrezalsia, a telokhranitel perevernulsia . . ." *Vecherniaia Kazan,* October 14.

Chesnokov, Oleg. 2002. "Tsirk na vode: Zakrytie sezona?" *Birzha,* July 15.

Chowdhury, K. Shyamal. 2004. "The Effect of Democracy and Press Freedom on Corruption: An Empirical Test." *Economic Letters* 85 (1): 93–101.

Collier, David, and Steven Levitsky. 1997. "Democracy with Adjectives: Conceptual Innovation in Comparative Research." *World Politics* 49 (3): 430–51.

Collins, Kathleen. 2006. *Clan Politics and Regime Transition in Central Asia.* Cambridge: Cambridge University Press.

———. 2004. "The Logic of Clan Politics: Evidence from the Central Asian Trajectories." *World Politics* 56 (2): 224–61.

Colton, Timothy. 2000. *Transitional Citizens: Voters and What Influences Them in the New Russia.* Cambridge, MA: Harvard University Press.

Colton, Timothy, and Michael McFaul. 2003. *Popular Choice and Managed Democracy: The Russian Elections of 1999–2000.* Washington, DC: Brookings Institution Press.

———. 2001. "Are Russians Undemocratic?" *Carnegie Endowment for International Peace Working Papers* 20. June.

"Constitutional Watch: A Country-by-Country Update on Constitutional Politics in Eastern Europe and the Ex-USSR." 1999. *East European Constitutional Review* 8, no. 3 (Summer).

Coulloudon, Virginie. 2002. "Russia's Distorted Anticorruption Campaigns." In *Political Corruption in Transition,* ed. Stephen Kotkin and Andras Sajo. Budapest: Central European University Press.

Curran, James, and Michael Gurevitch, eds. 1991. *Mass Media and Society.* New York: Oxford University Press.

Dahl, Robert A. 1971. *Polyarchy: Participation and Opposition.* New Haven: Yale University Press.

D'Anieri, Paul. 2006. *Understanding Ukrainian Politics: Power, Politics, and Institutional Design.* Armonk, NY: M. E. Sharpe.

————. 2001. "Democracy Unfulfilled: The Establishment of Electoral Authoritarianism in Ukraine." *Journal of Ukrainian Studies* 26 (1–2): 13–36.

Darden, Keith. 2003. "Graft and Governance: Corruption as an Informal Mechanism of State Control." Paper presented at the Center for Democracy and the Third Sector, Georgetown University, October 16.

————. 2001. "Blackmail as a Tool of State Domination: Ukraine under Kuchma." *East European Constitutional Review* 10 (2–3).

"Deiatel'nost' prezidenta RT, pravitel'stva i parlamenta v otsenkakh izbiratelei." 1997. Paper prepared by the Informational-Analytical Department of the Cabinet of Ministers, RT. Vypusk II, April, Kazan.

"Diagnostics of Corruption in Russia: 2001–2005." 2005. INDEM Foundation. http://indem.ru/en/publicat/2005diag_engV.htm. Last accessed May 23, 2007. [Preliminary report, "Corruption Process in Russia: Level, Structure, Trends."]

Dobrynin, N. M. 1998. "Problemy regulirovaniia otnoshenii kraia (oblasti) s vkhodiashchimi v ikh sostav avtonomnymi okrugami." *Gosudarstvo i Pravo* (7).

Dolgodvorov, Vladimir. 2002. "Delovaia informatsiia: Nizhnii v otkliuchke." *Trud,* June 19.

"Dolgozhdannaia aktsiia." 2002. *Tatarstan* (4).

Easter, Gerald. 2008. "The Russian State in the Time of Putin." *Post-Soviet Affairs* 24 (3): 199–230.

————. 2000. *Reconstructing the State: Personal Networks and Elite Identity in Soviet Russia.* New York: Cambridge University Press.

Eggers, Andrew, Clifford Gaddy, and Carol Graham. 2004. "Well-Being and Unemployment in Russia in the 1990s: Can Society's Suffering Be Individuals' Solace?" CSED Working Paper 35. www.brookings.edu/es/dynamics/papers/russiaunemp.htm.

Ekiert, Grzegorz, Jan Kubik, and Milada A. Vachudova. 2007. "Democracy in the Post-Communist World: An Unending Quest?" *East European Politics and Societies* 21 (1): 7–30.

"Election Reform: What Will Russian Political Spin Doctors Do?" 2004. #10, Johnson's Russia List 8375. (RIA Novosti, September 20, 2004.) www.cdi.org/russia/johnson/8375-10.cfm. Last accessed May 15, 2007.

"Electroenergetics." www.ifs.ru/body/memo/2002/Apr/e150402.htm.

Elgie, Robert, and Sophia Moestrup, eds. 2006. *Semi-Presidentialism in Central and Eastern Europe.* Manchester: Manchester University Press.

Evans, Alfred B., Jr., and Vladimir Gel'man. 2004. *The Politics of Local Government in Russia.* Lanham, MD: Rowman and Littlefield.

Faizullina, Guzel. 2000. "Regionalnyi egoizm ekonomicheski tselesoobrazen." *Expert,* February 10.

Fak, Alex. 2004. "S&P Issues Authoritarian Warning." *Moscow Times,* March 10.

Farukshin, Midkhat Kh. 2004. "Regionalnye politicheskie elity: smeny rolei." In *Vlastnye elity sovremennoi Rossii v protsesse politicheskoi transformatsii.* Rostov-na-Donu: n.p.

———. 1999. "New leaders for Tatarstan's Main Enterprises." *Russian Regional Report* 4 (25).

———. 1994. "Politicheskaia elita v Tatarstane: vyzovy vremeni i trudnosti adaptatsii." *Polis* (6): 67–79.

Farukshin, Midkhat Kh., and Valentin V. Mikhailov. 2002. *Chto khotel by znat' izbiratel' Tatarstana o vyborakh (no ne znaet gde eto sprosit').* Kazan: GranDan.

Fatullaev, Milrad. 2001. "Mintimerizm kak forma razvitiia. Tatariia predlagaet Tsentru svoiu ispytannuiu na praktike model ekonomicheskogo razvitiia." *Nezavisimaia gazeta,* March 30.

Feduta, Aleksandr. 2005. *Lukashenka: Politicheskaia Biographiia.* Moscow: Referendum.

Feigenbaum, Harvey, Jeffrey Henig, and Chris Hamnett. 1998. *Shrinking the State: The Political Underpinnings of Privatization.* Cambridge: Cambridge University Press.

Filippova, Iana. 2002. "Stroit' gorod—delo azartnoe." *Vostochnyi Express,* July 5–11.

Fish, Steven. 2005. *Democracy Derailed in Russia: The Failure of Open Politics.* Cambridge: Cambridge University Press.

Fleron, F., Jeffrey Hahn, and William Reisinger. 1997. "Public Opinion Surveys and Political Culture in Post-Soviet Russia." *Kennan Institute for Advanced Russian Studies Occasional Paper* 266.

Fomenko, Olga. 1992. "Nizhegorodskaia oblast: Obshchaia situatsiia." Politicheskii Monitoring (April), Institut gumanitarno-politicheskikh issledovanii (Moskva). www.igpi.ru/monitoring/1047645476/1992/0492/52 .html.

Freeland, Chrystia. 2000. *Sale of the Century: Russia's Wild Ride from Communism to Capitalism.* New York: Crown Publishers.

Gaddy, Clifford G., and Barry W. Ikes. 1998. "Russia's Virtual Economy." *Foreign Affairs* 77 (5): 53–67.

Galeev, Marat. 1993. "Tatarstan i problemy reform." *Nezavisimaia gazeta*, December 28.

Galkin, German, and Irina Nagornykh. 2001. "Vybory po-kremlevski." *Kommersant-Daily*, March 30.

Ganev, Venelin. 2006. *Preying on the State: The Transformation of Bulgaria after 1989.* Ithaca: Cornell University Press.

———. 2005. "Post-Communism as an Episode of State-Building: A Reversed Tillyan Perspective." *Communist and Post-Communist Studies* 38: 425–45.

Garifullina, Sof'a. 2000. "Tatneft' vozrozhdaet rodinu predkov." *Rossiiskaia gazeta*, April 28.

Gazizova, Evegeniia. 2006. "Strakhovka ot 'banka kachestva.'" *Expert-Volga* 23 (September 25). www.expert.ru/printissues/volga/2006/23/tatarstanskaya _neft/.

Geddes, Barbara. "Sources of Popular Support for Authoritarian Regimes." *American Journal of Political Science* 33 (2): 319–47.

Geddes, Barbara, and Artur R. Neto. 1992. "Institutional Sources of Corruption in Brazil." *Third World Quarterly* 13 (4): 641–61.

Gel'man, Vladimir. 2006. "Vozvraschenie Leviathana? Politika retsentralizatsii v sovremennoi Rossii." *Polis* 2: 90–109.

———. 2004. "The Unrule of Law in the Making: The Politics of Informal Institution Building in Russia." *Europe-Asia Studies* 56 (7): 1021–40.

———. 2003. "Institutsional'noe stroitel'stvo i neformal'nye instituty v sovremennoi rossiiskoi politike." *Polis* 4: 6–25.

———. 2000. "Subnational Institutions in Contemporary Russia." In *Institutions and Political Change in Russia*, ed. Neil Robinson, 85–105. New York: St. Martin's.

———. 1999. "Soobshchestvo elites i predely demokratizatsii: Nizhegorodskaia oblast." *Polis* 1: 79–97.

Gel'man, Vladimir, Grigorii Golosov, and Elena Meleshkina. 2002. *Vtoroi elektoral'nyi tsikl v Rossii: 1999–2000.* Moscow: Ves' mir.

Gel'man, Vladimir, et al. 2003. *Making and Breaking Democratic Transitions: Comparative Politics of Russia's Regions.* Lanham, MD: Rowman and Littlefield.

Gel'man, Vladimir, et al. 2000. *Rossiia Regionov: transformatsiia politicheskikh rezhimov.* Moscow: Ves' mir.

"General Elections in Latvia, 7 October 2006." 2006. European Elections Monitor, Robert Shuman Foundation. www.robert-schuman.org/anglais/oee/lettonie/legislatives/default2.htm.

Giddens, Anthony A. 1981. *A Contemporary Critique of Historical Materialism.* London: Macmillan.

Giuliano, Elise. 2006. "Secessionism from the Bottom Up: Democratization, Nationalism, and Local Accountability in the Russian Transition." *World Politics* 58, no. 2 (January): 276–310.

———. 2000. "Who Determines the Self in the Politics of Self-Determination?" *Comparative Politics* 32 (3): 295–316.

Glaeser, Edward L., Rafael La Porta, Florencio Lopez-de-Silanes, and Andrei Shleifer. 2004. "Do Institutions Cause Growth?" *Journal of Economic Growth* 9 (3): 271–303.

Glikin, Maxim. 2001. "Kak ukroshchali Volkova." *Obshchaia gazeta,* October 18.

Gogolev, Andrei, and Aleksandr Volynets. 1997. "Vsia rossiiskaia vodka stanet tatarskoi." *Vecherniaia Kazan,* February 14.

Goldman, Marshall. 2003. *The Piratization of Russia: Russian Reform Goes Awry.* New York: Routledge.

Gomez, Edmund, ed. 2002. *Political Business in East Asia.* New York: Routledge.

Goode, Paul. 2007. "The Puzzle of Putin's Gubernatorial Appointments." *Europe-Asia Studies* 59 (3): 365–99.

Gorenburg, Dmitry. 2001. "Nationalism for the Masses: Popular Support for Nationalism in Russia's Ethnic Republics." *Europe-Asia Studies* 53 (1): 73–104.

———. 2000. "Not with One Voice." *World Politics* 53 (1): 115–42.

———. 1999. "Regional Separatism in Russia: Ethnic Mobilization or Power Grab?" *Europe-Asia Studies* 51 (2): 245–74.

"Goskomsviazi ulichen v narushenii zakona." 1988. *Vecherniaia Kazan,* May 6.

Graham, Thomas. 1995. "The New Russian Regime." *Nezavisimaia gazeta,* November 23.

Grammatchikov, Aleksei. 2007. "U nego poluchilos'." *Expert* 36 (October 1).

Graney, Katherine. 1999. "Projecting Sovereignty: Statehood and Nationness in Post-Soviet Russia." Ph.D. diss., University of Wisconsin.

Gravingholt, Joern. 2002. "Bashkortostan: A Case of Regional Authoritarianism." In *Regional Politics in Russia*, ed. Cameron Ross, 177–92. Manchester: Manchester University Press.

Gray, Cheryl, Joel Hellman, and Randi Ryterman. 2004. "Anticorruption in Transition 2: Corruption in Enterprise-State Interactions in Europe and Central Asia, 1999–2002." *World Bank Report*. www.publications.worldbank.org/ecommerce/catalog/product?item_id=3788605.

Groner, Chris. 2006. "The Post-Communist Media: Comparative 'Oligarchisation' and After." *Slovo* 18 (1): 5–41.

Grzymala-Busse, Anna. 2006. "The Discreet Charm of Formal Institutions: Post-communist Party Competition and State Corruption." *Comparative Political Studies* 39 (3): 271–300.

———. 2003. "Political Competition and the Politicization of the State in East Central Europe." *Comparative Political Studies* 36 (10): 1123–47.

Gubenko, Olga. 2000. "Srednevolzhskie stradaniya. Reforma energetiki nachnetsia na Volge." *Izvestiia*, November 17.

"Gutseriev Says Goodbye to It All." 2007. *Kommersant*, July 31. www.kommersant.com/p791333/r_500/tax_enforcement/. Accessed September 10, 2007.

Haber, Stephen, et al. 2002. *Crony Capitalism and Economic Growth in Latin America: Theory and Experience*. Stanford, CA: Hoover Institution Press.

Hagopian, Frances. 1996. *Traditional Politics and Regime Change in Brazil.* New York: Cambridge University Press.

Hahn, Gordon. 2003. "The Impact of Putin's Federative Reforms on Democratization in Russia." *Post-Soviet Affairs* 19 (2): 114–53.

Hale, E. Henry. 2006. *Why Not Parties in Russia? Democracy, Federalism, and the State*. Cambridge: Cambridge University Press.

———. 2005. "Regime Cycles: Democracy, Autocracy and Revolution in Post-Soviet Eurasia." *World Politics* 58 (1): 133–65.

———. 2004. "The Origins of United Russia and Putin's Presidency: The Role of Contingency in Party-System Development." *Demokratizatsiya: Journal of Post-Soviet Democratization* 12 (2): 169–94.

———. 2003. "Explaining Machine Politics in Russian Regions: Economy, Ethnicity and Legacy." *Post-Soviet Affairs* 19 (3): 28–63.

———. 2000. "Will Elections Erode Russia's Democracy?" *Fletcher Forum* 24 (January): 123–36.

———. 1999. "The Regionalization of Autocracy in Russia." *Program on New Approaches to Russian Security Policy Memo Series (PONARS)* 42. www.fas.harvard.ed/~ponars/.

Hanson, Philip, and Michael Bradshaw, eds. 2000. *Regional Economic Change in Russia.* Cheltenham, UK: Edward Elgar.

Heidenheimer, Arnold J., Michael Johnston, and Victor T. LeVine, eds. 1989. *Political Corruption: A Handbook.* New Brunswick, NJ: Transaction Press.

Heilbrunn, John. 2003. "Oil and Water? Elite Politicians and Corruption in France." Unpublished manuscript.

Hellman, Joel. 1998. "Winners Take All: The Politics of Partial Reforms in Post-Communist Transitions." *World Politics* 50 (2): 203–34.

Hellman, Joel, Geraint Jones, and Daniel Kaufmann. 2000. "Seize the State, Seize the Day: State Capture, Corruption and Influence in Transition." *World Bank Policy Research Paper 2444.*

Hermet, Guy, Richard Rose, and Alain Rouquie, eds. 1978. *Elections without Choice.* London: Macmillan.

Herrera, Yoshiko. 2005. *Imagined Economies: The Sources of Russian Regionalism.* New York: Cambridge University Press.

Hoffman, David. 2002. *The Oligarchs: Wealth, Power, and the New Russia.* New York: Public Affairs.

Holmes, Leslie. 1997. "Corruption and the Crisis of the Postcommunist State." *Crime, Law and Social Change* 27 (3–4): 275–97.

Huntington, Samuel P. 1991. *The Third Wave: Democratization in the Late Twentieth Century.* Norman: University of Oklahoma Press.

Hutchcroft, Paul D. 1998. *Booty Capitalism: The Politics of Banking in the Philippines.* Ithaca: Cornell University Press.

Hutcheson, Derek. 2004. "Disenchanted or Disengaged? The Vote 'Against All' in Post-Communist Russia." *Journal of Communist Studies and Transition Politics* 20 (1): 98–121.

Idiatullin, Shamil. 2001. "Tatarstan. Sam sebe kreditor." *Kommersant-Vlast,* February 20.

Inkin, Aleksandr. 1993a. "Privatizatsiia v svobodnom polete ili smozhem li my vkusit' ot plodov reformy." *Nizhegorodskie novosti,* January 16.

———. 1993b. "Territoriia bez sobstvennosti." *Nizhegorodskie novosti,* February 6.

Ioffe, Grigory. 2004. "Understanding Belarus: Economy and Political Landscape." *Europe-Asia Studies* 56 (1): 85–118.

Ionov, Vladimir. 2002. "Vymyt' ruki nechem." *Birzha,* July 1.

———. 2001. "Primor'em pakhnet." *Birzha,* May 7.

Isaev, Georgii A. 2005. "Politicheskie otsenki i orientatsii izbiratelei respubliki v preddverii vyborov v munitsipalnye organy vlasti v Tatarstane." Kazan.

"Islamilov poslushalsya prem'era." 2010. www.gazeta.ru/business/2010/04/03/3346949.shtml. Accessed May 7, 2010.

Iudin A. A., N. N. Ivashinenko, and D. G. Strelkov. 1998. *Nizhnii Novgorod: vybory mera' 98. Sotsiologicheskii analiz.* Nizhnii Novgorod: NISOTs.

Iudin A. A., N. N. Ivashinenko, D. G. Strelkov, et al. 2001. *Politicheskaia kul'-tura i politicheskoe povedenie nizhegorodskikh izbiratelei.* Nizhnii Novgorod: NISOTs.

Ivanov, A. 1998. "Respublika Tatarstan v noiabre-dekabre 1998 goda." *Politicheskii monitoring,* no. 12.

Iwata, Edward. 2006. "Enron's Legacy: Scandal Marked Turning Point." *USA Today,* January 29.

Jack, Andrew. 2004. *Inside Putin's Russia: Can There Be Reform without Democracy?* New York: Oxford University Press.

Johnston, Michael. 2006. *Syndroms of Corruption: Power, Wealth and Democracy.* New York: Cambridge University Press.

———. 2000. "The New Corruption Rankings: Implications for Analysis and Reform." Paper presented at the World Congress of the International Political Science Association, Quebec, Canada. http://departments.colgate.edu/polisci/papers.

———. 1986. "The Political Consequences of Corruption: A Reassessment." *Comparative Politics* 18 (4): 459–77.

Jowitt, Ken. 1983. "Soviet Neo-Traditionalism: The Political Corruption of a Leninist Regime." *Soviet Studies* 35 (3): 275–97.

Kang, David. 2003. "Transaction Costs and Crony Capitalism in East Asia." *Comparative Politics* 35 (4): 439–59.

———. 2002. *Crony Capitalism: Corruption and Development in South Korea and the Philippines.* New York: Cambridge University Press.

Karklins, Rasma. 2005. *The System Made Me Do It: Corruption in Post-Communist Societies.* Armonk, NY: M. E. Sharpe.

Kaufmann, Daniel, Aart Kraay, and Pablo Zoido-Lobaton. 1999. "Governance Matters." Policy Research Working Paper 2196, World Bank.

Kertman, Grigorii. 2006. "Institut vyborov i elektoral'noe povedenie rossiyan." January 12. http://bd.fom.ru/report/cat/policy/elections/attitude_to_election_/d0600110. Accessed May 4, 2007.

Khairullin, Airat. 2002. "Komu krivo ot kazanskogo piva." *Vecherniaia Kazan,* March 26.

Khakimov, Rafael. 1998. "Tatarstan's Model for Developing Russian Federalism." Center and Periphery in Russian Politics. *The Development of Russian Federalism 235,* pp. 43–52. www.kazanfed.ru/authors/khakimov/publ4/.

————. 1997. "Rossiia i Tatarstan: u istoricheskogo perekrestka." *Panorama-Forum* 1 (Summer): 34–63.

————, ed. 1996. *Belaia kniga Tatarstana: Put' k suverenitetu (Sbornik ofitsialnykh dokumentov) 1990–1995.* Kazan: Tatpoligraf.

Kirkow, Peter. 1998. *Russia's Provinces: Authoritarian Transformation versus Local Autonomy?* New York: St. Martin's Press.

Kitschelt, Herbert. 1999. "Accounting for the Outcomes of Post-Communist Regime Change: Causal Depth or Shallowness in Rival Explanation." Paper presented at the Annual Meeting of the American Political Science Association, Atlanta, GA, September 1–5.

Klebnikov, Paul. 2000. *Godfather of the Kremlin: Boris Berezovsky and the Looting of Russia.* New York: Harcourt.

Kliamkin, Igor. 2000. "Tenevoi obraz zhizni (Sotsiologicheskii avtoportret sovetskogo obshchestva)," *Politicheskie Issledovania* (5): 121–32.

Kliamkin, Igor M., and Lev M. Timofeev. 2000. *Tenevaia Rossiia: ekonomiko-sotsiologicheskoe issledovanie.* Moscow: RGGU.

Kofanova, Elena N., and Vladimir V. Petukhov. 2006. "Public Opinion of Corruption in Russia." *Russian Social Science Review* 47 (6): 23–45.

Konitzer, Andrew. 2005. *Voting for Russia's Governors: Regional Elections and Accountability under Yeltsin and Putin.* Baltimore: Johns Hopkins University Press.

Konitzer, Andrew, and Stephen K. Wegren. 2006. "Federalism and Political Recentralization in the Russian Federation: United Russia as the Party of Power." *Publius: Journal of Federalism* 36 (4): 503–22.

Kononczuk, Wojciech. 2007. "Belarussian-Russian Energy Conflict: The Game Is Not Over." Batory Foundation Policy Brief, January. www.batory.org.pl/doc/belarusian-russian-energy-conflict.pdf.

Kornai, Janos, and Susan Rose-Ackerman, eds. 2004. *Building a Trustworthy State in Post-Socialist Transition.* London: Palgrave Macmillan.

"Korruptsia—norma zhizni." 2006. http://wciom.ru/arkhiv/tematicheskii-arkhiv/item/single/2861.html.

Kotkin, Stephen, and Andras Sajo, eds. 2002. *Political Corruption in Transition: A Skeptic's Handbook.* Budapest: Central European University Press.

Kovaleva, Elena. 2001. "Regional Politics in Ukraine's Transition: Donetsk Elites." Unpublished manuscript. www.sunderland.ac.uk/~os0hva/kova.htm.

Krotov, Pavel P. 2001. "Resource Rent and Regions: The Case of Komi." In *Explaining Post-Soviet Patchworks: The Political Economy of Regions, Regimes and Republics,* ed. Klaus Segbers, 99–122. Aldershot: Ashgate.

Kryshtanovskaia, Olga. 1996. "Finansovaia oligarhiia v Rossii." *Izvestiia,* January 10.

Kryshtanovskaia, Olga, and Stephen White. 2005. "Inside Putin's Court: A Research Note." *Europe-Asia Studies* 57 (7): 1065–75.

———. 2003. "Putin's Militocracy." *Post-Soviet Affairs* 19 (4): 289–306.

Kubichek, Paul. 2000. *The Unbroken Ties: the State, Interest Associations, and Corporatism in Post-Soviet Ukraine.* Ann Arbor: University of Michigan Press.

Kuzio, Taras. 2003. "Is Ukraine Any Nearer on Gongadze's Killing?" *RFE/RL Media Matters* 3, no. 8 (February 28).

———. 2002. "'Kuchmagate' Saga Continues." www.ukrweekly.com/Archive/2002/400206.shtml.

Kuznetsov, Georgii. 1997. "Goskapitalism kak vysshaia stadiia kommunizma." *Vecherniaia Kazan,* August 1.

Lambsdorff, Johann G. 1999. "Corruption in Empirical Research—A Review." *Transparency International Working Paper.* http://legacy.transparency.org/working_papers/#L.

Lani, Remzi, and Frokk Cupi. 2002. "The Difficult Road to the Independent Media: Is the Post-Communist Transition Over?" *Journal of Southeast European & Black Sea Studies* 2 (1): 75–90.

Lankina, Tomila. 2002. "Local Administration and Ethno-Social Consensus in Russia." *Europe-Asia Studies* 54 (7): 1037–54.

Lapidus, Gail W. 1999. "Asymmetrical Federalism and State Breakdown in Russia." *Post-Soviet Affairs* 15 (1): 74–82.

Lapidus, Gail, and Edward Walker. 1994. "Nationalism, Regionalism, and Federalism: Center-Periphery Relations in Post-Communist Russia." In *The New Russia: Troubled Transformation,* ed. Gail W. Lapidus. Boulder, CO: Westview Press.

"Latvia (2006)." Country Report by the Freedom House. www.freedomhouse.org/template.cfm?page=47&nit=393&year=2006.

Lau, Richard, Lee Sigelman, Caroline Heldman, and Paul Babbitt. 1999. "The Effectiveness of Negative Political Advertisements: A Meta-analytic Review." *American Political Science Review* 93 (December): 851–76.

Lazarev, Andrei. 2001. "Suschestvuiut li "shaimievskie reformy?" *Vremia i dengi,* February 7.

Ledeneva, Alena. 2006. *How Russia Really Works: The Informal Practices That Shaped Post-Soviet Politics and Business.* Ithaca: Cornell University Press.

———. 1998. *An Economy of Favours: Informal Exchanges and Networking in Russia.* Cambridge: Cambridge University Press.

Levitsky, Stephen, and Lucan Way. 2002. "The Rise of Competitive Authoritarianism." *Journal of Democracy* 31 (2): 51–65.

Linz, Juan J., and Alfred Stepan. 1996. *Problems of Democratic Transition and Consolidation: Southern Europe, South America, and Post-Communist Europe.* Baltimore: Johns Hopkins University Press.

Lipset, Seymour Martin. 1963a. "Values, Education and Entrepreneurship." In *Elites in Latin America,* ed. Seymour Martin Lipset and Aldo Solari, 3–60. New York: Oxford University Press.

———. 1963b. *Political Man: The Social Bases of Politics.* New York: Anchor Books.

———. 1959. "Some Social Requisites of Democracy: Economic Development and Political Legitimacy." *American Political Science Review* 53 (1): 69–105.

Liubarev, Arkadii E. 2003. "Golosovanie 'protiv vsekh:' motivy I tendentsii." *Polis* 6: 104–13.

Locke, John. 1980. *Second Treatise of Government.* Indianapolis: Hackett.

Lugovoi, Sergei. 1997. " 'Volga' v poiskakh Kaspiiskogo moria." *Birzha,* December 5.

Lysov, Viktor. 1998. "Pered vyborom: sub'ektivnye zametki." *Birzha* 8.

———. 1997a. "Nizhegorodskie provintsialy." *Birzha* 49.

———. 1997b. "Chto nemtsu zdorovo, to russkomu vo vred." *Birzha* 36.

Magomedov, Arbakhan. 2001. "Regional Ideologies in the Context of International Relations." *CSS Russian Working Papers,* vol.12. Center for Security Studies (CSS), ETH Zurich.

———. *Misteriia regionalizma.* Moscow: MONF.

Mainwaring, Scott, Ana M. Bejarano, and Eduardo P. Leongomez. 2006. *The Crisis of Democratic Representation in the Andes.* Stanford, CA: Stanford University Press.

Makarkin, Alexei. 2001. "Nepotopliaemyi khadzhi." *Segodnia,* March 22, 4.

Makarychev, Andrei. 2002. "Ot 'rezhima Skliarova'—k 'rezhimu Khodyreva': Institutsionalnye osnovy regionalnoi politiki v kontektse nizhegorodskikh vyborov 2001 g." In *Regionalnye vybory i problemy grazhdanskogo obshchestva v Povolzhie,* Carnegie Moscow Center, Working Papers no. 3: 128.

———. 2001a. "The Region and the World: The Case of Nizhnii Novgorod." *CSS Russian Working Papers,* vol. 6. Center for Security Studies (CSS), ETH Zurich.

———. 2001b. "Ten Years of Integration to the Global World: The Case of Nizhnii Novgorod's International Adjustment." OSI Policy Paper.

———. 1999. "Problemy upravlenia Evrozaimom: Opyt Nizhegorodskoi Oblasti." Paper presented at the seminar "Vneshneekonomicheskaia deiatel'nost' regionov: rol' v federalizatsii Rossii," Kazan, Russia, November 30.

———. 1994. "Ot dekabria k martu: pochuvstvuite raznitsu." *Birzha* 11 (March).

Maksymiuk, Jan. 2005. "Ukraine: Why Are Ukrainians Disappointed with the Orange Revolution?" Radio Free Europe/Radio Liberty feature article, November 21.

Malikov, Anvar. 2001. "Alfa-bank obiavil, chto do kontsa goda otkroet v Kazani dochernii bank." *Vecherniaia Kazan*, October 16.

Mandelstam-Balzer, Marjorie. 1994. "From Ethnicity to Nationalism: Turmoil in the Russian Mini-Empire." In *The Social Legacy of Communism*, ed. James R. Millar and Sharon L. Wolchik. New York: Woodrow Wilson Center Press and Cambridge Press.

Mann, Michael. 1986. *The Sources of Social Power.* New York: Cambridge University Press.

March, James G., and Johan P. Olsen. 1984. "The New Institutionalism: Organizational Factors in Political Life." *American Political Science Review* 78 (3): 734–49.

Marsh, Christopher. 2000. "Social Capital and Democracy in Russia." *Communist & Post-Communist Studies* 33 (2): 183–99.

Markowits, Andrei, and Mark Silverstein, eds. 1988. *The Politics of Scandal: Power and Process in Liberal Democracies.* New York: Holmes and Meier.

Markus, Stanislav. 2007. "Capitalists of All Russia, Unite! Business Mobilization under Debilitated Dirigisme." *Polity* 39 (3): 277–304.

Marples, David. 2004. "The Prospects for Democracy in Belarus." *Problems of Post-Communism* 51, no. 1 (January–February): 31–42.

Marsh, Christopher. 2000. "Social Capital and Democracy in Russia." *Communist & Post-Communist Studies* 33 (2): 183–99.

Matsuzato, Kimitaka. 2005. "Semipresidentialism in Ukraine: Institutionalist Centrism in Rampant Clan Politics." *Demokratizatsiya* 13 (1): 45–58.

———. 2004. "A Populist Island in an Ocean of Clan Politics: The Lukashenko Regime as an Exception among CIS Countries." *Europe-Asia Studies* 56 (2): 235–61.

———. 2001a. "From Ethno-Bonapartism to Centralized Caciquismo: Characteristics and Origins of the Tatarstan Political Regime, 1990–2000." *Journal of Communist Studies and Transition Politics* 17 (4): 43–77.

———. 2001b. "All Kuchma's Men: The Reshuffling of Ukrainian Governors and the Presidential Election of 1999." *Post-Soviet Geography and Economics* 42 (6): 416–39.

———. 2000a. *Regiony Rossii: Khronika i rukovoditeli.* Vol. 7. Sapporo: Hokkaido University, Slavic Research Center.

———. 2000b. *Regions: A Prism to View the Slavic-Eurasian World: Towards the Discipline of "Regionology."* Sapporo: Hokkaido University, Slavic Research Center.

Matsuzato, Kimitaka, and A. B. Shatilov, eds. 1999. *Regiony Rossii: Khronika i rukovoditeli (Nizhegorodsksia oblast, Ulianovskaia oblast).* Occasional Papers on Regional/Subregional Politics in Post-Communist Countries, no. 1. Sapporo: Hokkaido University, Slavic Research Center.

Mauro, Paulo. 1997. "Why Worry about Corruption?" *IMF Economic Issues* 6. www.imf.org/external/pubs/ft/issues6/index.htm#Consequences.

———. 1995. "Corruption and Growth." *Quarterly Journal of Economics* 110 (3): 681–712.

McAuley, Mary. 1997. *Russia's Politics of Uncertainty.* New York: Cambridge University Press.

McCann, James A., and Jorge I. Domingues. 1998. "Mexicans React to Political Corruption and Electoral Fraud: An Assessment of Public Opinion and Voting Behavior." *Electoral Studies* 17 (4): 483–504.

McCann, Leo. 2005. *Economic Development in Tatarstan: Global Markets and a Russian Region.* London: Routledge Curzon.

McFaul, Michael. 2006. "Political Transitions: Democracy and the Former Soviet Union." *Harvard International Review* (Spring): 40–45.

———. 2002. "The Fourth Wave of Democratization and Dictatorship: Noncooperative Transitions in the Postcommunist World." *World Politics* 54: 212–44.

———. 2001. *Russia's Unfinished Revolution: Political Change from Gorbachev to Putin.* Ithaca: Cornell University Press.

———. 1997. *Russia's 1996 Presidential Election: The End of Polarized Politics.* Stanford, CA: Hoover Institution Press.

McFaul, Michael, Nikolai Petrov, and Andrei Ryabov. 2004. *Between Dictatorship and Democracy.* Washington, DC: Brookings Institute Press.

McMann, Kelly. 2006. *Economic Autonomy and Democracy: Hybrid Regimes in Russia and Kyrgyzstan.* New York: Cambridge University Press.

McMann, Kelly M., and Nikolai V. Petrov. 2000. "A Survey of Democracy in Russia's Regions." *Post-Soviet Geography and Economics* 41 (3): 155–82.

Melvin, Neil. 1998. "The Consolidation of a New Regional Elite: The Case of Omsk (1987–1995)." *Europe-Asia Studies* 50 (June): 619–50.

Mickiewicz, Ellen. 2008. *Television, Power, and the Public in Russia.* Cambridge: Cambridge University Press.

Migacheva, Olga. 2002. "Khronika vyborov." *Birzha,* September 16.

————. 2001a. "Vitok spirali," *Birzha,* August 2.

————. 2001b. "Finishnaia priamaia." *Birzha,* July 5.

Mikhailov, Valentin V., V. A. Bazhanov, and Midkhat Farukshin, eds. 2000. *Osobaia zona: Vybory v Tatarstane.* Ulianovsk: Kazanskoe Otdelense Mezhdunarodnei Pravozashchitnoi Assamblei.

Minnikhanov, Rustam. 2002. "Vremia nestandartnykh reshenii." *Tatarstan* (3).

————. 2001. "Ekonomika Tatarstana: itogi polugodiia." *Tatarstan* (8).

Mishler, William, and Richard Rose. 2001. "What Are the Origins of Political Trust? Testing Institutional and Cultural Theories in Post-Communist Societies." *Comparative Political Studies* 34 (1): 30–62.

Mishler, William, and John P. Willerton. 2000. "The Dynamics of Presidential Popularity in Post-communist Russia." Studies in Public Policy 355. Center for the Study of Public Policy, University of Strathclyde, Glasgow.

Mite, Valentinas. 2005. "Ukraine: Yushchenko Goes to Brussels to Ask EU for Membership Talks." *RFE/RL Newsline,* February 21.

Mocan, Naci. 2004. "What Determines Corruption? International Evidence from Micro Data." *NBER Working Paper,* no. 10460 (May).

Moore, Barrington. 1966. *Social Origins of Dictatorship and Democracy: Lord and Peasant in the Making of the Modern World.* Boston: Beacon Press.

Moraski, Bryon. 2006. *Elections by Design: Parties and Patronage in Russia's Regions.* DeKalb: Northern Illinois University Press.

Moraski, Bryon, and William M. Reisinger. 2003. "Explaining Electoral Competition across Russia's Regions." *Slavic Review* 62 (2): 278–301.

Morris, Stephen D. 2004. "Political Corruption in Latin America: A Research Note." Unpublished manuscript. www.southalabama.edu/internationalstudies/sdmweb/research.html.

————. 1999. "Corruption and the Mexican Political System: Continuity and Change." *Third World Quarterly* 20 (3): 623–43.

Moses, Joel. 2002. "Political-Economic Elites and Russian Regional Elections, 1999–2000: Democratic Tendencies in Kaliningrad, Perm, and Volgograd." *Europe-Asia Studies* 54 (6): 905–932.

————. 1999. "Rethinking Political Typologies of Russian Regions." Paper presented at the Annual Meeting of the American Association for the Advancement of Slavic Studies, St. Louis, Missouri, November.

Mukhamadiev, Rinat. 2001. "Tatarstan pered vyborami: nabliudeniia pisatelia." *Sovetskaia Rossiia,* February 24.

Mukhametshin, Farid Kh. 2000. *Respublika Tatarstan: Osobennosti sotsial'no-ekonomicheskogo razvitiia na rubezhe vekov.* Kazan: Idel-press.

Mukhametshin, Farid Kh., and G. A. Isaev. 1998. *Respublika Tatarstan v zerkale obshchestvennogo mneniia: 90-e gody, sotsiologo-ekonomicheskii aspect.* Kazan: Cabinet of Ministers of the Republic of Tatarstan.

Mukhariamov, Nail'. 2000. "Khronika politicheskogo protsessa (1988–1998gg.)." In *Rossiia Regionov: Khronika i rukovoditeli,* vol. 7. Sapporo: Hokkaido University, Slavic Research Center.

Mungiu-Pippidi, Alina. 2006. "Corruption: Diagnosis and Treatment." *Journal of Democracy* 17 (3): 86–99.

Myers, Steven Lee. 2005. "Putin's Reforms Greeted with Street Protests." *New York Times,* January 16.

Nechaev, Vladimir. 2000. "Regional'nye politicheskie sistemy v postsovetskoi Rossii." *Pro et Contra* 5 (1): 80–95.

"Neft—vsemu golova." 2001. *Vremia i Dengi,* March 1.

Nelson, Candice J., David A. Dulio, and Stephen K. Medvic. 2002. *Shades of Gray: Perspectives on Campaign Ethics.* Washington, DC: Brookings Institution.

North, Douglass C., William Summerhill, and Barry Weingast. 2000. "Order, Disorder, and Economic Change: Latin America vs. North America." In *Governing for Prosperity,* ed. Bruce Bueno de Mesquita and Hilton Root, 17–58. New Haven: Yale University Press.

North, Douglass C., John J. Wallis, and Barry R. Weingast. 2009. *Violence and Social Orders: A Conceptual Framework for Interpreting Recorded Human History.* New York: Cambridge University Press.

———. 2006. "A Conceptual Framework for Interpreting Recorded Human History." Working Paper 12795, National Bureau of Economic Research.

Noskov, Vladimir. 2002. "Kak bodaiutsia gubernator s polpredom." *Novye izvestiia,* August 15.

"OAK razvorachivaetsya." 2009. *Expert,* April 23.

O'Donnell, Guillermo, Philippe Schmitter, and Laurence Whitehead. 1986. *Transitions from Authoritarian Rule: Tentative Conclusions about Uncertain Democracies.* Baltimore: Johns Hopkins University Press.

"O polozhenii v respublike i osnovnykh napravleniiakh sotsialno-ekonomicheskoi politiki v 2004 godu." 2004. *Vremia i den'gi,* March 30.

"O polozhenii Respubliki Tatarstan i osnovnykh napravleniiakh sotsialno-ekonomicheskoi politiki v 2002 godu." 2002. [President Shaimiev's address to the State Council, February 28.] www.rt-online.ru/text/1-03-2002/doklad.htm.

"Ob obshchikh printsipakh organizatsii mestnogo samoupravleniia v Rossiiskoi Federatsii." 2003. #131-FZ, *Rossiiskaia gazeta,* October 8.

Offe, Claus. 2004. "Political Corruption: Conceptual and Practical Issues." In *Building a Trustworthy State in Post-Socialist Transition,* ed. Janos Kornai and Susan Rose-Ackerman, 77–99. London: Palgrave Macmillan.

O'Flynn, Kevin. 2005. "A Book about Putin through His Dog's Eyes." *Moscow Times,* July 19.

Okmianskii, Vladimir. 2002. "Pogoriachilis." *Nizhegorodskie novosti,* October 1.

Olson, Mancur. 2000. *Power and Prosperity: Outgrowing Communist and Capitalist Dictatorships.* New York: Basic Books.

"One Year after the Orange Revolution: An Assessment." 2005. A Panel at the Carnegie Endowment for International Peace, November 22. www .carnegieendowment.org/events/?fa=eventDetail&id=830. Accessed July 24, 2010.

Oosterbaan, Gwynne. 1997. "Clan-Based politics in Ukraine and the Implications for Democratization." In *Perspectives on Political and Economic Transitions after Communism,* ed. John S. Micgiel, 213–33. New York: Columbia University Press.

Orlova, Olga. 2002. "Pochemu nizhegorodtsev ostavili bez kholodnoi vody?" *Delo,* June 21.

Orttung, Robert. 2006. "Business-State Relations in Russia." *Russian Analytical Digest,* no. 8 (October 17).

———, ed. 2000. *The Republics and Regions of the Russian Federation: A Guide to Politics, Policies, and Leaders.* Armonk, NY: M. E. Sharpe.

———. 1995. *From Leningrad to St. Petersburg: Democratization in a Russian City.* New York: St. Martin's Press.

Orttung, Robert W., and Phyllis Dininio. 2005. "Explaining Patterns of Corruption in the Russian Regions." *World Politics* 57 (4): 500–529.

"Otchet po resul'tatam otsenki pravil'nosti otsenki velichiny ustavnogo kapitala pri privatizatsii tselliulozno-bumazhnogo kombinata v g. Balakhne Nizhegorodskoi oblasti (Aktsionernoe obshchestvo 'Volga')." www.ach .gov.ru/bulletins/1999/arch12/2.doc.

Oversloot, Hans, Joop van Holsteyn, and G. P. van der Berg. 2002. "Against All: Exploring the Vote 'Against All' in the Russian Federation's Electoral System." *Journal of Communist Studies and Transition Politics* 18 (4): 31–50.

Panfilov, Oleg. 2005. "Putin and the Press: The Revival of Soviet-style Propaganda." Foreign Policy Center, London. http://fpc.org.uk/fsblob/495.pdf. Accessed May 3, 2007.

Pazderka, Joseph. 2005. "Russia: End of a Messy Affair." *Transitions Online* (June 1).

Pechilina, Galina, and Aleksei Ptichii. 1998. "Nizhnekamskshina' ishchet strategicheskogo partnera." *Russkii Telegraf,* April 29.

Peev, Evgeni. 2002. "Ownership and Control Structures in Transition to 'Crony' Capitalism: The Case of Bulgaria." *Eastern European Economies* 40 (5): 73–91.

Peregudov, Sergei. 2001. "Krupnaia rossiiskaia korporatsiia v sisteme vlasti." *Polis* 2: 16–24.

Petelina, Katerina. 1997. "Kto platit vovremia, tot platit menshe." *Birzha* (12).

Petrov, Nikolai. 2003. "Russia's 'Part of Power' Takes Shape." *Russia and Eurasia Review, Jamestown Foundation* 2 (16).

Pinsker, Dmitrii. 1997. "Anti-Davos in Moscow." *Itogi*, September 23.

Pipes, Richard. 2005. *Russian Conservatism and Its Critics: A Study in Political Culture.* New Haven: Yale University Press.

Polikanov, Dmitry. 2005. "Izbiratel'noe pravo prezidenta." *Vremia novostei,* March 30.

Politicheskaia kul'tura i politicheskoe povedenie nizhegorodskikh izbiratelei. 2001. Nizhnii Novgorod.

Politicheskoe razvitie Nizhegorodskoi oblasti v predstavleniakh regional'noi elity: nastoiashchee i budushchee. 2001. Nizhnii Novgorod: Nizhegorodskii Issledovatel'skii Fond.

Pop-Eleches, Grigore. 2007. "Between Historical Legacies and the Promise of Western Integration: Democratic Conditionality after Communism." *East European Politics and Societies* 21 (4): 142–61.

Popov, Igor. 2002. "Belarus under Lukashenko." *Contemporary Review,* January.

Postnova, Vera. 1999. "Tatarstan mog by stat Kuveitom." *Nadezhda Tatarstana* #1, March. http://scripts.online.ru/misc/newsreg/99/03/19_585.htm.

"Potomki detei leitenanta Shmidta." 2001. *Trud,* no. 241 (September 21).

Power, Timothy. 1991. "Politicized Democracy: Competition, Institutions, and 'Civic Fatigue' in Brazil." *Journal of Interamerican Studies and World Affairs* 33 (3): 75–113.

"Power and Money Rule Latvian Politics." 2007. www.allaboutlatvia.com/article/590/power-and-money-rule-latvian-politics.

"Pravitel'stvo Tatarstana reshilo zagruzit' neftekhimicheskie predpriiatiia syr'em v dobrovol'no-prinuditel'nom poriadke." n.d. http://elemte.bancorp.ru/koi/press/press00567.

"Pribavlenie v semeistve bankov." 2003. *Vremia i dengi* 75 (April 24).

Prokof'ef, Yuri. 2002. "Likvidatsiia vetkhogo zhil'ia: sud vynes reshenie, kotoroe nichego ne reshaet?" *Vremia i dengi* 35 (February 21).

Protsyk, Oleh. 2005. "Constitutional Politics and Presidential Power in Kuchma's Ukraine." *Problems of Post-Communism* 52 (5): 23–31.

Pryadilnikov, Mikhail. 2001. "Federalism and Interregional Conflict in Russia: The case of Tiumen Oblast and Khanty-Mansiisk and Yamalo—Nenetsk

Autonomous Okrugs." Paper presented at the Annual Meeting of the American Association of Slavic Studies, Arlington, VA, November 15–18.

Przeworski, Adam. 2000. *Democracy and Development: Political Institutions and Material Well-being in the World, 1950–1990.* Cambridge: Cambridge University Press.

———. 1991. *Democracy and the Market: Political and Economic Reforms in Eastern Europe and Latin America.* New York: Cambridge University Press.

Przeworski, Adam, and Henry Teune. 1970. *The Logic of Comparative Social Inquiry.* Malabar, FL: Krieger Publishing.

Puglisi, Rosaria. 2003a. "Clashing Agendas: Economic Elite Coalitions and Prospects for Co-operation between Russia and Ukraine." *Europe-Asia Studies* 55 (6): 827–45.

———. 2003b. "The Rise of the Ukrainian Oligarchs." *Democratization* 10 (3): 99–123.

Putin, Vladimir. 2006. "Address to the National Coordination Meeting of Law Enforcement Agency Directors." Kremlin, Moscow, November 21. www .kremlin.ru/eng/sdocs/speeches.shtml?type=82913. Accessed December 10, 2006.

Pynzenyk, Viktor. 2000. "How to Find a Path for Ukrainian Reforms." *Russian and East European Finance and Trade* 36 (1): 59–77.

Radnitz, Scott. 2010. "The Color of Money: Privatization, Economic Dispersion and the Post-Soviet Revolutions." *Comparative Politics* 42 (2): 127–46.

Raspopov, Nikolai P. 1997–99. "Nizhegorodskaia oblast." Politicheskii Monitoring [monthly], Institut gumanitarno-politicheskikh issledovanii. www .igpi.ru/monitoring/1047645476/.

Reddaway, Peter, and Dmitri Glinski. 2001. *The Tragedy of Russia's Reforms: Market Bolshevism Against Democracy.* Washington, DC: United States Institute of Peace Press.

Reddaway, Peter, and Robert Orttung, eds. 2005. *The Dynamics of Russian Politics: Putin's Reform of Federal-Regional Relations* II. Lanham, MD: Rowman and Littlefield.

———. 2004. *The Dynamics of Russian Politics: Putin's Reform of Federal-Regional Relations* I. Lanham, MD: Rowman and Littlefield.

"Regional'nyi egoizm ekonomicheski tselesoobrazen. Eksperimenty Tatarstana v ozhidanii effektivnogo sobstvennika." 2000. *Expert,* October 2.

Remington, Thomas. 2001. *The Russian Parliament: Institutional Evolution in a Transitional Regime, 1989–1999.* New Haven: Yale University Press.

Reuter, Ora John, and Thomas F. Remington. 2009. "Dominant Party Regimes and the Commitment Problem: The Case of United Russia." *Comparative Political Studies* 42 (4): 501–26.

Rigby, T. H. 1981. "Early Provincial Cliques and the Rise of Stalin." *Soviet Studies* 33 (1): 3–28.

Rivera, Sharon Werning, and David W. Rivera. 2006. "The Russian Elite under Putin: Militocratic or Bourgeois?" *Post-Soviet Affairs* 22 (2): 125–44.

Rose, Richard. 2004. "Russian Responses to Transformation: Trends in Public Opinion Since 1992." Studies in Public Policy no. 390, Center for the Study of Public Policy, University of Strathclyde, Glasgow.

———. 2002. "A Decade of New Russian Barometer Survey." Centre for the Study of Public Policy, University of Strathclyde, Glasgow.

Rose, Richard, and Neil Munro. 2002. *Elections without Order: Russia's Challenge to Vladimir Putin.* Cambridge: Cambridge University Press.

Rose, Richard, Neil Munro, and William Mishler. 2004. "Resigned Acceptance of and Incomplete Democracy: Russia's Political Equilibrium." Studies in Public Policy no. 392, Center for the Study of Public Policy, University of Strathclyde, Glasgow.

Rose-Ackerman, Susan. 1999. *Corruption and Government: Causes, Consequences, and Reform.* New York: Cambridge University Press.

"'Rosoboronexport' garantiroval obespechit' ne menee 50% ezhegodnoi vyricchki zavoda." 2007. *Kommersant* 111 (June 28). www.kommersant.ru/doc.aspx?DocsID=777800. Accessed May 7, 2010.

Rossiia Regionov: Statisticheskii ezhegodnik. 2001. Moscow: Goskomstat Rossii.

"Rossiiane ob otmene vyborov gubernatorov i deputatov." 2004. *Press-vypusk,* Levada Tsentr, September 29. www.levada.ru/press/2004092902.html. Accessed May 15, 2007.

Rost, Andrei. 1996. "Gromkie dela o bankrotstve mogut okazatsia ne takimi uzh gromkimi." *Neft i Kapital,* October 24.

"'Rostehnologii' ruliat." 2009. *Expert,* September 10.

Roudakova, Natalia. 2008. "Media-Political Clientelism: Lessons from Anthropology." *Media, Culture and Society* 30 (1): 41–59.

"Russian Elections." 1999. December 17. www.pbs.org/newshour/bb/europe/july-dec99/russian_elections_12-17.html.

Rutland, Peter, ed. 2001. *Business and State in Contemporary Russia.* Boulder, CO: Westview Press.

Saakashvili, Mikheil. 2006. "The Way Forward: Georgia's Democratic Vision for the Future." *Harvard International Review* 28 (1): 68–73.

Sal'nikova, Yiulia. 2004. "Rossiia strana mazokhistov." http://wciom.ru/arkhiv/tematicheskii-arkhiv/item/single/916.html?no_casche=1&c Hash=06de8810d1. (September 21).

Sakwa, Richard. 2009. *The Quality of Freedom: Khodorkovsky, Putin, and the Yukos Affairs.* New York: Oxford University Press.

———. 2002. *Russian Politics and Society.* London: Routledge.

Sapozhnikov, Petr, and Gulchachak Khannanova. 1998. "Neftianiki ne priznaiut dolgov pered biudzhetom." *Kommersant-daily,* July 9.

Satarov, Georgii, ed. 2001. "Anticorruption Diagnostics in Russia: Sociological Analysis." INDEM Foundation, Moscow. www.anti-corr.ru/awbreport/index.htm. Accessed December 10, 2006.

Schatz, Edward. 2005. "Reconceptualizing Clans: Kinship Networks and Statehood in Kazakhstan." *Nationalities Papers* 33 (2): 231–54.

———. 2004. *Modern Clan Politics: The Power of Blood in Kazakhstan and Beyond.* Seattle: University of Washington Press.

Schumpeter, Joseph. 1976. *Capitalism, Socialism, and Democracy.* London: George Allen & Unwin.

Scott, James C. 1972. "Patron-Client Politics and Political Change in Southeast Asia." *American Political Science Review* 66 (1): 91–113.

Scott, John. 2000. *Social Network Analysis: A Handbook.* Thousand Oaks, CA: Sage.

Seligson, Mitchell. 2002. "The Impact of Corruption on Regime Legitimacy: A Comparative Study of Four Latin American Countries." *Journal of Politics* 64 (2): 408–33.

Semeniuk, Mikhail, and Yurii Shukov. 1997. "A gorod podumal: investor idet." *Rossiiskaia gazeta,* June 5.

Shaimiev, Mintimer. 2002. *Tatarstan: Progress Cherez Stabil'nost'.* Kazan: Idel-press.

Sharafutdinova, Gulnaz. 2010. "What Explains Corruption Perceptions? The Dark Side of Political Competition in Russia's Regions." *Comparative Politics* 42 (2): 147–66.

———. 2006. "When Do Elites Compete? The Determinants of Political Competition in Russia's Regions." *Comparative Politics* 38 (3): 273–93.

———. 2001. "Concentrating Capital Helps Tatarstani Leaders in Battle with Putin's Centralization." *East West Institute, Russian Regional Report* 6, no. 36 (October 17).

Sharafutdinova, Gulnaz, and Andrei Makarychev. 2009. "Gestalt Shift in Russian Federalism: Where Has the Regional Power Gone under Putin?" Unpublished manuscript.

Shepsle, Kenneth. 1991. "Discretion, Institutions, and the Problem of Government Commitment." In *Social Theory for a Changing Society,* ed. Pierre Bourdieu and James S. Coleman, 245–65. Boulder, CO: Westview Press.

Shevtsova, Lilia. 2007a. "Povestka dnia: Doktrina Samoutverzhdeniia." *Vedomosti,* January 18 (1781).

———. 2007b. "Total'naia logika gibridnoi sistemy." www.polit.ru/analytics/2007/01/15/shevzova.html.

———. 2004. "The Limits of Bureaucratic Authoritarianism." *Journal of Democracy* 15 (3): 67–77.

———. 2003. *Putin's Russia.* Washington, DC: Carnegie Endowment for International Peace.

———. 1999. *Yeltsin's Russia: Myths and Reality.* Washington, DC: Carnegie Endowment for International Peace and Brookings Institution Press.

Shinkichi, Fujimori. 2004. "Ukraine's Gastraders: A Case of Political Economy in a Transition Country." Paper presented at the Slavic Research Center winter symposium "Emerging Meso-Areas in the Former Socialist Countries: Histories Revived or Improvised?" Hokkaido University, January 28–31.

Shlapentokh, Vladimir. 1996. "Early Feudalism: The Best Parallel for Contemporary Russia." *Europe-Asia Studies* 48: 393–411.

Shukan, Ioulia. 2004. "The Presidential Patrimonialism in Contemporary Belarus: A Case Study of the Direction of Presidential Affairs under Alexandr Loukachenka's Regime." Paper presented at the 9th Annual World Convention of the Association for the Study of Nationalities, New York, April.

"Sibneft and Production Control." 2005. *Kommersant,* September 29. www.kommersant.com/p613189/r_1/Sibneft_and_Production_Control/. Accessed September 10, 2007.

Sigelman, Lee, and Eric Shiraev. 2002. "The Rational Attacker in Russia? Negative Campaigning in Russian Presidential Elections." *Journal of Politics* 64 (1): 45–62.

Sil, Rudra, and Cheng Chen. 2004. "State Legitimacy and the (In)significance of Democracy in Post-Communist Russia." *Europe-Asia Studies* 56 (3): 347–68.

Silitski, Vitalii. 2006. "Still Soviet? Why Dictatorship Persists in Belarus." *Harvard International Review* 28, no. 1 (Spring).

———. 2005. "Has the Age of Revolutions Ended?" *Transitions Online,* January 13.

————. 2001. "Personalist Autocracy in Belarus: Mechanisms of Functioning, Control, and Maintaining Public Support." Unpublished manuscript.

Singer, Eleanor. 1981. "Reference Groups and Social Evaluations." In *Social Psychology*, ed. Morris Rosenberg and Ralph H. Turner, 66–93. New York: Basic Books.

Slider, Darrell. 2008. "Putin's 'Southern Strategy': Dmitry Kozak and the Dilemmas of Recentralization." *Post-Soviet Affairs* 24 (2): 177–97.

————. 2007. "Putin and the Russian Electoral System: 'Reforms' to Prevent Regime Change." *Soviet and Post-Soviet Review* 34 (1): 55–68.

Smith, Benjamin. 2005. "Life of the Party: The Origins of Regime Breakdown and Persistence under Single-Party Rule." *World Politics* 57 (3): 421–51.

Smolin, Stanislav, and Vladimir Volkov. 2005. "Russia: Wave of Protests against Welfare Cuts." www.wsws.org/articles/2005/jan2005/russ-j27.shtml.

Smyth, Regina. 2006. *Candidate Strategies and Electoral Competition in the Russian Federation*. New York: Cambridge University Press.

————. 2002. "Building State Capacity from the Inside Out: Parties of Power and the Success of the President's Reform Agenda in Russia." *Politics and Society* 30 (4): 555–78.

Snyder, Richard. 2001. "Scaling Down: The Subnational Comparative Method." *Studies in Comparative International Development* 36 (1): 93–110.

Solnick, Steven. 1996. "The Political Economy of Russian Federalism." *Problems of Post-Communism* 43 (6): 13–26.

Sparks, Colin. 2000. *Communism, Capitalism and Mass Media*. Tirana: AMI.

Stark, David, and Laszlo Bruszt. 1998. *Postsocialist Pathways: Transforming Politics and Property in East Central Europe*. New York: Cambridge University Press.

Stavrakis, Peter J., Joan DeBardeleben, and Larry Black. 1997. *Beyond the Monolith: The Emergence of Regionalism in Post-Soviet Russia*. Washington, DC: Woodrow Wilson Center Press.

Steinmo, Sven, Kathleen Thelen, and Frank Longstreth, eds. 2002. *Structuring Politics: Historical Institutionalism in Comparative Perspective*. New York: Cambridge University Press.

Stern, Jonathan. 2006. "The Russian-Ukrainian Gas Crisis of 2006." *Oxford Institute for Energy Studies*. www.oxfordenergy.org/pdfs/comment_0106.pdf.

Stiglitz, Joseph. 2002. "Crony Capitalism American Style." *Project Syndicate* (February commentary). www.project-syndicate.org/series/.

Stoner-Weiss, Kathryn. 2006. *Resisting the State: Reform and Retrenchment in Post-Soviet Russia*. New York: Cambridge University Press.

————. 1997. *Local Heroes: The Political Economy of Russian Regional Governance*. Princeton: Princeton University Press.

Sushko, Oleksandr, and Oles Lisnychuk. 2005. "The Election Campaign and Ukraine's Political Evolution." In *Presidencial Elections and Orange Revolution Implications for Ukraine's Transition*, ed. Helmut Kurth and Iris Kemke. Center for Applied Policy Research, University of Munich. www .cap.lmu.de/download/2005/2005_ukraine.pdf.

"TAIF budet opredeliat' ekonomichskuiu strategiiu Nizhnekamskneftek-hima." 2005. *Tatar-Inform*, November 23. www.tatar.ru.

Taran, Elena. 1998. "Tatariia prodaet telefonnuiu kompaniiu." *Vremia MN*, October 21.

"Tatneft' sdala neftepererabotku." 2005. *Kommersant*, September 2.

Thornhill, John. 1996. "The Island of Pragmatism in Russia." *Financial Times*, February 20.

Thurber, James A., and Candice J. Nelson, eds. 2000. *Campaign Warriors: The Role of Political Consultants in Elections*. Washington, DC: Brookings Institution Press.

Tilly, Charles. 1985. "War-Making and State-Making as Organized Crime." In *Bringing the State Back In*, ed. T. Skocpol, P. Evans, and D. Rueschemeyer, 161–91. Cambridge: Cambridge University Press.

"To li Lukashenko, to li Nazarbayev." 2005. *Novye izvestiia*, November 18.

Tolz, Vera. 2004. "The Search for National Identity in Yeltsin's and Putin's Russia." In *The Fall of Communism in Europe*, ed. Jonathan Frankel and Stefani Hoffman, 160–78. Cambridge: Cambridge University Press.

————. 2001. *Russia: Inventing the Nation*. New York: Oxford University Press.

Tompson, William. 2005. "Putting Yukos in Perspective." *Post-Soviet Affairs* 21 (April): 159–81.

Treisman, Daniel. 2008. "The Popularity of Russian Presidents." Unpublished manuscript. www.sscnet.ucla.edu/polisci/faculty/treisman/Put_Pop.pdf. Accessed August 20, 2009.

————. 2007. "Putin's Silovarchs." *Orbis* 51 (1): 141–53.

————. 1997. "Russia's 'Ethnic Revival': The Separatist Activism of Regional Leaders in a Postcommunist Order." *World Politics* 49 (2): 226–28.

Trifonova, Svetlana. 2001. "Upravliat energetikoi budut otlichniki." *Nizhegorodskie novosti*, July 13.

Tsyganov, Yurii. 2001. "Farewell to the Oligarchs? Presidency and Business Tycoons in Contemporary Russia." In *Russia after Yeltsin*, ed. V. Tikhomirov, 79–102. Aldershot: Ashgate.

Tumber, Howard, and Silvio R. Waisbord. 2004. "Introduction: Political Scandals and Media across Democracies." *American Behavioral Scientist* 47 (8): 1031–39.

Turovskii, Rostislav, ed. 2002. *Politika v regionakh: Gubernatory i gruppy vliianiia.* Moscow: Tsentr politicheskikh tekhnologii.

"Ukraine's Parliamentary Elections: March 29, 1998." 1998. CSCE Report, April. www.globalsecurity.org/military//library/congress/1998_rpt/1998Ukraineelections.pdf. Accessed May 23, 2007.

Vachudova, Milada A. 2006. *Europe Undivided: Democracy, Leverage and Integration after Communism.* New York: Oxford University Press.

———. 2001. "The Leverage of International Institutions on Democratizing States: The European Union and Eastern Europe." In *RSCAS Working Papers* no. 2001/33. European University Institute, Fiesolana, Italy.

Vanhanen, Tatu. 1997. *Prospects of Democracy: A Study of 172 Countries.* New York: Routledge.

Van Selm, Bert. 1998. "Economic Performance in Russian Regions." *Europe-Asia Studies* 50 (4): 603–19.

Van Zon, Hans. 2000. *The Political Economy of Independent Ukraine.* New York: St. Martin's Press.

Varese, Frederico. 2001. *The Russian Mafia: Private Protection in a New Market Economy.* Oxford: Oxford University Press.

Verdery, Katherine. 1999. "What was Socialism, and Why Did It Fall?" In *Revolution of 1989,* ed. Vladimir Tismaneanu, 63–88. New York: Routledge.

Viktiukov, Nikolai. 2000. "Vlast i pressa. Kardinal iz polpredstva." *Novaia gazeta,* December 4.

Vitebskaia, Tat'iana. 2002. "Izdevatel'stva nad nami energetikov—eto trenirovka Chubaisa." *Delo,* July 12.

"Vnedrenie vysokikh tekhnologii—osnova dinamichnogo razvitiia ekonomiki Tatarstana." 2001. *Vremia i dengi,* June 28.

Volkov, Vadim. 2002. *Violent Entrepreneurs: The Use of Force in the Making of Russian Capitalism.* Ithaca: Cornell University Press.

———. 1999. "Violent Entrepreneurship in Post-Communist Russia." *Europe-Asia Studies* 51 (5): 741–55.

Wallis, John J. 2006. "The Concept of Systematic Corruption in American History." In *Corruption and Reform: Lessons from America's Economic History,* ed. Edward L. Glaeser and Claudia Goldin. Chicago: University of Chicago Press.

Way, Lucan. 2005a. "Authoritarian State Building and the Sources of Regime Competitiveness in the Fourth Wave: The Cases of Belarus, Moldova, Russia, and Ukraine." *World Politics* 57 (January): 231–61.

———. 2005b. "Rapacious individualism and political competition in Ukraine, 1992–2004." *Communist and Post-Communist Studies* 38 (2005): 191–205.

———. 2005c. "Kuchma's Failed Authoritarianism." *Journal of Democracy* 16 (2):131–45.

Way, Lucan, and Stephen Levitsky. 2006. "Pigs, Wolves and the Evolution of Post-Soviet Competitive Authoritarianism, 1992–2005." Center for Democracy, Development and the Rule of Law Working Paper, Stanford University, June.

Weber, Max. 1950. *General Economic History.* Glencoe, IL: Free Press.

———. 1947. *The Theory of Social and Economic Organization.* New York: Free Press.

Wedel, Janine. 2001. "Corruption and Organized Crime in Post-Communist States." *Trends in Organized Crime* 7 (1): 1–60.

———. 1998. *Collision and Collusion: The Strange Case of Western Aid to Eastern Europe: 1990–1997.* London: Palgrave Macmillan.

Wegren, Stephen K. 2000. "Socioeconomic Transformation in Russia: Where Is the Rural Elite?" *Europe-Asia Studies* 52 (2): 237–71.

———. 1998. *Agriculture and the State in Soviet and Post-Soviet Russia.* Pittsburgh: University of Pittsburgh Press.

———. 1997. "The Political Economy of Private Farming in Russia." *Comparative Economic Studies* 39 (3–4): 1–24.

———. 1994a. "Building Market Institutions: Agricultural Commodity Exchanges in Post-Communist Russia." *Communist and Post-Communist Studies* 27 (3): 195–224.

———. 1994b. "Farm Privatization in Nizhnii Novgorod: A Model for Russia?" *RFE/RL Research Report* 3, no. 21 (May 27): 16–27.

Weingast, Barry. 1997. "The Political Foundations of Democracy and the Rule of Law." *American Political Science Review* 91 (2): 245–63.

White, Stephen, and Richard Rose. 2001. "Nationality and Public Opinion in Belarus and Ukraine." Studies in Public Policy no. 346, Centre for the Study of Public Policy, University of Strathclyde, Glasgow.

Willerton, John. 1992. *Patronage and Politics in the USSR.* Cambridge: Cambridge University Press.

Wilson, Andrew. 2005. *Virtual Politics: Faking Democracy in the Post-Soviet World.* New Haven: Yale University Press.

Woodruff, David. 2005. "Bloom, Gloom, Doom: Balance Sheets, Monetary Fragmentation, and the Politics of Financial Crisis in Argentina and Russia." *Politics & Society* 33 (1): 3–45.

———. 2004. "Property Rights in Context: Privatization's Legacy for Corporate Legality in Poland and Russia." *Studies in Comparative International Development* 38 (4): 82–108.

———. 2003. "The Extremely Hostile Takeover: Russian Lessons on Law, Property, and Politics." Paper prepared for the Annual Conference of the American Association for the Advancement of Slavic Studies, Toronto, November.

———. 1999. *Money Unmade: Barter and the Fate of Russian Capitalism.* Ithaca: Cornell University Press.

Yasmann, Viktor. 2005. "2005 In Review: The Tranformation of Television in Russia." Radio Free Europe/Radio Liberty feature article, December 27. www.rferl.org/content/article/1064193.html.

Young, John. 2000. "The Republic of Sakha and Republic Building: The Neverendum of Federalization in Russia." In *Regions: A Prism to View the Slavic-Eurasian World Towards a Discipline of "Regionology."* Sapporo: Hokkaido University, Slavic Research Center.

Zassoursky, Ivan. 2004. *Media and Power in Post-Soviet Russia.* Armonk, NY: M. E. Sharpe.

Zlotnikov, Leonid. 2002. "Into the Noose of Populism." In *Ten Years in the Mirror of the Belorusski Rynok.* www.br.minsk.by/book/zlot.htm.

Zubarevich, Natalya V. 2005. "Krupnyi biznes v regionakh Rossii: territorial'nye strategii razvitiia i sotsial'nye interesy." Working Paper. Moscow.

Zudin, Aleksei. 2001. "Neokorporativizm v Rossii?" *Pro et Contra* 6 (4).

Zyla, P. Roman. 1999. "Corruption in Ukraine: Between Perceptions and Realities." In *State and Institution Building in Ukraine.* New York: St. Martin's Press.

INDEX

Abramovich, Roman, 142
agriculture
  in Nizhnii Novgorod, 50, 53–54, 55
  in Tatarstan, 80–81
All Russia (Vsia Rossiia) party, 146–47, 153
Altynbaev, Rafgat, 73, 215n16, 219n120
Aristotle, 36
Aushev, Ruslan, 216n18
authoritarianism
  in Belarus, 21, 171, 180
  in Orel and Kemerovo, 95
  political parties and, 153
  popular support for, 4, 6, 9
  under Putin, 5, 6, 20–21, 139, 165, 173
  in Tatarstan, 16, 95, 118
  in Ukraine, 194–95
Aven, Pyotr, 207n2
AvtoVAZ, 143

bankruptcy law, 63
Barnes, Andrew, 35
Bashkortostan, 69, 135–36, 231n11
Bedniakov, Dmitrii, 59, 99–100, 220n8
  in 1998 elections, 105, 221n28, 221n30

Beetham, David, 8
Bekh, Nikolai, 216n26
Belarus, 178–82, 232n26
  authoritarianism in, 21, 171, 180
  crony capitalism in, 181–82
  privatization in, 178, 179, 232n27
  public opinion in, 193–94, 203–4
  as Putin's model, 180–81
  relations with Russia, 173, 188
  state economic control in, 21, 179, 180–81
Belgorod, 124
Berezovsky, Boris, 228n43
  media empire of, 150, 152, 230n110
  and Putin, 149–50
  and Yeltsin, 22, 141, 146
Berlin, Isaiah, 34, 200
Bernard, Claude, 1
Bessarab, Vladimir, 56
Bismarck, Otto von, 96
black PR. *See* electoral trickery
Bogachev, Evgenii, 81
Bonde-Nilsen, Johan, 220n124
Brevnov, Boris, 56, 212n31
Briansk, 124
bribes, 162

GULNAZ SHARAFUTDINOVA
is assistant professor of political science at Miami University.